ANCIENT SPRINGS AND NEW INDIA

Ancient Springs and New India

Convocation Addresses and Tributes

KAPILA VATSYAYAN

ADITYA PRAKASHAN
New Delhi

First published: 2018

ISBN 978-81-7742-165-1

Published by Aditya Prakashan, 2/18, Ansari Road, New Delhi – 110 002.

email: contact@adityaprakashan.com
website: www.adityaprakashan.com

Printed at Replika Press Pvt. Ltd.

Contents

SECTION I

Convocation Addresses

1.

North-Eastern Hill University, Shillong

Allow me first of all to express my deep gratitude to you for having invited me on this auspicious occasion of the 1983 Convocation of this unique University. I said 'unique' university and, for a moment, I want you to concentrate on three, or may I say four, words which constitute the name of this university. 'North', 'Eastern', 'Hill' and 'University', and perhaps I should add here 'Shillong'. In naming this university, the vision of its founders is clear. It points to a geographical feature of the region to which you belong as also the very words—'North Eastern' and 'Hill'—already points to a very special feature of the region to which you belong. The name points at its specificity as also at the inter-connections that the region has with the rest of India. So, connected to the North-West, you are distinctively the North-East. The word 'University' almost makes a leap in time because from the natural environment, the ecological situation, the zoological situation, the flora and the fauna, the inanimate but vital life which is contained in the hills of this place, and the most variegated animate life of the people of these regions, is lifted or transported into a new structure, namely the University. Am I labouring on the obvious? But the obvious contains a secret of the culture of India and of the very specific and unique nature of the people of the North-Eastern region of India and their contribution to that which is known as the totality of the Indian culture and civilization in time and space, as also the changes which are inherent in containing a great and vast civilization within the modern institutional framework of schools and universities.

Having said this, let me proceed further with what I have noticed in the contents of the courses which this university offers. My attention was drawn to the vast range of subjects offered here; behind this vast range of subjects is a pointed attention to the uniqueness of the region and, therefore, of the university. Let me begin with what you call the Department of Geography and what I would call the basic ecological situation in which you find yourselves—unique and specific, but in continuous dialogue with different regions of India. Rightly, your own report says: 'The main thrust of the Department is towards better understanding of the various dynamic process of both physical and cultural which are constantly working to shape the regional aspects of India as a whole and North-Eastern India in particular." Rightly so, your publications include problems of hill slopes, of land use, of soil erosion, of geo-morphology and rural settlements of Meghalaya and other such related subjects. Have you thought for one minute how this geography of the hill regions is a continuity, that the great Himalayan ranges extending from Afghanistan and Kashmir to Nagaland form one ecological system? Here, although many changes have taken place in the flora and fauna in the geological and zoological situation, there is a continuity from what one would call from the North-West to the North-East.

This same continuity has been responsible not only in geographical terms, but also in cultural terms, of the great migrations which have taken place from the North-West to the North-East, and may I say, perhaps from South-East into the North-East. This one basic geographical feature of your area has determined life styles and cultural patterns. Again, there is this Department of Zoology and Life Sciences, which is concentrating its attention on the regional needs of the hill States and studying life in this area—life as distinguished from the human life. The wide variety of what you call micro and macro fauna, the wide variety of climatic conditions ranging from warm at the foothills to cold at the higher altitudes, the wide variety of fish, animals and plants and insect life have also conditioned the cultural patterns. Similarly, there is the Department of Botany. Once again, your curricula draw attention to the special significance of the area, its rich forests and forest resources. Its uniqueness, you yourself have pointed out, lies in its being one of the richest geographical regions both from floristic and faunastic point of view. You also pointed out that the region has the unique problems of rapid degradation of its forest resources and germ plasm, etc., due to cutting down of its trees for timber and firewood. These Departments may seem very insular and my mentioning these Departments to you in a Convocation Address may seem trite. However, perhaps much later in life, you will remember that these very courses gave you a sense of rootedness and belonging to a cultural security which will be an asset to you.

Now, I would like to relate your concerns in these Departments as also the Department of Khasi language and literature and that of Creative Arts. All this has to be put together. For me, the Departments which you call the Departments of Geography, Botany, Zoology and the Departments which you call those of the Human Sciences and those you call of Humanities and the Arts, Languages and Literature, are all inter-related parts of a total personality which I would like to call the unique personality of the North-Eastern region of India. It contains for me the clue to the understanding of the cultural development of man and what one would term as the cultural experience—an experience which manifests itself in diverse media—be it that of science, physical or social or the humanities or the arts of poetry or of music or of dance or of sculpture or of painting or of weaving or of bamboo work or of cane work or of bronze or pottery and the innumerable other forms. All this is the essential culture given a form, a shape, colour and finally the giver of a power of communication for the maker and the participator alike.

Many definitions have been given of culture and civilization. An equal number of definitions are found of art and the creative experience. However, discarding all these conventional definitions, let us go back to where I began, namely, the North, Eastern, Hill and University. The ecological situation, the extensive Himalayan ranges, the equally pervasive river systems beginning in the North-East, flowing into the South-East, the flora and fauna, the multiplicity of the races, the plurality of the languages, the diversity of the religious faiths, the multitude of social systems and ultimately, basically and finally, their relationship of water, earth, space, fire and sky, are the determinants of what one would call the cultural experience and cultural manifestation both in space and in time. In other words, the cultural experience is the amalgam of the physical, natural environment in which man lives, the outer environment of space and the man-given environment, of his society which he nurtures through cultivation of the senses, feeling, mind and spirit. Cultivation in its primary meaning points not only at agriculture of *Krishti*, but also the web of human relationships that man develops. All these, individually and collectively, are part of one pervasive sensibility what one calls the cultural experience. For its full growth, there is the necessity also of the cultivation of the individual self which looks perhaps inwards. This too is perhaps determined by man's daily, weekly, monthly, annual and life cycles and yet it is something within man and constitutes his inner environment. It is the coming together of both these—the outer and the inner—which makes the artistic experience possible and the artistic expression a reality. In either case, whether in the collective experience of a group or the individual, silent experience of one alone or many together, it is heightened. It is a moment which differentiates man for that time and space from all that which is without. The dialectic of this process in exactly this, the multitude of environmental factors digested, churned in the inner psyche, when for a moment, short or long, specificity is submerged in the universal. Then, neither South-East or the North-West, the North or South, the West or the East, the tribal or the rural, the urban or the industrialised, have meaning because the ultimate expression of the totality of this experience is no longer particular; it is universal. Thus, while in a university situation, there are different departments and different disciplines and different intensive enquiries into the nature of matter and the elements, the flora and the fauna, the animal and the human life, the societal structures and the expressions through language, literature and the arts, all these together constitute a cultural personality. It is on one level tangible, measurable, specific, unique, on another, it is beyond it because it is in the very nature of the cultural experience for that, in momentary flashes or for a longer duration, gives rise to an experience which is intangible and immeasurable. This cultural experience is not restricted then to a single set of elements, natural, physical, social, economic, religious, individual or collective. It can be any of these—singly or together.

Let me make my point clearer by taking the case of a natural environment—an environment unrelated to a specific mountain or hill, its high peaks or its particular ascending lines or turfs, but just a mountain or a hill and many of you here have perhaps experienced the beauty of the mountain and the hill to which you belong under the clear blue skies of the horizon. Whether it is Kailash or the hill peaks of the Himalayas or the hills in and around Meghalaya, Nagaland or Mizoram if you watch with concentration, there is awe, there is fear, and there is joy. The very movement of the physical self of the human being looking up, the eyes and the head moving up, there is the invariable ascension of the spirit. For that moment of looking up figuratively, the pull of gravity is loosened and the self-rises above, up, as if to meet the horizon itself. Perhaps some of you have experienced this joy; others have perhaps been attracted by the challenge of climbing those hills so that you could reach the top. The cultural process and the cultural experience is both that moment of joy and that moment of ascension of the spirit—that physically you may be below, but spiritually and mentally you wish to climb to that top where you may meet the horizon of the skies. It is not the joy of the particular peak, it is the joy of ascension. So the study of geography becomes a cultural experience, a cultural experience born of the specific looking and experiencing the special contours of the hills of the Meghalaya, but the hills of the Meghalaya become the mountain peaks of the Himalayas. In one word, the experience of this simple experience of looking at the mountain can become a cosmic experience of knowing that there is the vertical that rises from the vortex of the earth to reach the skies.

Let us take another experience, this time of the waters. Now the eyes do not reach or travel upwards. This time it is a horizontal dimension when one stands near a sea-shore and looks with concentration at the unending rhythm of the rise and fall of the tides and the eyes try to reach or merely to experience shoreless beyond. This is the moment of again reaching out the infinity, to an unknowable beyond. For that moment and duration, there is the blending of oneself with that ocean of the beyond. The realisation that the ocean is made up of the fish and other organism, the variety of life, all that is lost. All is submerged in that one experience of being with the shoreless beyond. This is a heightened experience, a heightened experience which perhaps one knows when one has watched with concentration also the constant incessant flow of a river when the flow itself is not consciously known perhaps, but it is the rhythm of the flow of the water, with which one identifies oneself. There are other common place experiences, specific and eternal. The most common place experience and the wonder of wonders is the rising and the setting sun, the cycle of the bright and dark moon, and yet this daily experience can contain within itself mysteries beyond words. One could go on adding examples of fire and of light. But in each case, the perceptions of the individual are unfettered moments though subscribed in physical time and space. For those moments, the duality dissolves and the individual becomes one with this vaster, bigger, undefined infinity which is the universal. This is the release here and now and this is the freedom and the beauty. This is what in India is termed as being *Vimukta*.

The heightened experience of culture is not restricted to these moments of release and freedom, but extends to the collective life of man. I do not have to tell you—you who are surrounded by this joy and beauty and celebration of each moment of impregnating this earth with seed and the auspicious moments of fruition of a cycle of vegetative growth. Now, both man's conscious effort of whether scattered seed or slash and burn or plough cultivation is expressed not through individual moment of complete wonder, mystery or joy, but it is collective in nature. The joy is the shared experience. Design, in line, design in movement, and design through song and music, is another aspect of reflecting the design and coherence of society revolving round material culture born from the effort of man. Now the simple task of making a living together assumes cosmic proportions. The heightened experience is not one in aloneness. It is collective. Here the individual loses himself in a group activity. Differentiations are lost. Function and ideation are hand in hand and the socio-cultural and artistic faces are almost indistinguishable. Thus what you would call the Human Sciences and the Departments of Literature, Language and the Creative Arts, and those of perhaps Agriculture, come together to provide the basis for understanding and, more, participating in this collective life where a heightened experience of harmony is possible. This is truly the aesthetic experience which India has recognised in the Sastras.

The uniqueness of India, I believe, lies in understanding this life phenomenon at the individual level, at the moment of complete silence and aloneness in communion with the natural environment and all other living matter and its perception of the collective harmony possible through human endeavour. Exactly as the outer and the inner environment of living matter and energy are dependent on each other, so also is the individual and the society. The efficacy of culture lies in arriving at a beautiful balance between these so that artistic experience and expression are possible. Life and art are not two but one continually renewing each other. The lesson Indian culture teaches us is perhaps the lesson of modern science. The findings of empirical modern science were the intuitive perceptions of the seers of India. They conceived of all life, all matter and energy as interdependent, convertible and were aware of a cosmic order which is possible only through the intricate interweaving of diverse elements in a total design. The design or the paradigm was not linear, hierarchical as is often believed or other-worldly, as has sometimes been said. It was holistic with clearly defined contours of the parts and the separate components, but they had all to be brought together in one total design. No part had an individuality or was capable of survival in isolation or in insularity. Repeatedly the question is asked: can the part live without the whole? And repeatedly the answer is that although the whole may be divided into parts, no part can live or survive in isolation.

The cultural heritage of India can be summed up then in just two sentences. It lies in the recognition of sustaining an inner landscape of man, which is the centre unseen, and the recognition that it expresses itself in an outer landscape of man comprising myriad petals of a lotus flower. Whenever and however this vision may have to come to this country, it is clear that had this not been the guiding star of this civilisation and culture, it would not have been possible for it to sustain the staggering multiplicity of races, languages, religions, philosophical systems, social structures, artistic expression. The proverbial staggering multiplicity of this nation is held together as planets are held together in an astronomical orbit. Each planet has its own life and distinctiveness. However, its life depends on its being part of an astronomical orbit. Stated differently, whether it is the North-East or the North-West, the North or the South, the East or the West, the Himalayas or tribals or the rural populations, or the cosmopolitan cities of India, these are all the rainbow colours of a single white luminosity which we may call the Indianness of India. The real Indianness is perhaps unseen, intangible, almost like that heightened experience of the shape of the mountain or the ocean or the river flowering, but it is a real experience. The recognition of this inner unseen, but real Indianness, articulated itself in many aesthetic theories which could be applied uniformly to all regions and periods because these were really born out of the experience of the Indian at all levels of society cutting across the differentiation which we often talk about in terms of tribal, rural and industrialised or urban India. Whether it is the oral poetry of tribal India, of the Todas, or the Khasis, the Garos, the Nagas and the Mizos, or the oral sophisticated system of communication of Vedic poetry, there was an underlying unity, the underlying unity was in its perception in regard to the wholeness of the universe, man and nature relationship, man and nature being interdependent and not hostile. Myths of the tribal India grew into mighty archetypes of classic India, and classical India impregnated rural and tribal India.

What appears to the ordinary layman as great differentiation in architectural styles ranging from the lonely huts, the machans of your area, the architectural schools known throughout Indian history, whether of the *stupas* or the temples or even the mosques and the churches, underlying them all is this world-view. The mud walls, the brick and stone ground or elevation plans, are an orchestration of multiple form flowing out and flowing into a centre. Invariably, there is the centre. Invariably domestic or high architecture begins with a point of unity and manifests itself through a spectrum of multiple form which in turn invokes harmony and equanimity. Perhaps the experience of the mountain, the hill and the experience of the ascension to the heavens gives rise to the idea of the Meru in Indian culture and known to other cultures. In its totality, humble or grand architecture represents this heaven on earth, the central mountain. It represents also a cosmic order on earth arousing wonder in man, the same wonder as that wonder which the lonely man knew when he looked at the mountain. Then this is a transcendental experience of bliss. The observer, participator or pilgrim, in the case of the mountain, moves from his inside to the outside of the mountain and rose above in a moment in which almost gravity was lost. In the man-made mountain, the temple or the *stupa*, the church or the mosque, he moves from the outside to the inside, circumambulates the *stupa* or the temple or the mosque until he reaches that centre which represents that ultimate—the *Shunya*, the *Nirvana*, or the *Moksha*. Figuratively, he is always ascending that pinnacle whether in the austere simplicity of the spherical dome or the *stupa* or the masjid or the crowded multiplicity of the temple. Impersonality and intensity are the twin paradoxical demands of this experience which is life-bound and beyond it. The architectural heritage of India exemplified by dwellings, high or low, bear testimony of the concretization of this vision through a perfect language of art which was universal, pan-Indian as specific in time, region or locality and yet universal. One could go on to give other examples from Indian sculpture, painting, music and above all dance. But this vision which I have been speaking about, the vision of a totality born and determined by the outer environment, but experienced through the inner environment, gives rise to something which you are familiar with, but the significance of which perhaps you have not thought about. It was only in this culture that gradually over a period of time was evolved the concept of the multiple faces and the multiple arms of single deities. Why was this? And it was this paradigm of the multiple armed images and the multiple faces which repelled the European and the Westerner including a Goethe. Looked at more closely, it was the concretisation of an inner abstract vision. It was and is also almost an ecological statement, a geographical statement, a statement of zoology and botany, a statement of psychology, and a statement of the inner perception of unity as it expresses itself in multiple concrete form. These images are not historical portraiture of the specific. They do not belong to time and space, a particular region. Yes, they are clearly identifiable and distinguishable. However, each image is an embodiment of a dominant abstract and personalised state of mood in a given stance or pose evoking at the same moment stasis and dynamism together. Each is a complete world unto itself, related to life around it, born of that life, part of the specific cultural fabric, but not it. Buddha is Buddha, the historical prince Siddhartha and Sakyamuni. But perhaps that was only the beginning. He is more compassion, pathos, grace in the absolute. The spirit and soul of the cosmic infinite is contained in the body particular but in impersonal form. But Buddha is without many arms. Let us take the image of Shiva, Vishnu or other countless images which are made in tribal India throughout. Each image contains within itself both the benign and the demonic, both the static and the dynamic, both the moment of birth and the moment of death, or more particularly the whole process of creation, of involution, evolution and devolution. Each sculptural form in India ranging from a particular stock of lotus or vegetative growth or animals, or Gandharvas and the Apsaras, and the human form in different poses with diverse arms in standing, sitting, flying poses, is but the vehicle of a totality, a soul meaning a concrete embodiment of an innermost stratum of a human value in its universal validity and meaning. Each image is a juxtaposition of the various cosmic forces ranging from the flora and fauna, the animal life, the water, earth, space, fire, sky principles, the terrestrial and celestial, and a manifestation of multiplicity of human endeavour. Just as collectively in the dance, the individual was lost, so also conversely in these images, through the one, the collective in communicated.

Let us come nearer home to something perhaps which you have participated in but which you have just considered as a presentation art in your Creative Arts Department. That is all that you do by way of a dramatic experience in music and dance. This music and dance emerges out of the outer environment. The North and the East, the hill and the flora and fauna, and the animal life and the vegetative patterns, the Jhum culture and sowing of seeds, the matrilinear system of the Khasis, of the Garos, and yet in its ultimate expression is the expression of a totality, of an impersonalised emotion and dominant mood with a multiplicity of sound, movement and rhythm and for that one moment, the collective dance becomes eternal and universal. This dance, whether it consecrates the moment of the sowing of the seed or that of the harvest or the clearing of forests through fire or the consecration of the deity of the snake, or the loud and tempestuous sounds of the drums of the Garos, is a part and parcel of this outer environment, but it becomes experience of beatitude. The two together are born of life, are life and yet different, almost transcendental. This is heightened aesthetic experience. There is no differentiation at that moment between the creator, the performer and the participator, and in that moment of collective experience of this song and dance, this drama, there is the re-enactment of the beginning of life in its eternal rhythm of stasis and dynamism, in its rhythm of creation of involution, evolution and devolution. This is what one would call man's ultimate worship.

Have I moved beyond the parameters of what I said I would talk about, namely, merely the name of your University and what it stands for? No. In this rather detoured manner of presentation, I have wanted to share some of my thoughts with you today at this moment of your life, when from the structured institutional university, you will now perhaps move out into the outer environment of life and life experience, first perhaps the North-East and then India and then the world. The University tried to bring the ecology, the flora and fauna, and the life styles into a modern structure. If that cerebral understanding becomes an experience of life, it will be true graduation. The test and challenge of the education you have received here will be only when through the very medium of this university, you will not restrict yourself to the courses, and information and knowledge gathered, but will communicate it in life experience when the inner self must necessarily inter-act with the outward environment, natural, human, social and artistic. In doing so, you will transcend the boundaries of both your region and your university. If this happens, then truly, the University is a university which has cultivated in you a universal mind and a universal spirit which belongs to you, transcending narrow barriers of fragmentation, a danger which we all face precisely because somewhere, somehow along the line, the cosmic balance of the parts and the whole, of nature and man, of the flora and fauna and the animal and the human, and the ecological and societal, have been disturbed. The modern educated mind, the educated individual self's only duty and *dharma* is the restoration of these balances so that Man may live. Never before in human history has man stood at the precipice of his own annihilation, and never before has he had more power to shape his destinies for a new universal order. If the inner and the outer can be sustained through a silent still centre and dynamic action, remembering finite limitations and yet the capacity for infinite possibilities of enlargement in harmony, there is hope. The future is in your hands, to shape, for survival and more for beatitude.

(19 November 1983)

2.

Manipur University, Imphal

Allow me first and foremost to express my sincerest gratitude for this rare honour you have bestowed on me today.

I have neither language, nor words, nor song, nor gesture to reciprocate adequately. As one who considers herself nurtured by the beauty of Manipur, this jewel of jewels, I am deeply aware that in 'my making', as in the making of perhaps many other Indians, Manipur, and what it stands for, has played a crucial role.

Today when the refined and sophisticated artistic expressions of Manipur scatter their fragrance in India and in all other parts of the globe, there is a sense of pride as also of gratitude. There was a time not in the remote past when the name of the word Manipur brought different images to people's mind. Some full of beauty, culture and refinement, others of a distant small land, disconnected with the hustle and bustle of what may have been termed as the mainstreams of plains of India. Within a few decades, these images have disappeared and have been replaced by a single image where Manipur stands as an example of the processes of Indian culture at its finest and most refined. As in its natural environment where the mountains, lakes and valleys come together to make a beautiful whole, so in its human environment and culture, traditions going back to unmeasured antiquity, along with a young and dynamic youth, Manipur is in the forefront of many dimensions of contemporary India—be its sports, music, dance, drama, theatre, literature, handicrafts, women movements, scientific achievements in the field of earth and natural sciences and much else. For all this you must be complimented. Moreover, other communities of India have a lesson to learn from the manner in which you have been able to create a symbiosis between the past and the present, tradition and modernity, regional identity and national unity.

The Manipur University, though young as an institution, appropriately incorporates the richness of an ancient tradition which permeates into the lifestyle of every hamlet and home, tree and forests, Umang Lais temples and *Sankirtana Mandapas*. It is not therefore surprising that one of the first aims of this University should be to foster the composite culture of India and to establish such departments or institutions as may be required for the study and development of languages, arts and culture of India and in particular those in the north-eastern region of the country. Equally important is its goal to promote an awareness as an example of a happy blending of the cultures of both India and Southeast Asia and provide for the study of culture of Manipur in this wider context.

Today at this moment when my young friends are leaving the University to enter into the life of work and activity, it is perhaps necessary to articulate once again even, at the cost of some repetition, universal aspirations as also the specific goals of education and national integration in the context of India. Fundamental to both these is the perennial quest of man to move from the gross to the subtle, from the individual to the collective, from the narrow parochial to the universal, from the mortal to the immortal. Let me then begin perhaps with identifying what are the most fundamental crisis facing humanity before we go on to the question of how education and the processes of education can be the single most important human tool of averting the threat to survival.

At this moment of world civilization when man has delved more deeply and extensively into the nature of phenomena, as never before in human history, he also stands at the brink of a precipice which can cause disaster to the earth he stands upon and he himself threatens the life of the human species.

Natural and environmental pollution and ecological imbalances created by Man and penetration into space and nuclear arms are imminent threats to survival. In India while the second many seem distant, the first surrounds us along with the prospects of dealing with vast numbers of a new generation. In such a situation of gravity, internationally and nationally education as *Shiksha* (learning) and education as *Vidya* (science to explore, to know) is the single most crucial aspect of development which will enable *Humanity* to have the perceptivity, the *vivek*, to ensure survival of life on this planet, and create conditions, physical and psychical, for a harmonious future.

Never before the wisdom of ancient India of the concepts of *rta* (a cosmic order, celestial and terrestrial), of the inter-relationship of man and nature, of the juxtaposition of freedom and discipline, the balance between the life of reflection and action, of harmony between the inner stillness and outer dynamic energy for the good of all *buhurjan hitaye*, of the inter-dependability of the twin birds on a single branch of the Svetasvare and Manduka Upanishad (of the *bhokta* and *drsta*, the experiencer and the vigilant alert observer) become more pertinent than today. Education is the instrument through which this imbalance can be corrected once again to establish man-nature dialogue.

Ancient and even medieval India had evolved a system of education which aimed at developing full potential of the human being in varying contexts and situations. A judicious balance of refinement of sensibility, working with hands, of inculcating ability for creative expression and sharpening of intellect was maintained.

The spirit of questioning, of a quest for knowledge, is reflected most powerfully in that dialogue between Nachiketa and Yama in the Katha Upanishad. The dialogue between Nachiketa and Yama symbolises, in one intense moment, Man's quest for knowledge and that which lies beyond the pale of physical death.

In India, education was this quest for the unknown, unknown in the deepest recesses of the individual human psyche, and unknown in the formless beyond the world of multiple forms. The spirit of enquiry enshrined in ancient India was the scientific temper we speak of today. Had it not been for this spirit of enquiry and of the fundamental commitment to the principles of co-existence, it would not have been possible for this culture to contain the staggering multiplicity of races, languages, religions. The principle of a unity permeating all manifestation, plural and diverse, is illustrated time and again in the questions and answers between teacher and pupil. Of these, the dialogue between Shvetaketu and his son assumes great pertinence and significance, be it the famous story of "breaking the fig" or "putting salt into water" empirical experiments.

Dedication to duty, of relating knowledge to action, was crucial in such a system.

It was these ideals which enabled India to sustain a continuity despite political vicissitudes and conquests. However, as we all know, in course of time a cleavage took place between the speculative and the empirical, the written and the oral, the regional and the national, the sophisticated urban and the rural, the *margi* and the *desi*. A model of inter-connectedness of inter-webbing unity and oneness of goal and plurality of forms and expressions was replaced by a fragmentation and aggregation. The indigenous model of both education and culture was of defined roles, recognition of differentiation and the relationship of the parts to the whole. Inter-connectedness and inter-dependence, consensus, co-existence were its mechanism of cohesiveness. Alas, this was replaced by fragmenting the parts, placing them in a hierarchical order and replacing the consensus model by a conflict model. Resultantly, during the last 200 years Chasm and Schism of many kinds developed, not the least between the formal systems of education and the rich and varied artistic and cultural traditions of India. The few educated and the large human resource outside the system communicated but not fully with each other. Manipur, as some other parts of India, has also faced this problem and perhaps the measure of the success of this University will lie in its ability to create these bridges of communication between the institutional formal system and the pervasive cultural and technical richness which lies all over.

I have no doubt that in your curricula and in your programmes you have already created the environment of this fusing to take place. Perhaps the crucial test of your education will be when those of you who are entering into life will ask yourself this question more pointedly and more consciously, i.e., what is it that I can give and what is it that I can receive from the large human reservoir of community resources?

Before we move from this fundamental level of the crises facing humanity and education as a tool for restoring balances, let me take the liberty of drawing your own attention to how this man-nature dialogue and communication is re-enacted in Manipur in the vast number of fairs, festivals and rituals. Whether it is the totality of the *Lal Haraoba* or the *Rasa* dances or the *Sankirtana*, it is a symbolic re-creation of life from the seed in the waters to vegetative life, herbs, and trees. This principal re-creation is enacted month after month, year after year, only so that the community is reminded through a collective performance of the symbiosis between the man and nature. It would be presumptuous on my part to analyse at some length the significance of these rituals in terms of the sacred plants, songs of music, the gestures of dance and processes, through a number of days, when the relationship of sun, moon and the stars, water, earth, fire, forests and human life is re-created. Some of you are aware of it, other perhaps go through it as mere ritual and some others only as an entertainment. The revoking of the essential symbolism of such community participation in all its speculative and scientific dimensions is a task which only a University can fulfil.

Perhaps there will be another occasion to suggest ways and means of studying as also rejuvenating the essence of these traditions of great antiquity and significance. Their validity is increased on account of man's facing these primary crises of having cut himself away from processes of the vegetative, of animal and natural world which sustain human life.

Now let us turn our attention to another problem, a problem which is recent but has begun on ugly proportions in India, and I refer here to what constitutes national integration in the context of India.

When Tagore wrote that famous poem, sometimes called a Utopian Prayer, beginning: "Where the mind is without fear and the head is held high"........ or when he composed that other poem which is India's National Anthem, "Jana Gana Mana", or earlier when Bankim called out to Mother India, "Vande Mataram.... Sujalam, Suphalam, Malayala Shitalam".... or when Bharathi spoke of "breaking the fetters", or when Iqbal called out "Sare Jahan Se Achha", or earlier further back in history when the Rig Vedic seers spoke of concord of the community of men and the coming together of many, of *Vasudeva Kutumbakam*, were these men and seers speaking of education or national integration? Did they have in mind, a dichotomy or a dialogue between the human individual or a soul belonging to this earth, here and now, and yet making the fulsome communion with nature, earth, the spirits of the trees, and joy of the experience of the incessant movement of the Sun and the Moon, night and day, or were they calling out for a kind of an arbitrary, an artificial national integration as an intellectual effort of bringing together intrinsically disparate heterogeneous units in a moment of great emotional and political crisis?

No. The answer clearly is, No. Because for them, as for others in India—leaders, thinkers, seers, poets, musicians, saints—ancient and modern life and the process of human growth and development was a continuous education, learning and experience of the totality. This basic and fundamental difference in approach towards both education and national integration will make it clear that in the Indian situation or in the situation of all plural cultures, which have been held together by a community of ideas and a cohesive life style, education is the touch-stone by which life is measured. Education then is not a matter of individual attainment of specific skills but is a ceaseless process of expanding the self, to embrace larger and larger areas of human consciousness and to contain differentiations. Education first and last is the growth of the total personality where the inner and outer are harmoniously balanced, where the movement is from the gross to the subtle and from the understanding of the one within to the many without. The process is continuous, beginning with birth, going on and culminating in the wisdom and experience before the moment of death.

Where does Education begin then? It begins at the moment of birth. The warm security provided by the mother in biological terms, is transmuted into emotional security given to the child for life. This sense of security, physical and emotional, is his first sense of birth identity, the first lesson at attuning himself as a separate being to that other—the mother. This is an educational experience. From this moment to the next of perceptions through sensory and motor responses to darkness and light, to taste and smell, movement and stillness, awakening and sleeping, the educative experience is full every minute before any formal education begins. Gradually it all falls into place and we understand that as simple routine but it is not so simple, because it is these first moments of education which provide the basis for a life-long journey of learning. The two together, the human and the natural environment, then enlarge themselves into the environment of kinship patterns, on the one hand, and making adjustments with the natural, physical, ecological environment and then, later, societal environment. These fundamental experiences are the core, involving an assertion or recognition of a distinctive identity and yet the indispensable need of communication, atonement and harmony. These remain always. When enlarged to individuals, societies, regions or nations, they call for two fundamental demands of the human psyche, one freedom and the other discipline. Freedom born out of discipline and discipline or order born out of the very freedom of the spirit.

Now, let's come to national integration comprising both the concept of a nation as also integration. What is meant by this? The notion of national integration for some implies challenges of the incompatible, the creation of a conceptual or a superimposed uniformity in the mistaken belief that a multi-racial, multi-linguistic, multi-caste, multi-regional culture can only be integrated by a code of external conduct or an artificially nurtured uniformity which eschews differentiation. Perhaps this was the reason for some to come to the conclusion that in the Indian context the notion of a nation itself is a western gift of the 19th century. However, a closer look will reveal that different races, languages, communities, castes, religions in this country of ours have all been a single unified organism which has its different parts. National integration in the Indian context is only or should only be the opening of that third eye of perception which can see the reality of this organism, the process of growth behind what appears as a staggering multiplicity of races, languages, social structures, regions, art forms, life-styles. How then can education be the single tool or the most important vehicle for opening this third eye of perception where differentiation or respect for that other can be cultivated without a loss of freedom or identity, yet with a sense of not only deliberate or matured tolerance but joy, and therefore create a milieu of harmony?

Let's take the analogy of the human body. Does one ever talk about the integration of a little finger with the heart, or the integration of a circulatory system with the digestive system? Is it not a fact of life that each of these are inter-connected and inter-dependent in all the diverse and distinct systems by which the anatomy and physiology of our body is governed? Each has its own identity, place, important function in the body. It cannot exist without the other. It was this image of man which was used as a basic philosophic concept in the Indian tradition—*Purusha* as the microcosm and *purush* as the macrocosm. These concepts brought home repeatedly the message that while each part is important, clearly differentiated, it has no place and identity unless seen in its function as a whole.

The education of the young and old, men and women, was then a continuous process but through different paths. Sometimes, it was the transmission of the sacred word, the *shruti* from the teacher to the pupil, from the Guru to the *sishya*, at other times it was the written word and simpler still and more potent, it was through the strategies which this country evolved, through pilgrimages, festivals, functions, daily, weekly, annual calendar, the fairs and melas; these were and are the milestones of the educational experience outside the formal system but equally, if not more, important for integration.

But we are no longer either in ancient India or in medieval India where at all times arose both integrators and creators, such as the saints, gurus, pirs, fakirs drawn from the highest to the lowest classes. They ignored all precepts of standardisation, classification, purism and pietism in the fields of whether it was worship or language, sound, meaning, music, social conduct and metaphysical belief. These were the great integrators of this culture, whether it was Farid or a Khusro, a Jayasee or a Tulsi, or a Sur, or a Nanak. These were the integrators in some ways who brought about the bridges of communication between the tribal, the rural and urban levels of society. This problem continues in India, and in terms of integration, without harking back to the past, one might identify the tensions that exist on four levels despite all conceptual unity. One, the seething tension between or amongst tribal, rural and urban levels of society, second, tension which arises as aberrations amongst languages; three, tension which arises sometimes again as aberrations amongst religions and four, tension which arises because of the disperate level of economy or education in rural agricultural levels and urban industrialised levels.

What part can education play in not only resolving this but making it into a creative effort? Delicate balances have to be found, new orders have to be maintained between the full flowering of regional identity and an equally strong perception of mutual dependence of regions and a continuous sustained awareness of being parts of a single whole. This is inculcation of a sense of community and the enlarged self which can contain differentiations of 650 million. The task is both challenging and difficult. It is no different than the challenge that was faced by Arjuna when he went into the war of Mahabharata. And therefore it became important for Krishna to reveal himself as the *Vishvarupa* in the 11th Chapter to show that whether it was regional identities, egos, languages, societies, religions they were all contained in that one.

The educational process is perhaps that moment where the Arjuna saw the vision of Krishna in his *Viratarupa*. Then the two identities are known and the path of action is clear. Nearer home let us recall a speech of Jawaharlal Nehru delivered as a Convocation Address in 1949 which is relevant today, and I quote:

> A university stands for humanism, for tolerance, for reason, for progress, for the adventure of ideas and for the search for truth. It stands for the onward march of the human race towards even higher objectives. If the educational institutions discharge their duties adequately, then it is well within the nation and the people. But if the temple of learning itself becomes a home of narrow bigotry and petty objectives, how then will the nation prosper or a people grow in stature?.....

And then he goes on to say. I quote:

> Let us be clear about our national objective. We aim at a strong, free, democratic India where every citizen has an equal place and full opportunity of growth and service, where present day inequalities in wealth, status and educational opportunities have ceased to be, where our vital impulses are directed to creative and cooperative endeavour. In such an Indian communalism, separatism, isolation, untouchability, bigotry and exploitation of man by man have no place and while religion is free, it is not allowed to interfere with the political and economic aspects of a nation's life. If that is so, then all this business of Hindu and

> Muslim and Christian and Sikh must cease in so far as our political life is concerned and we must build a united but composite nation where both individual and national freedom are secure.

Indeed Jawaharlal Nehru was articulating a perennial truth expressed in the Rig Veda:

> "United your resolve
> United your hearts
> may your spirits be one
> that you may long together dwell
> in unity and concord."

However, much has happened even between 1949–87. Despite the Commissions and the efforts made by national and State Governments, the comprehensive report of the Kothari Commission, the Educational Policy of 1968, the clarion calls of our political leaders, the inspiration of our poets, the achievements of our scientists and the inspirations of the masses of India, there was the need of enunciating the New Educational Policy. And what has this policy enunciated and why?

New Educational Policy: Recognising both the goals of an accelerated pace of development as also the need to maintain a continuity with the rich and varied cultural traditions of India, the new educational policy seeks to:

1. Bridge the gap between the formal educational system and the diverse and multiple systems of cultural experience still alive and obtainable in the community.
2. The goals of this cultural and artistic component in education is to inculcate a perception of the totality of India with all its plurality and multiplicity of natural and cultural phenomenon, races, religions, languages where each is a part of a whole.
3. To develop a sense of individual, local and regional identity along with an equal ability to respect and appreciate differentiation, in short, tolerance and catholicity of views.
4. To refine sense perceptions individually as also collectively with a view to experience joy and fulfilment in both solitude and participation, i.e., harmony and peace, inside and outside.
5. To develop manual and cerebral skills which enable the individual and social group to explore the past with discrimination in its aspects of validity in contemporaneity, in short, discrimination, "vivek".

6. To develop attitudes of questioning exploration, adventure, be it in the sphere of natural phenomenon, physical sciences or the cultural heritage.
7. To develop capacity to innovate, improvise and be creative in all situation and milieus.
8. To develop a capacity to perceive the inter-relationship and inter-dependence of levels of society (affluent and impoverished), rural, urban, regions, nations as also the world of science and the world of refined culture, of knowledge, of speculative thought as also action and above all a consistency between precept and conduct.
9. To utilise the arts not so much as professional skill but more as instruments of fostering human values, especially of harmony, balance and non-violence.

Strategies for achieving these goals can be diverse responding to the specific needs of the different cultural regions, stages of education, the different systems, formal and non-formal and the diverse institutional systems. Modifications in the content of curricula, training of teachers, awareness programmes have to be carried out. Zonal centres, institutions of higher education in the fields of humanity, i.e., science and technology, archaeology, languages, have to be systematically utilised to evolve programmes to meet these goals.

In this context the young University of Manipur has a significant role to play. It can use its regional natural and human resources, to the maximum to bring about a meaningful symbiosis between ancient and modern knowledge, the rich oral traditions and means of communication and textual and archaeology, evidence, natural sciences and humanities, and between the wisdom and rigour of disciplines of the older generation and fresh energy of the younger generation.

This valley, always a jewel of natural beauty and human sensibility and the incredibly regional artistic traditions, is indeed '*Mani*' (pearl) rare and pure for the entire subcontinent. It is in your hands to make the future by nurturing the roots and allowing fresh leaves to continually bloom and flown, never forgetting that the roots, the trunks and the branches and the ever changing leaves are integral to the essential oneness of not only India but the world in perpetual stillness and flux.

(14 May 1988)

3.

National Institute of Design, Ahmedabad

Thank you for inviting me to be with you on this auspicious day. The honour you have bestowed upon me is undeserved and I feel inadequate to address so distinguished a gathering comprising men of distinction from so many disciplines; all converging, inter-meshing in the single total discipline of 'Design'.

What can I say to you at this moment, when you have mastered the skills of form, industrial or visual communication, and when you have explored in some depth and breadth of perception of the user's needs, evolved new modes of production and communication?

Although unnecessary and repetitive, perhaps a brief historical overview of the changed milieu and context in which the need for a new discipline of 'Design' emerged as distinct from 'art', 'craft', 'life-style' and life process, would be pertinent, specially a century or two before Charles Eames emerged.

Although I shall not burden you with dates and figures, much of it you know, but it is pertinent to recall that the tacit philosophic premise of the emergence of such an all-encompassing concept lay in the breakdown of a coherent cultural life-style. As we know, life function and art and craft were not dissociated in pre-industrialised societies: this is still true of traditional societies or whom we choose to call backward in socio-economic terms. In each of these culturally cohesive societies 'creativity' was recognised as essential and ordinary, as the act of breathing. Art-creations of things and product was intrinsic to the act of living. From birth to death life was punctuated with key moment of time when objects, products created were given meaning and significance as 'signifiers' and symbols beyond their form. This ranged from the process and expressions in all 'media', from song to movement, from floral design to floor and mud paintings, to mobiles of toys to the making of rattles and 'cots'. All sense perceptions came to play and a totality was created by cultivating a distinctive sense of sight, hearing, scent, touch and taste. Each sense perception was sought to be refined in singleness and confluence in a manner that the sense perception became the vehicle of 'experience'. In turn they were tools of manifestation, containers of the vitality of the 'creations' and herein was embedded their power of communication between creator and audience. The manifestation in diverse media was conditioned in part or whole by a cultural context of man and nature inter-relationship, mother-child, individual-society, inter-webbing and an avowed faith in a world-view where a system of correspondence was recognised between the micro and macro. In artistic terms we called it the language of myth and symbol. At each moment 'form' was both functional and symbolic. It was in time, place, context, historical, social, economic, religions concurrently. Consequently significant 'form' was a micro-model of a macro-universe. Object was also signifier of process and experience. 'Function'—'Utility' and 'Beauty' were not disconnected. No quantitative hierarchical categorisation of Fine Art and 'Craft' was necessary or viable.

This is the history of cultures throughout the world, not restricted to the developed or underdeveloped world. The life-death life-cycle was complemented by the awareness of another cycle of the movement of the earth the solar and lunar astronomical orbit. Life function—daily, monthly, annual time—was not mere passage from one to other second in a sequential linear order, but was instead only a reminder of the incessant movement of the planets in cyclicity. Man's needs from food gathering to sowing, harvesting, making of utensils, clothes, modes of transportation, harnessing of natural resources were all organised on a tacit acceptance and sometimes clearly articulated awareness of an eco-system of the micro-man and macro universe. Naturally everything fell into place because there was a multi-layered concurrency of 'form', meaning and value of the physical and metaphysical, space, circumscribed or free at micro-macro dimensions. While the levels and layers could be differentiated, the experience was of the 'whole', the total in its multi-layered inter-webbing and inter-relatedness. Logically no absolute categorisation could be made between the secular and sacred, the terrestrial and celestial or time past, present and future. Transmutation/transubstantiation was the norm, and not the exception.

Beginning with the European Renaissance, itself the product of many influences from West Asia and East Asia, and developments in the fundamental sciences, the first disjunction took place, because no longer was 'man-in-nature' one amongst all living beings interrelated to inorganic and organic matter. He was the centre of the universe, the conqueror of nature. Without recalling all that happened in history of mankind during this period, it is necessary to note that two important developments took place which effected the 'arts' and notion of 'creativity' and function. Individuation or individual as 'creator' apart, distinct from others not 'creative', was recognised. The communication between the earth and the sky, the 'waters' of eternity and the fire energy within the waters was defranchised. It was not primary or secondary forms in conjunction; each element began to be isolated. Disjunction and aggregation and a linear order of cause and effect came into being. Material Earth, not planet earth, was the beginning of physical and psychical bipolarities.

The industrial revolution although coming three centuries later was not unlinked with the beginnings made during the European Renaissance. Man was no longer in Nature. He perceived and objectified 'nature'. Earth was no longer giver, sustainer, but resource to be exploited, water no longer the symbol of the relationship of the ocean and the sky. Disjunction —and fragmentation—had begun. The extension of man's limb was the 'machine' and the machine in turn brought about the unrevocable disjunction between function and art, life-function and beauty, and the great divide between 'producers' and 'consumers'. The human condition was not an isolated phenomenon in what we call industrialised societies, but reflected a much deeper fissure in the mind of Man. The moment of dissociating life function and art/craft was the moment of also accepting the dissociation of Senses, Body, Mind, Intellect and Spirit from each other. Sense-perceptions in one stroke, and all that they stood for as the instrumentality of refinement of the gross to the subtle, became a matter of gratification, titillation of profanity. Senses and Body stood disjointed from the life of the mind and consciousness. Both at the individual level, as also collective level, isolated islands or particles in competition rather than complementary were recognised. The moment of disregard or non-acceptance of mutual interdependability of the elements of man and nature, of individual and society, became the moment of making a multi-layered system into a 'unidimensional' phenomenon in defined time. 'Art' was 'product' dissociated from life function. It was decontextualized. Naturally a culture of wastage replaced the culture of eco-recycling. Individual creations dissociated from life-perception became Art, collective or community creations in a coherent social group Craft. The first aspired to the universal by transcending context, the latter became an object of decoration when torn out of its context of life-function—life-symbolism. The *lota*, your 'symbol', was reduced from the great *purnaghata* representing void and fullness to a pitcher or pure utility. The background of the breakdown of the holistic multi-layered multi- discipline system into fragmented moments of time and units of 'space', could not but result in *products* being totally 'decontextualized' at mundane and sacred levels.

The debate in the early part of the twentieth century spearheaded by Coomaraswamy and Eric Gill, etc., was the first outcry against the loss of the whole and the holy tradition of working and the lamentable disjunction between function and art. Article after article, essay after essay is an outburst against the gradual but sweeping impact of the movement of fragmentation. Perhaps the following quotes from the volume 'A Holy Tradition of Working—Passages from the writings of Eric Grill', Golgonooza Press, Suffolk, UK, 1983, will recall the anguish of these prophetic voices:

> "With the division of 'art' from 'work' and 'beauty' from 'use' in the modern world, art comes out of the artist and gets attached, so to say, to the work of art itself. The creator of 'art', now called an 'artist', personifies art and is given the sole prerogative of its production. Beauty too comes out of the thing made to be an aesthetic sensation desired for its own sake. No longer the property of a thing that shows forth the fullness of integrity, harmony and intelligible clarity due to its being; no longer identified with goodness and truth, beauty is now associated with a select category of things made. As an aid to emotional stimulus, beauty is freed from the process of rational manufacture so that art has become 'pure' or 'fine' and as such is treated idealistically. The workman is no longer expected to be in *possession* of his art; 'art' and 'work' are distinct, even opposed, orders of making. Moreover, 'art' becomes a snob value and the word 'art' actually comes to denote the objects that comprise this artificially isolated category of things whose value is maintained in the interests of social prestige. Indeed, the modern world speaks of 'art' instead of 'works of art' because this artificial isolation makes it necessary to distinguish 'art' from 'non-art' in the category of things made."

Blake had anticipated Eric Gill by a century in a memorable poem, he wrote:

> .... all the Arts of Life they chang'd into the arts of Death in Albion.
> The hour-glass contemn'd because its simple workmanship
> Was like the workmanship of the ploughman, and the water wheel
> That raises water into cisterns, broken and burn'd with fire
> Because its workmanship was like the workmanship of the shepherd;
> And in their stead, intricate wheels invented, wheel without wheel,
> To perplex youth in their outgoings & to bind to labours in Albion

Of day & night the myriads of eternity; that they may grind
And polish brass & iron hour after hour, laborious task,
Kept ignorant of its use: that they might spend the days of wisdom
In sorrowful drudgery to obtain a scanty pittance of bread,
In ignorance to view a small portion & think that All,
And call it Demonstration, blind to all the simple rules of life.

The questions asked were about man and nature:

There is a thing called Man and there is a thing called Nature—nature environs man.
Is man one with his environment?
Is he *precisely* one with it?
That is the atheist affirmation.
I have assumed that we deny it.
It is in accord with all our experience to deny it.
Walk about in a place removed from civilization—some bare moorland, or polar ice cap.
The common verdict of man is that in spite of his material harmony with his surroundings, his sharing in the life of birds and grasses, his dependence on air and warmth, he also stands outside, above, beyond, independent and aloof.
This proves nothing—but we are not here concerned with proofs but with verdicts, with affirmation.
We affirm our nature, not by the faulty instruments of induction and ratiocination, but by the convictions of experience.
You know it is so.

Consequently the definition of art was questioned at a fundamental level:

"Skill in making, the thing called art, degenerates into mere dexterity, i.e. skill in doing, when the workman, for whatever reason (.....) ceases to be concerned for the thing made or, having become a mere tool, a 'hand' in the employ of another, has no longer any responsibility for the thing made and has therefore lost the knowledge of what it is that he is making (....) In many factories the 'hands' cannot even know what they are *supposed* to be making. All their acts are deeds. All their acts are prudential acts. They polish this or twist the other simply because they are told to do so. They obey because their wage depends on it and they depend on their wage. The factory hand can only know what he is *doing*. What is being made is no concern of his.

(...) Art is skill in making; but the thing to be made must first of all be known in the mind. If it be not known in the mind it is obvious that no degree of surface finish or juggling with tools will bring it into existence. The trouble in those times and places where technical dexterity takes the place of skill in making is not at all in the fact of technical dexterity, for dexterity is in itself good. The trouble is simply the degradation of the mind. In such times and places the artist, the responsible

> workman is without clear ideas and without desire. He does not know what he is making; he does not see it clearly in his mind or he does not desire above all things to make it. (….)
>
> Art is skill in making; the good work is the skilful work, the work in which the appropriate means have been employed to effect the desired end. If inappropriate means have been employed, the end will not, cannot be achieved. Everything depends upon the nature of the end desired and ends are many and various. It is obvious that the workman must know what he wants to make before he begins the work; it is equally obvious that he must be able to make it or the thing will not be made. Knowing what is to be made is one thing, and knowledge is a thing which may be acquired by anyone; it is connatural to man to know what he desires and all men in consequence are potentially artists; but the word art means skill in making and the name of artist is reserved to him who has the skill to make things and does actually make them.

A requisitioning of the distinction between art and fine art began:

> The distinction between art and 'fine art' is, in every sense but one, a superstition —many superstitions are widespread, so the mere popularity of the distinction need not concern us (….)
>
> The idea that the distinction between art and fine art is that art is skill applied to the making of useful things and fine art is skill applied to the making of things of beauty, is clearly unreasonable—because there is no reason why useful things should not be beautiful, and there is no reason to suppose that beautiful things have no use. Are tables and chairs and houses and pottery necessarily ugly? Are portraits and statues and church paintings and wall decorations necessarily useless?
>
> And the idea that the beauty of useful things is accidental whereas, in the fine arts, it is the usefulness that is accidental, is equally unreasonable, for you cannot have beauty by itself, any more than you can have art or culture by themselves.
>
> But there is one sense in which the distinction between art and fine art is a possible one, and that is when we distinguish between the necessary arts, the arts necessary to the business of living, and the arts of *recreation*, the arts whose purpose is mental and physical recuperation—so that we return again to the arts of living, revived and refreshed.
>
> But even though the distinction between the arts of living and those of recreation is a valid one; and apart from the fact that such a distinction only makes the fine arts more useful than ever (for what is more useful and good than something which enables us to return to work refreshed?), even so, it is obvious that the distinction is one of category: a scientific division rather than one of nature.

Hardly had we come to terms to a recognition of what industrialism and mechanistic science had brought on its wake, the two World Wars, and more developments in science and technology, threw us into another vortex of being a global village threatened by sheer physical proximity, into the dangers of a total loss of cultural identity. The slow pace of age-old cultural influences which brought about change gradually and imperceptibly was overtaken by an avalanche of international movements/products/manifestation, travelling at jet speed, de-contextualised. Isolated phenomenon pieces of mirror flew from one part of the world went to East, and East to West, 'Form' shorn of it value loaded context was exported as product—be it 'yoga' in the west or 'cowboys', Hamburgers and all else in the East. Immediate consumption and 'form' without feeling and 'meaning' became watchwords.

'*Design*,' the new word, was one answer amongst others to renew the perception and creation of '*form*' in a new context or, I may even say, *No Context*. We had accepted that symbol and form had been disjointed and a disjunction had taken place, producers and consumers were absolute categories and the world of form '*Rupa*' was of the senses, of the Body and intellect, but perhaps not of Mind, consciousness, spirit.

Fruits of this tacit recognition of de-contextualisation and of rapid and swift influences were many, and have been many, none to be negated. A fragmented decontextualized society no longer connected at a psychical plane to a transcendental intangible but real centre and 'axis' was still in need for significant 'form,' functional form and the tool of sense perception and manual skills.

A whole new species of man-made technologies came into being. It was not only machines as understood immediately after industrialisation, but it was much more an explosion of new technologies. Each part of an assembly of products and expressions demanded different level of skill and technique. The new technologies and the new environment call for a new insight, if a human being, Man, is still to be the centre in control and not to be devoured by the creations of his own intellect, namely, the machine and the technologies.

Logically, a new discipline comprising other disciplines and, if I may use the term, an interdisciplinary discipline came into being, today well recognised as the autonomous discipline of Design.

As has been stated time and again in your documents, Design is both old and a very new discipline. You have achieved remarkable success through dedication and sensitivity and have brought about a new consciousness in regard to the need for creating a sense of 'order' to this our new disparate environment beginning with the reviving and sophistication of the form of objects, things: understandably the vision of the discipline has been enlarged and widened to include not just products but place, space, complex and most of all process. A recognition of the interrelatedness of the parts and the whole is obvious in the adventure into redesigning living space, habitat and rejuvenation of the traditional centres of pilgrimage and cultural importance. The various projects undertaken, specially of Sravaṣti Braj etc. clearly articulate the recognition of interrelation and inter-webbing. In short, from disjunction you have moved to junction and conjunction. For this, the institution, its founders, and those who have given it vision and direction, skill and insight, must be congratulated. Fundamentally, it is the recognition and self-awareness that a viable design of life in all its dimensions is of pivotal importance. Through a variety of paths and plurality of approaches, through the disjunctions created by our historical conditioning, we are at the threshold of a crucial junction. Whether it is through developments in the post-industrial society at the level of social, economic, political dynamics or it is at the level of the pursuit of intellectual disciplines, or most of all at the level of the new insights gained on Astrophysics and Mathematics, we have come full circle to realise that once more, as in the beginning of organic life on earth, we must first and foremost subscribe, be aware and conscious of this our earth as the literal and metaphorical ground on which we stand. So far it sustained and nurtured us, we exploited it, devastated it, desecrated it, polluted it. This was the disjunction we caused to the eco-system within man and the eco-system in which man was related to the earth and the elements. Today, the consciousness of man, ancient, perennial, has to be and is being regenerated, renewed. Modern Science has brought us to the same recognition of the intrinsic inter-relatedness and the inter-webbing of the parts and the whole and the phenomenon of a continuous transmutation of matter and energy and transferability of time and space and the multi-layered and polyvalence of meaning and value to that which we label 'form'.

Where does this take us in the context of your concerns and the life adventure which lies before you? The vistas of your exploration for the future will be, as the Ahmedabad Declarations said, the total design of living, not restricted to any particular level of society, tribal, rural, urban, or only to function and utility, but will be humanity at large and man, man and his life of 'introspection,' interiority as also outward action, arriving at a new balance as a challenge of the future. This balance has to come from within not negating the modern human condition nor reviving as 'design' piece of antiquity but will be and can only be a positive and meaningful symbiosis of the extra-ordinary powers that Science and Technology has brought us and the equal, if not more potent, power and the human resources with indigenous skills, materials and traditions which lie before us in this rich and diverse land of ours. The search will be a deeper search for evolving a viable design of life not fragmented into hierarchies: instead emphasising inter-relatedness and interconnectedness through a complex network. No longer would be evolution of form be restricted to either function, utility or beauty, but 'form' so created will have its intrinsic value as creativity in context, but will also have the capacity and potentiality for communication beyond context. This will be its last test.

The tenth annual convocation of this Institute held on April 18th had begun with an invocation from the *Taittiriyopanisad*. The excerpt chosen brings back our attention to the need for conjunction, links and interlocking. We have travelled the path of Science and Technology to arrive at an awareness of the interrelatedness. The Nobel Laureate D. Bohm had said: "One is led to a new notion of unbroken wholeness which denies the classical idea of analysability of the world into separately and independently existing parts.... We have reversed the usual classical notion that the independent "elementary parts" of the world are the fundamental reality, and that the various systems are merely particular contingent forms and arrangements of these parts. Rather, we say that inseparable quantum interconnectedness of the whole universe is the fundamental reality, and that relatively independently behaving parts are merely particular and contingent forms within this whole." The Indian seers have articulated these very insights from the well springs of intuition and experience. The 'conjunction' and the 'links' which the *Taittiriyopanisad* invokes is the interlocking dynamic system of the universe. The context of the verse is important. The universe in the *Taittiriyopanisad* is conceived as the five-fold and the five-layered system in which the individual is placed. *Taittiriya*, like the other Upanisads, had drawn attention to the 'five-fold' as a whole world. It is within this context that the significance of the inter-locking has to be understood. *Samhita*, *Sandhi*, *Rupa* and *Akasa* are the crucial words. They unlock for us the codes of the most complex system of concepts evolved centuries ago and which have validity here and now and for the future of mankind. Each of these relates to process, manifestation and micro and macro. *Samhita* and *Sandhi* are the confluence, confluence of elements, of space and of time. At this moment may this notion of *Samhita* and *Sandhi* of the earth and the sky, of fire and water and of the passing of the knowledge, *Vidya*, from the teacher to the pupil, be yours. Concerned with *Rupa*, form, may the recognition that all form emerges from non-differentiation from *Arupa* to *Rupa* to *Pratirupa* only to lead to the experience of the beyond the

Pararupa—be yours. May this be your journey and finally to 'Space', i.e. *Akasa*, *Akâsa* the word with the five-fold meaning and the five levels of perception of the inner and the outer, the infinitesimally small and the infinitely expanded. May its experience be yours. The *Chhandogya Upanisad* had told us: "As far, indeed, as the vast space outside extends the space within the heart. Within it, indeed, are contained both heaven and earth, fire and wind, sun and moon, lighting and the stars, both what one possesses here and what one does not possess all is contained in SPACE."

Does this sound to you a lot of ponderous, pious, *asirvachan* at a time when life lies fractured and fragmented? Perhaps, yes; perhaps, not. This is this significant moment, the threshold of human knowledge and experience in which we are all participants. Fragmentation of the intellect, stratification, arbitrary classification has brought us to a point where we all need a discriminating eye and an internal perception so that art and design is not a product but it is process of man within man. It was Coomaraswamy who said that: "Art is not a special category of manifestation. Each man or person is a distinctive artist". I can only hope that your adventures of the future will be the instrumentality of creating, recreating a new order, order I mean in the sense of the Sanskrit word *Rta*. A new order will no doubt take different forms in different contexts, but its vision will be unitary, unified. Unity of vision and plurality of forms would be the conjunction. I hope also that your endeavours will ensure to bring back the *Sandhi* between life and art 'form', meaning and value and will give a new refinement to the design and pattern of our living. In the beginning life was punctuated from birth to death as a series of design festivals. Each of these is still observed, but not without pollution and dilution. We are keenly made aware of this at the normal Sanskar ceremonies of Indian life. Perhaps a new design is necessary for the *Sanskars* as it is also necessary to bring back and rejuvenate the highly refined structure of the design of congregational festivals interspersed throughout our land. Once we enter these areas of life, i.e. life cycle and moments which consecrate time and place, then maybe it will be the beginning of a new journey of redesigning from a fragmented fractured human condition to a renewed organic whole.

(14 April 1989)

4.

Rabindra Bharati University, Calcutta

First and foremost, I would like to thank you for this rare honour you have bestowed upon me by inviting me to this twenty-second Convocation of the Rabindra Bharati University. I had communicated to the honourable Vice-Chancellor, time and again, my sense of inadequacy and awe to address a gathering which symbolises in spirit and form one of the most versatile towering figures of our times, and of all times—Gurudeva Rabindra Nath Tagore. The Vice-Chancellor replied that he would not take 'no' for answer. And so here I am, to share with you this auspicious and touching occasion of when you will leave the sylvan security of the university to enter into a new world of challenges and, in our day and time, of many choices, not unmixed with a bewildering complexity, even confusion.

For me it is an opportune moment to acknowledge unhesitatingly and unambiguously, like other Indians of my generation, a deep and un-repayable debt you and I owe to this creative genius who moulded our character and shaped our minds in the most formative years and also to this city Calcutta with its Chitpur Road, Ballygunj and Chowringhee and Shyam Bazar to the adjoining near and far-away Bolpur and Shatiniketan and to the whole of Bengal. As I travelled from the B.T. Road campus to the Jorasanko Campus last month, my mind was crowded with memories of childhood, each more poignant, inspiring and sustaining, even after a lapse of many, many decades. The centre, *kendra bindu*, of these memories was undoubtedly the life and work, the sensitive and penetrating voice of Gurudeva Tagore. The regular weekly meetings with him in Shantiniketan and the visits of his associates, poets and painters, to Calcutta punctuated our life in this town with its Loreto Convents and St. Zaviers, College Square book-stores, and much else. Along with reading, Highways and Bye-Ways of English Literature, we read and recited passages of Anandamath and Vande Mataram and quoted lines of *Gitanjali*, particularly "Where the mind is without fear and the head is held high", back to Gurudev himself. To him, and that generation of Indians born here, I pay my tribute. For, truly it was said then "What Bengal says today, India will do tomorrow."

I along with countless others were enriched and made 'whole', thanks to their instilling undying insatiable thirst for knowledge and a search for a national identity. This search was coupled with respect and openness for the other and the outsider. Truly our minds were shaped to break the chains of dead habit.

Today nearly fifty two years after his passing away and the passing by of many historical moments of Calcutta, Bengal, India and the world, we cannot rest content by paying homage and tribute on ceremonial occasions to these pathfinders. The moment is ripe to reflect and retrospect not with only a sense of nostalgia but also with analytical hindsight and perspective, so that we can have prospective and a prospectus for the future.

There could perhaps be no better place to do this, than a university, founded in his name, which is striving to concretise his vision through a programme of intellectual critical discourse as also creative experience of the arts, literary, visual and performative, here called 'fine' and the 'visual arts,' along with Bengali literature and a department of Tagore studies. In keeping with his ideals and catholic open minded attitudes, the University embraces many disciplines from vedic studies to philosophy, history, economics, political science, literary sciences, information technology, and much else. Perhaps, in the near or distant future there will be departments of fundamental science and mathematics. When I visited the University last month, I was deeply impressed with the range of subjects, and the syllabus. Equally impressive was the intellectual vitality of the faculty. All this is welcome. I learnt much from this short visit, although I have had the pleasure of interacting earlier with many departments and core members of the faculty, particularly those of the departments of vedic and Sanskrit studies and those of the Faculty of the Arts. I would like to felicitate them for their many achievements, intellectual and artistic, and specially congratulate the Vice-Chancellor for providing leadership and guidance to a community of scholars, researchers and students.

Nevertheless, as I said, this is an opportune moment to reflect and introspect on the state of ourselves, the country Bengal, Calcutta and the University System and this University. As far back as 1906, 1908, 1911 and 1912, Gurudeva Tagore had spoken eloquently and meaningfully in a series of talks, later published in diverse journals and magazines on 'the vicissitudes of education', 'the problem of education', 'the unity of education', as also on 'the changing age', and 'crisis in civilisation'. The very titles of these essays, some included in the volume *Towards Universal Man*, brought out on the occasion of his centenary celebrations in 1961, make most educative and illuminating reading, even after a lapse of nearly nine decades. I have no doubt that all of you, in all faculties, are more familiar with these than I am. Nevertheless, even if it is, as they say in English, 'bringing coal to New Castle', I want to take hesitant courage to underline the importance of these ideals and views, not as the historical past of early twentieth century India, but as issues and problems which continue to be our pre-occupations in the nineties of the twentieth century and as we stand on the threshold of the entry into the next millennium of the twenty-first century.

Let me try and identify a few of these issues only to highlight the fact that the future is in your hands to reshape and remodel yourself, Bengal, the country, and the world. The vision was provided by those peers of yore, your peers of today have given you intellectual and artistic tools; but sculpting the future with conviction and determination, self-reliance and openness without being submerged in the tumultuous current of a homogenised global village is your challenge and destiny. In a manner of speaking, these are hard times, for never before had humanity been faced with the real prospect of its own annihilation, and perhaps never before had Indian civilisation and culture at the very moment of its ascendancy and political freedom been faced with deep questioning of the fundamental tenets of its thought and knowledge systems and sense of ambiguity with respect to itself. Also the country had known wars and invasions and external threats from time immemorial. However these could not destroy the security and surety of the core of the Indian self. For the first time somewhere there is a disturbance, we are unsure of and there is evidence of a fragmentation. Now it is an inner threat, not outer. Only a man, calm of mind, tranquil in thought and detached but active can have the discretion and resolve to withstand the twin blessing and curse of momentous changes in the human condition of our time.

To return to Gurudeva's perceptions on the problems of education and the quality of education, specially those that are relevant today, primary is his emphasis on the relationship of life and education. Gurudeva reminds us that "Man belongs to two worlds, one of which lies within him and the other outside. They give him life, health and strength and keep him ever-flowing by ceaselessly breaking upon him in waves of form, colour and smell, movement and music, and love and joy". Education is the instrumentality of inculcating these two worlds. Do we not find, as he did, that often our education continues to be a joyless journey of collecting a mass of information? Now, more than ever before, bourgeoning information clutters the mind, often enchains.

Resultantly we lose capacity for originality, repeat derived ideas and notions not applicable to the existential reality of our life, we are uprooted. If not uprooted, certainly lost and bewildered in a maze of concepts which we know by rote, not by experience.

The first benediction I can give is: May you have the capacity of nurturing the two worlds of the "inner" and the "outer". May the two faculties of the power of thought and imagination be yours forever. These alone will enable you to discharge your duties as real man and woman. Gurudeva had concluded his remarkable essay, written in 1892, with the words, "Let us pray that He would unite our language with our thought and our education with our life." With a slight amendment for the university system in the ninety-nineties, a hundred years later, we may say "May He (We) unite our language of thought with the realities of our life." This is not the occasion to dwell at greater length on the relevance and appropriateness and otherwise of the liberal arts programme of our universities which has sometimes shown anachronistic persistence of outmoded moulds and models. Perhaps when you become great teachers you will grapple with this problem. We have to prepare human beings, and not a number of human units, with special skills to man jobs.

In yet another essay, Rabindranath Tagore emphasizes the need for developing throughout life and especially through education, the indispensable and close contact with nature, and the desire to be one with animal and vegetable life. Gurudeva's insistence on Man and Nature dialogue was an article of faith which he expounded in his system of education and concretised in the institution he established. The *Vasantotsva* songs and *Varshamangal* and the songs of *Sisir* and *Hemanta* reverberate in our ears as they did then. But is there not a difference? The great poetry of 'nature' and the annual festivities around the seasons for him were not a matter of 'song' and 'dance'. They were the expression and outpourings of one who had awakened to the imminent disastrous consequence of dissociating matter from spirit and man from nature, body from soul. He realised the frightening prospects of mechanised age where, if this dialogue broke, it would be at man's own peril. We remember and recount his poems and songs, celebrate the *Utsavas*, but perhaps it is time now more than even before, to remember that this dissociation of Man from Nature and the five elements, Man from all living and non-living beings, may bring disaster upon himself, and threaten his very existence. The environmental pollution and the disturbance of the ecological balance of the Earth is real and imminent. It is not a distant threat from another planet to be read in books and journals; it is with us, every day in our lives, with our choked cities and polluted waters, deforested Himalayas. We have to not only remember but instead, through our lives, reinstate Gurudeva's poetry and song and message in this changed and even deteriorating state of our planet, country, towns, our rivers and our oceans. Perhaps had Gurudeva lived to see what man has made of Man and of Nature, he would have been sad and dismayed. Perhaps, he would give us another new 'mantra' and line of poetry and song to revivify our deadened sensibilities towards our environment. The School and the University system have a fundamental role to play for ensuring the survival of the Earth and the survival of humanity. Gurudev had said: "the four elements of earth, water, air and fire form a whole and are instinct with the universal soul", and had asserted that the blue sky, trees and flowers, vegetable and animal life were indispensable for the human. We need to remind ourselves of this, with or without education, act with fervour and faith to make the world a habitable globe.

My second benediction is a favourite chant of Gurudeva from the Upanishads:

> To the God who resides in fire and water, in trees and plants,
> Immanent in the world and the universe, we bow, we bow.

Today this bowing has to be translated into a programme of work and action, no matter in which sphere of work, whether as professional environmentalists or engineers, scientists or administrators or artists.

Gurudeva's concern with life-long education preceded any conferences in UNESCO forums and international conferences. He was at great pains to propagate and explain that the greatest art was the art of living. "Life", he said, according to India's ideals "must not only grow within itself but outgrow itself into a higher meaning beyond it as a flower outgrows itself into fruit. India's aim has been to guide life's current between its boundaries or banks towards an unbounded sea of freedom." In saying this, Gurudeva was drawing our attention to the need to ever enlarge ourselves for the greater good of other fellow beings. Gandhiji had spoken of 'oceanic circles'. Gurudeva speaks of the 'banks' and the 'rivers' and the 'journey to the ocean of emancipation and freedom'. Stated simply, he is urging us to go beyond our immediate narrow selfish concerns to the larger good of humanity. Now this is a tall order, because we are taught for the best part of dictum of 'each unto his own' and are propelled to act by external stimulus and demand in a world of competition, based on the principle of conflict, confrontation, protest on dissent. In contradistinction, Gurudeva and Gandhiji, both in their separate and distinctive ways, are calling us to overcome and outgrow our narrow selves to partake of a harmonious world based on the principles of interdependence, reciprocal relationships and mutual respect with love. While these are perennial abiding values, which have been voiced at many times by many people in all civilisations, we have to remember that in our world today this message has to be understood as reminder to ourselves that we cannot be isolated or insulated. Further, we have to eschew narrow parochial biases of caste, class, religion, language and territorial boundary, and endeavour to attain a greater degree of understanding and appreciation for that 'other.' Without him/her, their region, we ourselves will lose our identity as individual, society, religious sects or linguistic group. In India today while we are asserting a national unity, this very unity is being threatened by fragmentation on the basis of class, caste, religion or language, not to speak of socio-economic competition. It is right to repeat the beacon call of our political and cultural leaders that only by transcending and outgrowing our narrow selves that we shall attain the boundless freedom and peace of the collective 'self', called India, a civilisation, not merely a nation state created by the Nineteenth Century.

Time and again, Gurudeva quoted the Sanskrit couplet:

> For the family, sacrifice the individual;
> For the community, the family;
> For the country, the community,
> For the soul, all the world

While this ideal may be too high to attain for us, can we strive to balance the desires of the 'self' and the ambition of immediate achievement with an equal commitment to seeking a life harmony so that we can be at peace with ourselves and others?

Perhaps I have dwelt already too much, too long, on the lofty ideals of Gurudeva which seem remote and unattainable today, even though they represent the perennial stream of Indian thought and which have great relevance and meaning.

Let me turn now briefly to the great changes which have taken place in the realm of understanding the Universe and its systems, which have a bearing on the educational systems and the domains of knowledge. We know that post-Einstein science has given us a very different view of the Universe, space and time. It is not necessary for me to take the names of Heisenberg, Schrodinger, David Bohm and Ilya Prigogine. I mention these names, without their respective theories, only to remind us that the theories of implicate and explicate order, chaos and order, dissipative systems and self-organising systems, have brought about a radical change in perception. No longer can we talk of an objective Cartesian world.

(7 May 1997)

5.

Potti Sreeramulu Telugu University, Hyderabad

I am, indeed, grateful to the Vice-Chancellor, Prof. Nayani Krishnakumari, who has invited me to address you on this significant occasion of the Sixth Convocation of your University. I am particularly happy to be here in a University which is dedicated to the fields of the Arts and the Humanities, and a University which has encompassed other institutions and organisations which normally lie outside the sphere of Indian universities.

From the reports of the University since its inception, I have gathered that the University is truly unique because it is focussing on fundamental aspects of the Indian cultural tradition as embodied and expressed through Telugu language literature and allied languages and arts. I find from the profile and reports of the University that the University is not restricted and, rightly so, to a Centre in Hyderabad, but, it extends to the banks of the river Krishna at Srisailam and the banks of the river Godavari in Rajahmundry. In addition, I am delighted to find that the famous Siddendrakalakshetram, the traditional home of Kuchipudi, has been merged with the Potti Sreeramulu Telugu University. Equally significant is the constituting of the School of Folk and Tribal studies in Warangal. The location of these Centres in different parts of Andhra Pradesh and the programmes which have been instituted in these Centres, speak of the deep understanding of the fabric of different aspects of Telugu culture. It was only appropriate that a School of History, Culture and Archaeology should function from Srisailam, a School of Literature from Rajahmundry, Kuchipudi from Kuchipudi, Krishna District and Folk and Tribal studies from Warangal. These four units, along with the School of Language Development, Fine Arts and the Centre for Comparative Studies and Encyclopaedia, offer a rich programme for any student or researcher who wishes to understand the multidimensional and the multi-layered character of the Indian tradition as manifested in Andhra Pradesh.

I would like to felicitate those who had the vision for this University and those others who were responsible for conceptualizing the institutional framework for a unique University. The Schools and the Centres, the programmes, are obviously not a replication of conventional courses in the liberal arts and science in other Universities. It is quite obvious to me that a refreshingly new and challenging approach has been adopted for establishing the University which would take cognizance of the different aspects and facets of the culture and civilization related to the life of the people. As we know, for nearly a century and half the University system provided education which was largely dissociated from life. Education then became, and is still by and large, though not always, a de-culturising tool. In such a situation it was particularly gratifying for me to note that this University has concretised its education through so many well-conceived programmes. I find it is imparting education in 27 subjects, has conducted major national seminars on Lexicography, Kakatiya Art, Architecture, the Bhakti Movement. Most impressive is its record of publications. Few Universities succeed in bringing out a sustained programme of publications and to bring more than 150 standard works on different aspects of Telugu language, literature and the arts, is no mean achievement. Its programme of video-tapes of interviews has been acclaimed far and wide and I hope that these programmes will be available to other Centres. I could go on to congratulate the University, the faculty, the Vice Chancellor and the Chancellor for all that has been accomplished in this very short period.

My young friends who have just completed their studies and received their Degrees have been exposed to the diverse fields—be it archaeology, Telugu language, literature, music, dance, fine-arts, folk and tribal art. This is as it should be. The intense training that you have all received in your respective fields will be the vehicle of continuing your journeys in many directions. Today marks the watershed, a watershed of both achievement and future expectations.

Although you know it well, but perhaps it will not be irrelevant for me to underline the fact, that Andhra Pradesh represents a minuscule India with a plurality of traditions, multiplicity of languages, diversity of social levels, castes and classes, the concurrency of modes of behaviour. And yet there is an unmistakable Andhra identity. What is true of Andhra is true of India. The diversity emerges from a unified vision and life-style. Here interaction and communication is the norm, not the exception. Andhra Pradesh, like some other regions in India, but uniquely so, is surrounded by other States. From times immemorial it has been the cradle of many movements which have affected it and, in turn, it has effected and affected others. This is true of the landscape, the flora and the fauna, various tribes and castes which inhabit this region, and most of all the diverse philosophies, languages and artistic expressions. As in the case of the physical geography, so also in the matter of monuments, architecture, language, Andhra Pradesh has been the home of Buddhist, Jaina, Hindu and Islamic thought. It has a plural heritage of Sanskrit, Telugu, Urdu and Hindi. It has much strong links with Orissa and Oriya and Maharashtra and Marathi on the one hand and Karnataka and Kannada and Tamilnadu and Tamil, on the other. This complexity of a plural heritage in thought and language affects and permeates the nature of artistic expression in this land.

It is certainly not necessary for me to remind you that you are the inheritors of a great tradition of monumental architecture, an architecture which has affected the course of the Indian arts for millennium. The *stupas* of Amravati and Nagarjunakonda are the finest expressions of the faith, philosophy, architectural skill and sculptural dexterity. The ground plans of Amravati and Nagarjunakonda have been considered repeatedly as providing the fundamental basis of architecture in this country, be it Buddhist, Hindu or Jain. The chariot and the wheels-plan of these great *stupas* has a history of development far beyond the region of Andhra. Nor is it necessary for me to bring to fore the richness of the cave temples and the great achievements of the later architectural styles, especially of Alampur and Palempet, Kakatiyas and others.

And why do I mention all this to you at this time? Because these monuments embody in stone and brick a world-view of this country, a world-view which has sustained the Indian culture and civilisation. The world-view looks at life as a whole in which all aspects of life are interwoven and the levels of the sacred and profane, the mundane and the transcendental are not dissociated.

What is evident in concrete brick and stone becomes even more clear through the heritage of literature, be it the *Brihat Katha* or Hala's *Gatha Sapta Sati*. In each of these works, there is a sense of rejoicing of life, a rejoicing which is not unmixed with discipline and austerity. Through the continued interaction between Sanskrit and Telugu, the great names of Nannaya Bhattu and others—Tikkana and Errana—emerged. Kavitrayam, the Trinity of the classical Telugu literature, reflects this sense of creativity, a commitment to the values inherited and a desire for continually revalidating the heritage in contemporary terms. Most of all, this is apparent in the many versions of the Ramayana in the 13th and

14th Century. We are acquainted with the greatness of the *Ranganatha Ramayana* which interpreted the Ramayana theme in a unique way, as also the *Bhaskara Ramayana*, *Molla Ramayana*, *Uttara Ramayana*. Each of these Ramayanas is not mere copies but reflect of reinterpretation of a perennial theme which spread all over India, in each region. Through each language a new Ramayana was created and yet the fundamental message of this great epic remained constant. This capacity of the Indian tradition to constantly play with the perennial and the changing, the constant and the contemporary, is perhaps the secret of an ancient civilisation being still alive. Often we study these works but don't realise the dynamics of the flow of a culture. This is also true of the Andhra Mahabharatam and Andhra Mahabhagavatam. They are ancient and contemporary Pan-Indian and typically Telugu in character. The story continues until the tradition of the Panchakavyas in Telugu and the great efflorescence that took place during the period of other great poet among Kings and King among poets, Krishnadevaraya. The relationship of Andhra Nayak rulers of Thanjavur, Madurai and Pudukottai was responsible for the emergence of yet another school of Telugu literature, popularly known as the Southern School of Telugu Literature. I do not need to tell you about the talented women poets like Madhuravani, Rangajamma and Muddupalani and least of all about those great giants of music—Kshetrayya and Tyagaraja. They were great mountains of creativity which was produced by this region but were never isolated or insulated. These were the mountains which affected creativity not only in the valleys which lay close to them but also the rest of India. The creativity of this region as embodied in the word and the poem, the poetry and the drama, architecture, sculpture and painting is closely related to all else that happens to all that we understand of the folk arts. Andhra has been and is particularly rich in the creativity and vigour of the groups we recognise as the Chenchus, Gonds and others. Their creativity, as also of rural Andhra, has inspired many popular craft traditions and dramatic forms. The modern artist has utilised the techniques of Kalamkari in textiles, of Burra Katha in drama or Kuchipudi in dance.

However, underlying all these expressions, *Vak* the primary word, the first act, embodied in language containing a thought system, provides a foundation of creative expressions in the other arts. It is the creative mind which sees the natural phenomenon, the interaction of the Earth and the Sky, the water and fire, the Sun and the Moon and then creates those myths which have peopled the minds of the people of India for millennium. The myths, be they of *Shiva* or *Vishnu*, *Durga* or *Sakti* or the *Jatakas* and many others constitute the basis for a language of visual imagery, arresting, alluring, monumental edifices of Andhra Pradesh—be it Amaravati, Nagarjunakonda, Alampur or Srisailam and Ramappa. The sculptural visualisation and the painting, all are flowerings of a single vision contained in words but translated into stone or paint or again re-evoked through music or dance. The Indian arts thus reflect an inextricable inter-relationship of literature, architecture, sculpture, painting, music and dance. This inter-relationship is evident not only in the creative texts of literature but is evident in what we call *Sastras* of our tradition, be it those of *Vaastu*, *Silpa*, *Chitra*, *Natya* or *Sangeet*. Andhra Pradesh and South India has many such texts in which these inter-relationships are worked out as a system at the level of both form as also technique. Amongst the many *Sastric* treatises I would like to mention only two, which I hope all of you are acquainted with and have studied carefully during the course of your studies. I refer here to the work of Sarangadeva, the writer of *Sangitaratnakara*. The text moves from the most minute analysis of the body system to the centres from where sound emanates to the compositional structure of Indian music. The text has had a profound influence on the musical traditions of South and North. As you know it has a most important chapter on Dance. This is also true of the great text of Jayapasena. The *Nruttaratriavali* dwells at length on the nature of the body system, its articulation and, therefore, its relationship with the entire sculptural tradition. The great sculptures of Palempet and Ramappa temple are the kinetic image frozen in stone.

This heritage of the unified vision and diversified expression again culminates in a pattern of mobility between and amongst what we call classical and the folk arts of India. Although in the traditional division there was a stream of *Margi* and the *Desi*, the two were never insulated. The *Margi* could become *Desi* and the *Desi* could become *Margi*. I refer to these fundamentals of the Indian tradition on this occasion because often in the pursuit of a single discipline we forget or overlook these interconnections. It is, therefore, important that after mastering a single discipline, be it music, dance, drama as you have done, one should investigate the deeper roots of the particular art as also observe the many branches and off-shoots. This is not the occasion to dwell deeper into the dynamics of a tradition at its macro level or its micro level but it is an occasion to indicate the vast avenues of further exploration of this rich tradition which lie before you. The words are the true indicators of life both of reflection as also expression and communication. Today the challenge before you is to see how you can, through these arts, make a relationship with the rich heritage of India and Andhra Pradesh in particular, as also be in the present to make a new future. Neither fossilisation of the arts nor hybridisation of arts would be healthy.

However, you will ask me a question that: all that you have told us, we know; our education has facilitated access to these great sources and the heritage but, Madam, we are living in this age where nothing of what this unique University has taught us will enable us to get jobs, be in offices and climb up the ladder of careers which our contemporaries in the fields of science, technology, computer technology, business administration, etc. do so easily?

Since these are real questions which will arise in your minds, I think it is only appropriate that I take this occasion to tell you that these values, this heritage, this accomplishment in the skills and techniques of the visual and the performing arts is as important as pursuing any other discipline in a normal college or University. A little while ago, you will remember, I spoke about the textual tradition of the arts in India. Those of you who have been pursuing courses in the fields of architecture, languages and music have a vast field of scholarship lying in front of you. I mention only two texts. But are you not aware that there are thousands of texts in Indian architecture, sculpture, music, dance, literature, engineering lying in the manuscript libraries of India and many also in Andhra Pradesh itself? It is only the new generation that can take the dusts off all these great manuscripts, do textual criticism and bring out properly annotated, collated and definitive editions with modern commentaries. As you know, this has been done in the case of a few texts, such as *Mayamatam* and of course, *Nrittaratnavali*, but there are hundreds of other texts. I hope that some of you will investigate this field of textual criticism in relation to actual creativity. Although work has been done by archaeologists and historians on the temples of Andhra Pradesh of different periods, there is still enough scope for much greater studies in art history on the sculptural, the mural tradition and the painting traditions. Our critical literature on the temples and monuments of Andhra Pradesh is meagre. So also on the mural tradition: except for one major monograph on *Leepakshi*, there is none available. Now this whole field of research lies before you and there are opportunities through academic institutions for pursuing your teaching and research. There are many more opportunities today than twenty-five years ago.

But not all of you would be interested in research. You are, after all, practising musicians and dancers. Earlier, you would have learnt these arts through a single Guru through *Guru-Shishya* parampara. Today you have received training in these arts in an institutional framework. You would, naturally, wish to establish your own schools and academies, be it small organisation, in which you can give training to those who come to learn more about these traditional arts, or join an existing institution. The scope is much larger than it used to be a few decades ago both on account of Governmental and non-Governmental action. There is a scope for private entrepreneurship and you can branch out into so many different fields through mastery of music and dance, not only as dance teachers and music teachers. You can be associated with design institutions, films, multimedia and much else. Your education has empowered you to be on your own, not necessarily just seek a routinized white-collar job. I have no doubt that you will make full use of this training.

In today's world, specially in the world of new technology—information technology and computer technology—there is a close relationship between the multimedia aspects of Indian architecture and new technology. This aspect of inter-relationship which I have been speaking about, is remarkably suited for multimedia programming and evolution of software. The phenomenal support given to and rise in information technology in Andhra Pradesh, along with its rich heritage, makes this fertile ground for a creative dialogue between the traditional knowledge and computer technology. This is yet another field.

I could go on to tell you about how your training will enable you to also do social engineering in rural areas of Andhra Pradesh. After all, it is the arts, the fairs and the festivals, which have provided the age-old network of maintaining cohesiveness in traditional societies. Your understanding and analytical skills can enable you to be the first-rate leaders for reshaping and renewing rural culture in the light of developing programmes.

I hope that this heritage which you carry within yourself and the training which you have received here will give you strength and courage to embark confidently into the future that beckons you.

May I give you my good wishes and blessings for a challenging and fruitful future.

(15 December 1998)

6.

Banaras Hindu University

It is indeed a singular honour for me to be invited to deliver the convocation address this year. As I told the Rector and the Dean, I feel truly inadequate for this task, because I have considered myself only as a humble student of this great university and no more. Also, I feel sincerely humble when I recall the grand vision of the founding fathers of this university. It exemplified an idealist aspiration for reconstituting and rejuvenating the holistic Indian world-view at a time when some other universities had become centres of largely propagating and inculcating values and system of thought grounded only in western philosophy and system of thought of that time. Pt. Madan Mohan Malaviya and his illustrious son, Govinda Malaviya, with unflinching support of the Maharaja of Kashi later, succeeded in laying the foundations of a different university system where there would be an equal emphasis on the eastern and western, the scientific, technological, the philosophic and the aesthetic. Although today this is taken for granted, at that time fresh ground was broken by encompassing the faculties of Science, Engineering, Ayurveda, modern Medicine and, of course, the Humanities and the Arts within a single campus. This certainly required courage and resolute will and extra-ordinary organizing capacities to collect material and human resources. The vision was concretized through many unconventional methods of recruitment. As is well-known, most members of the faculty were hand-picked, almost invited, to join the university, whether they had formal qualifications or not. It was ensured that the best intellectual minds of diverse discipline and varying points of view came together. There was obviously a well-conceived programme which brought together some of the finest minds both in the Sciences as also the Humanities and the Arts. Successive Vice-Chancellors—a Dr. S. Radhakrishnan, a C.P. Ramaswamy Iyer—provided exemplary leadership. The founding fathers, the Vice-Chancellors, the faculty were no doubt fired with a nationalist spirit, but a nationalist spirit which sought to, and did, transcend narrow boundaries of region, religion, language, caste as also disciplines. The broad catholicity of vision was evident in all spheres.

It was thus no accident that the Faculty of Arts had luminaries of the order of T.R.V. Murty and B.L. Atreya in Philosophy, Shyam Sunder Das, Lala Bhagvandin, Acharya Ramchandra Shukla and Hazari Prasad Dwivedi in Hindi, a P.L. Vaidya and Baldeo Upadhyaya in Sanskrit, Bhikku Kashyap in Buddhist studies, and my revered guru Vasudev Saran Agrawala. Having known most of them, not all personally, I owe a deep debt to them for the knowledge they imparted and the values they personified. I pay my tribute to them. My diffidence and sense of inadequacy is naturally understandable. Compared to the contribution of these towering figures, I have wondered whether the generation following them has been able to match the depth and range of their scholarship and the commitment to teaching and learning in the Acharya *parampara*. These are perhaps pertinent questions to be asked with sincerity and humility?

The Faculty of Arts has no doubt had a distinguished history of accomplishments. Today I find that it has enlarged into twenty-two departments, with a faculty of over two hundred and a student enrolment of 2700. Many more subjects have been added, languages and vocational courses. All this is commendable and I would like to congratulate the faculty and the students for the many successes they have achieved. The publications, the journals and the seminars held bear testimony to the vigour and strength of the Faculty. My felicitations and good wishes.

Nevertheless, there continue to be some matters of approach and structure which perhaps need to be re-examined after a lapse of a few decades since the inception of the University. In this context, with some diffidence, let me recall that, at one point, there was a College of Indology here. I happened to be its first Ph.D., but this is not material. However, it is pertinent to re-assess the reasons for, first, establishing the 'College' (today called School or Centre) and subsequently dismantling it. The College of Indology was established, as far as I can remember, with the specific aim of promoting an inter- and multi-disciplinary approach for the study of what we would today term as Indic studies or Indic civilization as a whole, and not through the prism of a single discipline. The appellation 'Indology' no doubt carried with it a load of Orientalist discourse, which essentialized the East and West, the spiritual India and the material West, etc. etc., but in spirit and approach it was seeking to utilize the tools of investigation of many discipline, e.g., archaeology, anthropology, history, philosophy, literature and the arts, as also science and social sciences, for comprehending the multi-faceted, multi-layered and interlocked distinctive personality of Indian civilization. The creative arts—sculpture, painting, music and dance—were incorporated as essentials. The presence of a Rai Krishnadasa, a Pt. Omkar Nath, Alain Danie tou made a difference. The past and present, the historical and the contemporary were considered complementary. Gradually the pressure of the prioritization of disciplines took over, apart from the rejection of the appellation of Indology as an out-moded, anachronistic concept. Today, in many universities, including those in Europe and USA, tension between departments of disciplines and centres and schools continues. There are no easy solutions, but it is a fact that all recognize the need for an inter-disciplinary and multi-disciplinary approach, specially for the study of civilizations and cultures. Here in Banaras it is heartening to know that the Departments of Philosophy and Religion, Ancient Indian History, Culture and Archaeology have been identified for support under the special assistance programme by the University Grants Commission. This is welcome; however it also assumes importance, because the special assistance programme may well lay the foundations for structural modifications so as to give a fresh impetus to an inter-disciplinary approach, as these subjects constitute the ground for studying civilizations and cultures, specially the Indian civilization as a whole, and not in isolated parts. Today the study of Indian civilizations cannot be identified with the earlier model of Indology, which sometimes becomes backward-looking or even chauvinistic. However, a fresh look is necessary against the larger contemporary context of the world. Civilizational studies become pertinent and relevant because we are once again arriving at a stage where there is a tendency to equate civilization only with either religion or political and economic progress. Both essentialize, or at best are partial. The dynamics of a civilization is an inter-locked network, a spacio-temporal complex of the physical, material, scientific, technological, political, economic, social structure, knowledge and value systems, the artistic expressions and the living traditions. No single discipline can capture the complexity, nor can an aggregative exercise be effective. Alas, today we have economic, political, social histories, even histories of science and the art but no overarching framework or theory and model for the study of 'civilizations' and Indic civilizations in particular. Such centres could be conceived and established by BHU, or the BHU could be an important and indispensable partner in an inter-university programme of the UGC. It is understood that the UGC is actively considering the establishment of an inter-University centre for Indian civilization. I hope that the BHU will either establish such a centre, for which it is admirably suited, or will be an active participator in the UGC's envisaged scheme of an inter-university centre.

No doubt, all of you are aware and conscious of the on-going contemporary discourse on what is considered to be the inevitable clash of civilizations. The concept and theoretical position propounded has been debated and critiqued by many in different parts of the world, e.g., Iran, Greece and elsewhere. Many international conferences have been held under the auspices of several organizations, including UNESCO, on the Dialogue of Civilizations, as opposed to the clash of civilizations. This active and vigorous movement is indicative of humanity's need to re-assess the nature of civilizations as a whole in their dynamics of dialogue, interchange and reciprocity and not hegemony and dominance. It is my fervent hope that the University, the Faculty and the scholars will give this suggestion serious thought. The establishment of such a centre of launching of well-conceived programmes will necessitate an in-depth study of dialogue not only between diverse civilizations but also between the domains of fundamental science, specially theoretical postulates of new science, astrophysics and neuro-science, post-Einstein theories as also speculations in the schools of philosophy, western and eastern, ancient and modern. Only then aspects of the consanguinity of approach in the method of science and the method of speculative thought in the traditional knowledge systems, particularly Indian, can be made evident. It is not for me to refer to the work of scientists, such as E.C.G. Sudarshan, Subhash Kak, in the domain of sciences amongst others, and others from the philosophic schools. However, without further explication, I do wish to take this opportunity to make the suggestion as a future vista of academic pursuit through whatever structure.

An intrinsically related but distinct issue is of the prioritization or even exclusivity of the written/the textual over the 'oral'. Now, as inheritors of a long and continuous tradition of oral transmission, as complex, sophisticatedly-structured as the Vedic enunciation to the 'fluid' but perennial of the 'loka' (not to be confused with 'folk' of the English language), one is woefully conscious of the fact that the 'academia' of the university system, or more exactly the structure of the university system, does not take into cognizance the fact that the written and textual and the oral were and continue to be complementary, and they cannot be placed in a progressive scale of hierarchy. Except for what are euphemistically called 'field studies' and oral interviews, the knowledge and value systems of 'orality' which have given space and form, vigour, vitality and continuity to civilizations, particularly Indian civilization, have not been recognized as refined pedagogical tools of critical study. No longer can we subscribe to the progressive model of civilization from savagery, barbarism, village and urban, and from oral to the written. There is monumental, sizeable data from all parts of the world, specially the so-called 'developing' world, which provides the basis for a renewed or alternate model for the study of civilizations and cultures. This is also seminal concept relevant to the contemporary debate of diversity of cultures vs. mono-cultures. A forum within the University system would have the potential of evolving theoretical models more appropriate than those which have developed from the purely positivist's position.

This is a subject too vast and complex to be addressed at a Convocation address, but I am emboldened to mention it because I am concerned that Banaras, with its traditions of great antiquity and continuity, and the University, in which a vision is embedded, are ideally situated to take up this challenge. I also say this as a personal tribute to this place and the University which taught me after years in the USA to turn my gaze from models of progress and uniformity, from sharpening the sword of pure intellect and reasoning, to comprehending and experiencing at the level of thought and feeling, diversity, multi-layering of complex systems. I returned also to seek the inner centre of Indian civilization and culture.

My personal journey of 'return' but with wide open eyes would not be of any consequence but for the fact that now the personal 'I' can be appropriately replaced by the most recent endeavours of reflection on these issues by the thinking West and also the speculations of modern science. Both are, at a deep levels, searching desperately for an exploration of avenues of 'renewal' and rejuvenation of a fractured human, even universal, order. The perennial sources of knowledge and wisdom, or other knowledge systems and world-views, lie in and around us sometimes covered with dust, at other times desecrated and polluted, but they are still there. A future generation without bias or ideological predilections has the potential to bring about correctives which will be the new beginnings of a humane world order. This is my hope and prayer.

My *ashirvada* for all those who will today cross the threshold from learning to living. The future lies in your hands. It is given to you to reshape this society in which you live without falling prey to narrow boundaries of caste, creed, religion, political ideology. It is given to you to shape a future India on the principles enshrined in all its texts and still evident at many levels. It is given to you to demonstrate that the Indian civilizational model can be a future paradigm for the world. This will no doubt require courage, it will require more, that you should be rooted at home with yourself and yet be a citizen of India and the world.

(2005)

SECTION II

Tributes

7.

Dr. S. Radhakrishnan, the Teacher of Teachers

A hundred years ago was born in Tiruttani Dr. Sarvepalli Radhakrishnan, whose life and work, the ease and lucidity of his exposition and the vast spectrum of his concern, have left a deep impact on Indians and foreigners alike.

Teacher, first and last, at home in many languages and cultures, he was the perfect bridge builder in the realm of ideas, thoughts and religions, between the world of science and technology and religion and faith; between the East and the West. The ease of his expression, the lucidity of his style and the power of his oratory were matched by an unshakable faith in the innate goodness of Man.

No believer in idolatry and no blind follower of dead scriptures, he gave a new contemporary meaning and value to the 'truths and insights' of the perennial philosophies and religions of the world, as also developments in modern science and technology.

'Humanism' was the theme of the teacher, no matter what discipline, what forum, which audience. Like a true teacher, he wished not only to communicate seminal ideas of knowledge and power but to present a living example of conduct. Each piece of writing is a model lesson, each lecture an impeccable 'gem' of ideas, articulated with the simplicity of an aphorism.

Education was his 'passion' and his faith. The teacher-taught relationship was his vocation—whether in class, or in politics or as a statesman or head of State.

On Education he said:

> "The kind of education that is imparted must not only be broad but should also be deep. We are lacking in depth. We may become learned and skilled, but if we do not have some kind of purpose in our life, our lives themselves become blind, blundering and bitter. The Gita says: *vyavasayatmikabuddhirekeha.* For a truly cultured mind, there is a single mindedness, a dedication to a single purpose. For the uncultured mind, the whole life is scattered in many directions, *bahusakhahyanantasca*. Therefore, it is essential that education should give

not merely learning and skill but endow one with a definite purpose in life. What that purpose is, one has to define for oneself.

It is said that *vidya* gives *viveka, vimarsarupinividya* gives a sense of what is right and helps to avoid what is wrong. Therefore, the young men and women of this generation must try to find out what is required of them. A purpose which held good centuries ago may not hold good today in view of rapidly changing conditions of our country and of the world. So the purpose which young persons adopt in their lives must be adapted to the relevant needs of the present generation."

He taught us to value literature, the *Upanisads* and *Kavyas*. With phenomenal memory he could quote from primary sources. The epics and Kavya, specially Kalidasa, were his favourites. Of the need to read the Kavyas he said,

"There is a famous verse which tells us *samsara visa vrksasya*. In this imperfect world, *samsara*, there are two fruits of inimitable quality. They are the study of our great classics and communion with great minds. These two are the things which mould men's minds and hearts. I am anxious that our great classics should be studied, the classics of all countries of which we are the inheritors. It is in a small dialogue in an Upanisad that a question is put: what constitutes the essence of the good life? The teacher replies: didn't you hear the answer? There was a thunderclap: da dada. Immediately the teacher explained that these were the essence of good life—*dama, dana, daya*. They constitute the essentials of good life. You must have *dama* or self-control, restraint, which is the mark of a human being. In the Ramayana, when Lakshmana sets out for the forest, his mother tells him: "Look upon Rama as your father Dasaratha; look upon Sita as myself, as your mother; look upon the forest as Ayodhya; go, my dear."

The inaugural address on the establishment of the Sahitya Akademi was a lesson for writers and readers alike. In his inimitable style, he made the connection between the East and the West.

"Whatever gives the shock of intellectual and imaginative pleasure and says something fresh and stimulating is literature or *sahitya*. The Rg Veda, the first literary document in the world, is not merely religion and symbolism but poetry and literature. The Bible, the Avesta, and the Quran are not merely classics of religion but are works of literature. The seer of the Rg Veda clothes exalted thought in words of force and feeling."

Fond of music and dance and drama, connoisseur of sculpture and painting, he appreciated the arts for their ability to refine the quality of life.

"The dramatist or the playwright delights us by the perfection of his art, its variety, its music and its mood. He can do so if he is a man of *svadhyaya* and *tapas*, of learning and intensity of spirit.

> If drama is to be one of the most powerful manifestations of the human mind, there must be maturity of mind and greatness of soul. Without these we cannot win and hold the affection of people across distances of time and space. If any literary work is to have enduring quality, abiding power, the author should have magnificence of mind, and intensity of vision. If we work too much on the surface, the deeper and more obscure feelings of life will find no adequate expression. Rootlessness in our lives reflects itself in the lack of richness in our lives and the superficial character in our writings. Our plays may be striking and admirable in many ways but they will not touch the depths in us. They may excite a tumult in our minds but not touch the deeps. A great drama overwhelms, devastates, annihilates us and yet exalts us and makes us new."

The interest in painting, music, dance and drama was not something to his pivotal interest in *culture per-se*. And on this, he said, "Music and literature, dance and drama, sculpture and painting are intended to purge the soul of its defects and lead it to a vision of the Eternal. These arts cannot refine the soul unless they spring from the soul, unless the spirit of man raises itself above its usual routine level. The artist is a priest. The aim of art is to capture the inner and informing spirit and not merely the outward semblance. It is by integral insight or spiritual intuition rather than by observation and analysis of given objects that the sculptor or the painter attains to the highest power of artistic expression."

But concerned as he was with the beauty of artistic expression, it was his deep commitment to the world of speculative thought which gave body and substance to his teachings.

For him religion was not a dogma—a set of prescriptions. Repeatedly he quoted *Tattvamasi*, the *Upanishadic* view, to demonstrate the unity of all religions.

> "When the *Upanisads* proclaim the great truth, That art thou, when the Buddha teaches that each human individual has in him the power to grow into a Buddha or a Bodhisattva, when the Jews say that the "spirit of man is the candle of the Lord," when Jesus tells his hearers that the Kingdom of Heaven is within them, and when Muhammad affirms that God is nearer to us than the very artery of our neck, they all mean that the most important thing in life is not to be found in anything external to man but is to be found in the hidden strata of his thought and feeling. We must not look for it, lo here or lo there, for behold the Kingdom of God is within you, Know ye not that ye are the temple of God and that the spirit of God dwelleth in you.' In the words of II Peter, we are "partakers of the divine nature." Plotinus tells us that we can know the unknowable for we ourselves, in our deepest ground, are the unknowable. "This is the soul's true goal to touch that light and to behold it by means of that light itself, and not by any other light; even as we see

> not the sun by any light except its own." St. Augustine observes: "Thou art more inward to me than my most inward part." St. Thomas says: "The Holy Ghost inhabits the mind by his substance." Blosius, at the end of the Book of Spiritual Instruction, speaks of the hidden essence of the soul.
> It is far more inward and sublime than are the three higher faculties, for it is their origin. It is wholly simple, essential and uniform, and so there is not multiplicity in it, but unity, and in it the three higher faculties are one thing."

Although steeped in Hinduism, specially Vedantic, he was a teacher of all religions/faith. He decried "Intolerance and fanaticism marked the periods of our decline. We suffered when we became rigid and fanatical and prospered when we were tolerant and friendly. The misfortunes of our history teach us the need for the qualities of tolerance and goodwill."

> Ye may know each other
> Not that ye may despise each other.

Guru Granth Sahib in the spirit of the Indian tradition contains hymns from the Hindu and Muslim writings. A great Muslim saint Hazrat Mian Mir was invited to lay the foundation stone of the Golden Temple.

India is today the home of the living faiths of mankind and their followers live together in peace and friendship in spite of occasional setbacks and conflicts.

And it is against this background that we have to understand his definition of the concept of secularism in the Indian democracy.

> "When it is said that our State is a secular one, it means that the State is not identified with any one faith but protects and respects all faiths so long as their followers do not behave in a way which is an outrage on moral conscience or a danger to the integrity of the country. Secularism attempts to remove religious rivalries; it discourages the exploitation of religious beliefs for political purposes. Our Constitution gives freedom of worship to all, permits us to organize ourselves for religious purposes. It has abolished separate electorates and our election law provides that a systematic appeal to a voter on the ground of caste, race, community or religion is a corrupt practice for which a person elected may be disqualified.
> The test of a true faith is the extent to which it transforms the individual and the social order. It must illuminate the dark places of our social life and religious practices. The Rg Veda says that the human race is one, *ekaivamanusijatih*. All men are brothers: *bhrataromanavassarye*. All religions teach that the human being is of infinite worth, and deserves respect and loving kindness, especially the unfortunate ones. Those who bear the deepest wounds require our greatest sympathy."

But this teacher was interested in the making of a world citizen transcending narrow nationalism. In one conference he declared "All those who belong to a nation share certain ideals and purposes and work for general welfare of the community as a whole. A nation is not a casual association of men for the performance of certain political functions. It is a vital union. The sense of nationality is derived not from race, language or religion but from traditional values accepted by the members of the nation. They had a sense of honour, respect for indefinable obligations."

> "If conditions which prevail within a Welfare State are extended on a world scale, we should be prepared for a little sacrifice of national sovereignty, and be willing to accept peaceful methods of settling disputes, enforce peaceful legal solutions and avert violence, secure minimum economic conditions of well being and remove the grievances of large communities which suffer from political subjection and racial discrimination, and develop a moral community based on spiritual values. A proper appreciation of the duties and responsibilities implied in the world citizenship is necessary today. We have to lift the world off its hinges and transform the national man into a universal man.
>
> The United Nations Organisation is the first step towards the creation of an authoritative world order. It has not got the power to enforce the rule of law. It has used military force on occasions. There is talk about disarmament, inspection and control. The cold war is the result of the two power blocs facing each other in Europe, Asia and Africa. If the cold war is to end, the groups should abandon the armament race to annihilation. If the two sides seek all the time arms that would outmatch those of the other, suspect and distrust each other, war becomes inevitable. Even as national welfare requires us to give up the personal right to use force, international security requires the surrender of the right to use force on the part of nations."

Responsible for initiating the UNESCO Major Project for the Appreciation of Eastern and Wester Cultural Values, he said in 1954–56, "The sense of belonging together to the same nation is derived from a sense of sharing the same memories and hopes, the same historical experiences, the same artistic and cultural heritage. If membership of one world is to be developed, projects like the 'East and West understanding and cooperation' should help us to realise the cultural wealth and knowledge to which we are all heirs. When mischievous misunderstanding is at work, it is our duty to work for creative understanding among nations."

But this Teacher was no ivory tower scholar speaking from the cloistered rooms of his monumental library. Diplomat, statesman, chairman of Rajya Sabha, he was the impeccable towering teacher on all occasions. He could chide, admonish, young and old, politicians, administrators with love—love which empowers a teacher. In Moscow, in Paris, in London, Oxford, New York or Yugoslavia at a toast, at dinner or in casual conversation, his teaching was imbued with human and loving candour.

Not all the pomp and splendour, the awards and citations, the recognitions and felicitations would make him divert from his unshakable faith, faith in spirit and above all love.

An intellectual giant of his age, he held the intellect in a secondary position to the spirit. So whether it was in the context of science, civilization, religion and art, the teacher experienced within and taught without.

For him, all aspects of life were inter-connected. Always conscious of the inner, he was at pains to bring home the fact the inner was made valid by an equal concern, effort to radiate to the outer. Thus, "The aim of literature", he said, "is the good of the world *Visva Sreyah Kavyam.* Its purpose is not to neglect the world, but to redeem the world. It is not to mirror the glinting surfaces of the given but to recreate the experience. The literary artist must enter into solitude, glimpse the vision, bring it down to earth, shape it with emotion and carve it into words. Literature is the channel between spiritual vision and human beings. The poet is the priest of the invisible world, a divine creator, a Kavi. He is not a mere entertainer but is a prophet who inspires and expresses in varied ways the entire aspirations of the society to which he belongs", and added, "Unless the individual has the courage to be lonely in his mind, free in his thought, he is not capable of great writing. Great literature like true religion is what a man does with his solitariness."

A man steeped in Rg Veda, the *Upanisads* and the *Kavyas* was equally sensitive to the beauties of the visuals, the performing arts. Fond of music, promoter of classical dance, he responded to contemporary painting. Nandalal Bose and the Bengal School were naturally his favourities. In an inaugural address on the exhibition of Nandalal Bose's paintings, he gave a remarkable discourse, almost a moral capsule lesson on the history of Indian art. Once again he dwelt on the fundamental goals.

> "Music, dance, drama, sculpture and painting are intended to purge the soul of its defects and lead it to a vision of the eternal. These arts cannot refine the soul unless they spring from the soul, unless the spirit of man raises itself above its usual routine level. The artist is a priest. The aim of art is to capture the inner and informing spirit and not merely the outward structure."

Had Dr. Radhakrishnan written more on literacy criticism and theories of Indian art he would have been taught in universities along with Aurobindo and Coomaraswamy, who gave us a new vision to look at Indian art. Education, literature and arts were the teacher's themes, but he was at his most articulate best as the expounder of philosophy and religion.

His concern here was for the brotherhood of man, world solidarity, *lokasamgraha*, as he called it. He said, that it was no longer a pious dream, but a practical necessity. "The destructive power now in the hands of man has reached such terrifying proportions that we cannot afford to take risks." "The unity of the world is being shaped through the logic of events, material, economic and political. If it is to endure, it must find psychological unity, spiritual coherence. The world unified as a body is groping for its soul. If mankind is to save itself it must change the axis of its thought and life". And he went on to add:

> "The need for religion, for a system of thought, for devotion to a cause which will give our fragile and fugitive existence significance and value, does not require much elaborate argument. The question is what kind of religion? Is it a religion of love and brotherhood or of power and hate? .... The question is, therefore not, religion or no religion but what kind of religion?"

The rhetorical question asked by the teacher was answered by him in innumerable ways on countless occasions. Neither dogma nor exclusive revelation was acceptable to him. He pointed out that a sharp line between religion and social life could not be drawn, but recognised that although "religion is not a social reform movement and yet a large part of one's life is spent in society. A stable social order is the ground work of civilised life. Religion is a social cement, a way in which men express their aspirations and find solace for their frustrations." At another level while recognising the plurality of religions each with its own peculiar character and structure, he pointed at the transcendental unity of all religions. "The vital differences among the living faith of mankind are over-arched", he said, "by a fundamental unity of vision and purpose which embraces all mankind ..... The unredeemed situation of man, the longing for liberation, the recognition of the Divine Reality and the many ways to reach the real are found in all religions."

"All religions affirm that man is confronted by something greater than himself which in contrast to human nature and all other phenomenon is Absolute Reality—Absolute Reality is Absolute Good for which Man is athirst".

Quoting from scriptures and texts—Hindu, Buddhist, Islamic, Indian, Christian and Zoroastrian—he convincingly proved this fundamental unity and universal aspiration for liberation, as the realisation of life's fullest possibilities, the perfection of personality.

Religion to him was not only a way to god but a way to Man. It was not mere contemplation, the fight of the alone to the alone, but a way of active service. These insights into religion were a deep faith and he could not but be hurt and pained when he saw strife and conflict in the name of religion. In an impassioned tone, he admonished those who provoked communal violence and reminded them of Gandhiji's prayer of *Allah Isvar tera hi naam.*

On more occasions than one he took pains to define the meaning of secular state. Addressing a conference of a particular section he declared "Ours is a secular state. This does not mean that we believe only in material values and have scant regard for the spiritual. Happiness should not be confused with material comfort. It is really intellectual refinement and spiritual joy. The ideal of secularism means that we abandon the inhumanity of fanaticism and give up futile hatred of others. In a secular state there will be the spirit of true religion and the environment necessary for the development of a gentle and considerate way of life." True religion was no static notion for the teacher. He cautioned that if religion aspires to immortality it has to be constantly young, another way of saying that it must respond to the demand of the times.

His clarity and lucidity in clarifying the common confusion that secularism eschews the religious spirit is a lesson which has significance for us here and now. With unmatched perception he clarified that there was no absolute conflict between the religious spirit and the scientific temperament or science and technology.

> "The general impression that the spirit of science is opposed to that of religion is unfortunate and untrue." He argued, "There are many people who think on account of their intoxication with the developments of science and technology that matter is the most important thing. But if we scrutinize a little further we will realize that these great developments of science and technology, if they establish anything, establish the omnipotence of the human spirit and not the omnipotence of matter. It is the human mind that sits in judgment on nature. Whether it is scientific discovery or technological development or artistic creation, the human being does not regard himself as a single item in a series of objective happenings. He believes that there is an element of subjectivity, an element of spirit in man, which enables him to do the wonderful things which he is doing.
>
> What is science? Science is the pursuit of truth. And what is truth? Truth is not something which you manufacture from out of the resources of your mind; it is

pursuit of something which is extramental, which is objective, which is there, to which the human individual has to subscribe. All the great changes that have taken place from the time when men lived in primitive caves down to the time when we are trying to circle the earth, when we are trying to transverse regions of space—all these things are due not to mere mind or the senses but to that spirit in man. When the scriptures declare that man is made in the image of God, or an Indian scripture says that *deha* or body is *devalaya*, or the dwelling of God, they are trying to tell us that, whereas the cosmic happenings may take place, man is not to regard himself as a mere item in the series of objective happenings." And he concluded by saying "It is wrong to think that science and religion are opposed to each other. Science and religion represent two dimensions to the human being, the national and spiritual. These two things cannot be divorced from one another: they must be coordinated. They must be integrated, they must be correlated, if a human being is to become a real human being."

He wanted the barriers of religions, between science and religion, to be broken as also those between the East and West. "If we are to evolve into a universal society, we must break down the barriers separating East and West and build bridges." And finally the message of the teacher was 'Love' and compassion, qualities he cherished most. He wrote:

"Every time we start, we use our hymns and end with saying *santih, santih, santih.* The teacher and the pupils are expected to avoid hating each other. Compassion, *daya*, is the quality which is more characteristic of women than of men. I read recently a book which speaks about the decline of womanhood, and says that this is so because there is a decline in compassion. In other words, the natural quality of woman is compassion. If one does not have compassion, one is not human. It is, therefore, essential for every human being to develop the quality of considerateness, kindness and compassion.

Without these qualities we are only human animals, *nara Qasu*, not more than that.

Give us good women, we will have a great civilisation.

Give us good mothers, we will have a great nation."

To be with him was to bask in the sun-time of his warmth, a universal love which embraced all, big and small, young and old, men and women and children. The teacher gave of himself freely and generously but always with the strength of that intangible but real transcendental quality which made him as near as far, as towering as loving. The eternal spirit had truly touched the teacher, who taught as he walked or talked, conversed or debated or presided, as the maker of the destiny of the nation for many years.

8.

Maulana Azad, Educationist and Humanist

Perhaps it was at the Congress Session of 1937, that I saw on the dais a stately looking figure: awesome, impressive and with a commanding dignity. In succeeding Congress sessions, as volunteers, we watched a galaxy of leaders, delivering impassioned speeches, calling upon us to be equal partners in the struggle for freedom.

There was something in the air, but one did not quite know what exactly this freedom stood for other than a clear commitment for the removal of a foreign regime. Recitations of poems of Tagore, verses of Bharati, were as much part of our cultural education, as was the reading of the Old and New Testament, the tales from Shakespeare's plays by Charles Lamb, stories of Beowulf and Anglo Saxon poetry.

As students, either in the vanguard or rear guard of processions, we shared the fervour with inadequate comprehension. In the 1942 movement, there was a keener awareness of what bondage stood for and the freedom aspired for. Gradually, almost imperceptibly, came emotional fervour, the hero worshipping of leaders. By the 1942 movement this was juxtaposed with an intellectual and a critical understanding of the socio-economic, educational and cultural aspects of the bondage. By 1947 equally poignant was the reality and the challenging experience of the divisions of community from community and religion from religion which had been created and made real from the figments of distorted mind. We shouted slogans, saw riots, rehabilitated refugees as freedom came. As observers, participators in a smaller or greater measure, it came home that freedom was not merely from the external foreign regime, but freedom was the continuing, ever present challenge of creating harmony and balance within. No books, no poetry, no speeches, not even news of leaders going to jail, could bring this home more meaningfully with a charged, simple intensity than the memorable last prayer meetings of Mahatma Gandhi in January 1948.

The enthusiasm, the new inspiration and the hope and the desire of building a new India ushered in 1947 was present, but equally present was the pain and the anguish, the horror and the sorrow of a family divided and a Father of the Nation communicating his despair in words of childlike simplicity and wisdom which resonated then and they resonate now.

It was these emotionally charged encounters which were responsible for changing the course of normal flow of mundane desire for a career, to a commitment at a deeper level. Not without reason, therefore, when Maulana Abul Kalam Azad was appointed the first Minister for Education in independent India, he stood for us as a symbol of the freedom from bondage, not only at the political level but, more, at the socio-cultural and educational dimensions.

Little wonder that he mobilized around him no career administrators but a band of committed educationists: who shared his vision; who were committed to making education an instrument for transformation of the Indian socio-cultural reality.

Despite the great difference in personality, perceptions, Maulana was not a disciple, but certainly a follower of Gandhiji in two fundamental aspects. Here he would make no compromises. The first was the unity of undivided India and the other in respect of basic education at the primary and elementary level. Also, Maulana was a humanist first and last. His phenomenal scholarship, his extensive erudition and his mastery over theological issues did not blunt his sensibilities as a poet, and a connoisseur. Literature, poetry and music were closest to his heart. In jail and elsewhere he could sing out the verses:

> "No one tells me where my journey will end: I have traversed wilderness after wilderness, and there are yet more wildernesses to be crossed", and
>
> "In this garden, where spring and autumn are wrapped together in an eternal embrace, Time has a wine-cup in its hand and a coffin in its shoulder".

The silence of his inner poetic sensibility would be broken through couplets which followed with the same ease as his fiery passionate speeches in Congress pandals. Besides, as a man, Maulana was deeply immersed in the philosophic thoughts and literature of West Asia and the cross-cultural movements that took place throughout the centuries, inter-linking India with cultures adjacent and remote. All these qualities were combined into one personality in this first Education Minister whose faith in the unity and integrity of India was unshakable. For him education was an instrumentality for social transformation, a poetic sensibility, which verged on the mystical, was the inner journey, and outer action was the expanse which embraced all cultures of the world. As Education Minister, it was his prime responsibility to concretize these commitments into an educational policy of independent India and initiate plans and programmes. He set out to do this with great agility of mind and understanding of the constraints of the structures which had already come to be and which could not be demolished overnight.

Political freedom had been won, but the shackles of archaic and inappropriate structures were not so easy to shake off. He was committed to basic education; he drew upon the experiments of Zakir Saheb, called upon Saiyidain and others to establish a new system. However, both within Government and Parliament he was acutely aware of the fact that Basic Education would not be viable and effective outside the context of the socio-economic cultural plan and programme of a Mahatma Gandhi. His despair on this account is clear and unequivocal. Time was short and the spheres on which educational programmes had to be launched were many. In each meeting of the Central Advisory Board of Education, Maulana drew attention to this need of paying the utmost attention to primary and elementary education. However, this was not to be at the cost of the urgent need for vocational education and adult education. The appointment of the University Education Commission, and the Secondary Education Commission in 1952, reorganization of All India Council for Technical Education, the establishment of the chain of libraries of scientific research, the development of the Indian Institute of Science, the establishment of University Grants Commission, the establishment of the National Archives of India, the three Akademies, the National Museum, the nationalization of the Salar Jung Museum, the Indian Museum, were all the results of the initiative taken by Maulana as the first Education Minister. Contact with foreign countries was as essential, and thus it was his personal initiative which was responsible for the establishment of International Cultural Relations Cell and of course he was the founder of the Indian Council for Cultural Relations. On the achievements of his ten years in office, he said on 6th February 1958, "When I assumed charge of Education in 1947, I immediately saw that there could be no solution of our educational problems without the fullest co-operation of the Centre and the Provinces. Education was no doubt a provincial subject, but it was my considered opinion that this distinction could be maintained only when our educational targets have been achieved. Till such time, the Central Government should openly recognize that though education is a State subject, it must share this responsibility with the State Governments if we are to meet the challenge of the times".

And yet, as he looked back on his achievements of ten years in office, he remarked, "The progress which has been achieved in spite of these difficulties can be measured by the fact that when I assumed charge, the Central budget for education was only about Rs.2 crores and is today considerably more than Rs.30 crores. It is not only the financial allocation which has been increased, but there has been expansion in all types of activities".

Despite all these achievements, he was aware about the difficulties and often spoke of financial constraints, specially his inability, almost helplessness, in finding more monies. In reply to demand for grants, he had said in the Parliament in 1952,

> The question is whether this knot, which has come in the way of education and which is being lamented for the last five years, can be cut by complaints of this nature. My budget speech last year was not just a speech, it was an expression of my mental agony which thus found an outlet. I have stated in detail how the Government decided to go ahead in all directions in the educational field during the last five years and how they had to stop for sheer helplessness.
>
> With a full sense of responsibility I have been telling you and do so again that there is no aspect of the educational problem in the country which the Government have not considered and on which they have not made plans. Today, you have mentioned only a few matters connected with the educational problem. Four years have already rolled by since the Government not only considered these matters but finalised their policy about all these fundamental and important matters also. They appointed committees on almost every subject, considered the recommendations of these Committees and finalised plans for work. There is hardly any branch of education such as basic education, adult education, technical education, university education, physical exercise education, etc., etc. which has been ignored and for which a finalised scheme is not ready now. But when all the schemes were ready and the Education Ministry took final decisions to implement them, we came to know that the road was blocked and that we could not take even a single step in that direction. Why is the road blocked? The reason is that we require money to get every scheme implemented and unfortunately we have not got sufficient money. If we cannot provide money for this purpose it is obvious that we cannot do anything practical, no matter how many schemes we may work out on paper. Will any hon. Member out of five hundred Members of this House be pleased to suggest to me how to remove this impediment?
>
> Day before yesterday complaints were voiced that the various measures relating to education had not been taken. I assure you that there is no measure which Government has not fully considered and regarding which a complete blue-print has not been drawn up. If you can arrange for money today, I can assure you, Government would start the work tomorrow, for the consideration stage is already

> over. It is not the mind which is empty, but the pocket. You need not try to infuse intelligence or wisdom into the Government's mind. So far it has not felt any lack of it. What is lacking is money, which you should try to make available, if you can.

For Maulana Saheb, at no time, the system of education was to be dissociated from socio-economic life of today or tomorrow. At the first meeting of the Central Advisory Board of Education under his Chairmanship and at other subsequent meetings, he reminded us, 'Our system of education must not be formed in isolation from our social and economic life of tomorrow. Different sides of our life and activities must be correlated. The primary aim of any system is to create balanced minds which cannot be misled. We must be strong mentally before we can think of building a nation'.

Restructuring of secondary education was and is still difficult but Maulana gave it attention and concentration; but for him there may not have been a Central Board of Secondary Education. Of greater significance are the bold initiatives taken by Maulana in the matter of technical education and the establishment of the Council of Technical Education and it was through this modality that the higher technical institutes were established and which formed the bedrock of the development of technical education in the country.

Maulana undertook the unenviable and challenging task of introducing four Bills in Parliament relating to the Central Universities. As a young officer, writing notes on these Bills and listening to the debates in Parliament, one realised that the universities of Vishva Bharati, Banaras, Aligarh and Delhi aroused deep emotions. As a listener of these debates it was brought home once again that Maulana's commitments were unshakeable and he was a true follower of Gandhiji in more senses than one. Responding to some scathing criticisms on the Vishva Bharati Bill in 1951, he said as many as five times, 'that the objects of the Bill are to preserve and promote the ideals for which that great Institution was established. Further I had then referred to what had transpired between me and Mahatma Gandhi in January 1947 at the time I took charge of this Ministry. He had told me that Gurudev had left a great trust with him which he was going to entrust me thereafter. The Government of India, by introducing this Bill, had tried to preserve that trust and the passage of this Bill does not mean at all that any dishonesty will be practiced, instead of making efforts for its ideals for which this University had stood all along.

Doing that, I feel, will, instead of preserving it, mean sheer dishonesty and a betrayal of the trust.'

His ideas of what institutions of higher education might be, came through in the scintillating words that the institution does not need any building, 'nature provides us with the canopy of the sky and the open spaces where spirit will flourish. Brick and stone do not make institutions.'

Again in another context, responding to the criticism about the appropriateness of having schools associated with Shantiniketan, he was quite clear in his mind that the original character of the University would not be disturbed. Although Dr. S.P. Mukherjee and Maulana Azad differed on many fundamental matters, in this matter of preserving the intrinsic character of Vishva Bharati, Maulana Azad accepted all amendments suggested by Dr. S.P. Mukherjee and Dr. C.D. Deshmukh.

Maulana's wit and humour were unmatched. As a Parliamentarian, he replied with razor sharp retort. When one Member suggested that there should be a specific mention of civilizations and teachings of civilizations in the Act, Maulana's reply was brilliant. He said, 'The objective has been stated above and ends with the reference to caste and creed and this sentence in question is only a concluding one, when we generally utter the words "in the name of God" or "in the name of the Divine Being", " in the name of Bismillah" etc. They, therefore, do not form a part of the objects proper. It is not the position. I will again bring it to your notice that it has nothing to do with this issue. The object of the university ends with the words, "all religions and caste and creed."

The debate on the Aligarh University Bill was stormy, long and brought up many matters which went into the fundamentals of approaches in regard to the religion, culture, education. Each of these debates shows Maulana's catholic, open attitude. His tolerance and his total commitment to an education system of a secular Government being nothing but secular, at the same time he was anxious to assert that although the character of these institutions could not be changed, religious instructions could not be made compulsory. The passage of the Bills of Aligarh and Banaras Hindu University were concrete instrumentalities for bringing about socio-cultural transformation through education. He was clear that the universities as they had been established should continue. He insisted on the retention of the words Banaras Hindu University and Aligarh Muslim University but at the same time asserted throughout these debates that the curriculae should be international encompassing all civilizations and cultures. Of importance was also his awareness of the fact that the structures, whether of the University or the University Grants Commission, should continue to be *modelled* on patterns of the British system. Throughout the debates he made mention of the fact that at the moment, "we are following British system to a great extent and adapting it for our purpose. Later it will be necessary to have our own appropriate systems". A re-reading of these debates brings home the fact that Maulana's aspirations were for creating new models but he was also aware of the necessity on immediate action and therefore retention of the older models.

As deeply committed to arts, literature and the heritage, Maulana Azad took keen interest in the reorganisation of the Archaeological Survey of India, the establishment of the National Museum and the National Archives of India, the Council of Historical Records Commission. From amongst the many reminiscences, I recall one great learning experience. Maulana wanted an All India Council of Museums to be established. Museums as they were at that time were omnibus comprising art, geology and botany. A few were established by the British and there were a handful of private museums. In a room in the Ministry of Defence where tribunals had held meetings and freedom fighters had given evidence, the first meeting of the All India Council of Advisory on Museums was held. Maulana gave a speech in Urdu which was as full of gravity as full wit and humour. He punned on the word *ajaib ghar,* then held forth on what constituted the heritage, went into the riches of Asia, the export of art objects to the British Museum. The speech, its contents and the manner of its delivery left each of us stirred, inspired, because Maulana had given the call for another type of freedom: The freedom to know and recognize your intellectual past and to come to terms with it.

Rai Krishnadasa and Moti Chandra who sat and listened to the speech could not but come up to acknowledge the depth and perception of Maulana's speech.

Maulana in turn was a hard task master, wanting immediate action, even checking up on the promptness of writing the minutes of a meeting. It was his perseverance almost which enabled the Ministry of Education to have an administrative set up for museums. Archives, historical records were naturally very dear to his heart. He knew his material, knew his texts, could pinpoint the primary sources and could give instructions to the heads of archives and others to keep the records of the country in order. This aspect of his character, one could only know if one had worked with him. The poet in him expressed itself in many ways, not in the least when it came to preserving monuments like the Taj Mahal or declaring others as monuments of national importance. The revision of the 1904 Act was at his initiative.

The poet in Maulana and the writer in Jawaharlal Nehru, the philosopher in Radhakrishnan were the motivating forces behind the establishment of the three Akademies. Never before perhaps and never after has there been such a symbiosis of vision and power of creativity together, in recent history. These giants and men of letters sat at the very seat of power to *create institutions* which should foster imagination and which would not be shackled by the silken threads of the centres of power over which they themselves presided. Maulana Azad and Jawaharlal Nehru were the strongest exponents of giving freedom, autonomy to the Akademies. I recall that Maulana Azad was even reluctant to get the Akademies registered as autonomous bodies with a Constitution and framework and annual grants in any hurry. Each time this matter was brought up before him, with his beautiful, long tapering index finger, he would point out to you and say, "No hurry, poets, writers, philosophers will meet, they will discuss, they will reflect and they will find ways and means of governing themselves. Why are you in such a hurry to put them all into one solid framework?" The wisdom of these words one realizes when one looks on the history of the creation of inappropriate structures to contain foster and regulate creativity.

Maulana Azad was a champion of languages. His versatility in Persian, Arabic and Urdu was known but few recognized Maulana's inspiration behind the programmes of Sanskrit, the establishment of the Council of Scientific Technical Terminology and the impetus that he gave to several institutions for the propagation of Hindi, such as the Dakshin Bharat Hindi Prachar Samiti etc. The Parliamentary combat between Purshottam Das Tandon, Seth Govind Das and Maulana was familiar to us. We expected that knives would be sharpened, swords of ideological positions drawn and insinuations made. Each time Maulana stood his ground firmly. Never against Sanskrit or Hindi, he was equally opposed to the domination of any language over any other language. It was Maulana Azad who took the greatest interest in launching the scheme of the Sanskrit Dictionary based on Historical Principles. It was also Maulana Azad who repeatedly drew attention to the need for strengthening the study of classical languages.

In this respect, as in the matter of national integration and his being a true Indian, a true Muslim, he was a follower of Mahatma Gandhi, because for him the language of integration was Hindustani. This he wrote and spoke and in fact if one saw intolerance anywhere, it was when officers of the Government of India could not communicate with him in an Indian language. It was not uncommon for the Maulana to interrupt meetings if participants or officers begin to speak in highly Anglicized English. He understood the language well, but with a naughty glint in his eyes he would turn around to Saiyicain or Ashfaque and ask the question, "what is that person or woman saying in this English gibberish?" Those returned from Cambridge or Oxford were promptly put into their place. That was Maulana, the Hindustani first and last. However, his pain at insinuations hurled at him could not be contained. In one debate he burst out,

> "I want to tell you that you should not expect me to talk in a tone of flattery. Only that one indulges in flattery who has an axe to grind and who wants that everybody should be pleased with him and that he should not lose the office of a Minister. I have no self-interest. Forty years ago, when nobody had even heard of my friends sitting around here, I decided to dedicate my life to the service of the country. I am talking of 1907 when I was 18 or 19 years of age and joined the Revolutionary Party of Bengal. Since then my whole life has been an open book before the world. There is no desire left in me now. The larger part of my life is over. Whatever little remains will also end one day. I have no desire and no ambition now. I may tell you that when a man has no personal motive left in him, he loses his identity. I mean that such a man is immune from worldly setbacks. Such a man is unassailable by weapons because this body is assailable so long as there is self-interest in a man. Once this weakness for the self disappears, nothing can harm or injure a man. I may tell you frankly that for the misfortune that befell this country as a result of the two-nation theory and the establishment of Pakistan, this sort of mentality, this sort of attitude has been as much responsible as the misguided Muslims and the Muslim League."

Hindustani sure but equally international, Maulana Azad was familiar with the age-old cultural dialogue between India, the West Asia and the East. Like Mahatma Gandhi, he wanted the winds of all cultures to blow through India but without being uprooted.

One of the first actions of Maulana Azad as Education Minister was to set up Chairs of Indian Studies in West Asia. This included a Chair of Sanskrit in Iran, Iraq and what was then Egypt. It was at his initiative that Kalidasa's *Shakuntalam* and other works of Sanskrit were translated in Arabic for free distribution to the libraries and institutions in West Asia. In many meetings he referred to the close proximity of Avesta and Sanskrit and the need for Indians to know Pahalvi. A programme of receiving books from these countries and sending books to those countries was the first initial scheme which later came to be known as presentation of books scheme. South-east Asia and cultural ties with these regions also called for his attention. He was particularly interested in Indonesia and its heritage and the common ties between Indonesia, Malaysia and India. Long before the UNESCO General Conference in 1956, he had already established an Indian network of educational and cultural exchanges. The founding of the ICCR should be viewed in this larger context of Maulana Azad's vision of fostering ties between India and other cultures at a non-political, purely cultural and educational level. It is perhaps pertinent to recall at this moment that Maulana Azad was very clear in his mind that the culture and education dialogue must not be conditioned by exigencies of foreign policy, and it was at his instance that the cultural exchange programmes between India and other parts of the world remained in the administrative charge of Education and Culture, and not External Affairs.

As a scholar-savant he was anxious to ensure that the India Office Library returned to India. Reluctant though he was to take trips abroad, he undertook to visit London to discuss with the British Government the return of this Library. He said that in the eyes of the law, the contents of this Library belong to India and should be returned to India. However, in the interest of the dissemination of knowledge, copies should be given to British libraries as also libraries elsewhere. The Government of UK raised many legal issues and mooted the proposal of the division of this library into India, Pakistan and later they brought up the question of Mandlay papers of Burma. Maulana wanted the library back. It should have been returned to India on the eve of independence. Although Mualana had accepted the division of India with pain and defeat, but the division of this library into fragments he would not accept. A library he told us was but a totality, a person and at no time a library be dismembered because it would almost mean the dismembering of a personality, a human being. Committed to a united vision, whether in life or scholarship or education, Maulana stood for a unified vision.

This was the message and the lesson we learnt from him.

9.

Panditji—A Reminiscence

It is difficult to speak about someone whom you have considered an ideal and who has influenced not only your life but the life of a whole generation of Indians. Also much has been written on Panditji. What can I add which will be of any value? Let me therefore go back into memory lane and recreate the images of this man whose towering personality and his vision of the future of the humanity and of India has left an indelible mark. I belong to a generation of Indians who were brought up under the influence of Gandhi and Nehru. Our lives moved in the alternating rhythm of a pendulum of a British education and the calls *Jhanda uncha rahe hamara*. In Congress sessions, we were young volunteers who were sometimes shown how to carry ourselves with elegance and a neat turn out by no less a leader than Nehru. We were stirred with the inspiring speeches of those who spoke from platforms and instilled in us a commitment both to freedom and to discipline.

All this has been written about, so also perhaps of his deep commitment to the spirit of creativity, sensitivity and sensibility. In clear contradistinction to other political leaders, he stood out as a man of culture with a full rounded personality, full of fun and frolic, enthusiasm and zest for life. The earliest images are of a good horse rider, kicking his heels on a horse saddle and riding off in the mountains of Kashmir. The life of the mountains, the lakes and the rivers and the oceans were for him the symbols of a spirit of adventure as also the quiet inner flow which gave stability to his life of ceaseless dynamic action. Whether it was Kashmir or Ladakh, the Western or the Eastern Himalayas, mountains and snow scapes, were an eternal call. The Mansarover and Kailash dominated his life of reflection. He was perhaps spiritually there. The flow of the Ganga represented to him the foundations of not only Indian culture but the culture of the world. In a letter from prison written to his daughter in 1941, he articulates it in a manner which echoes in the hearts of every Indian:

> I can see the Garhwal foothills from here and a longish walk will take you to the district boundary. The knowledge of this surpassing beauty, so near us and yet so far from this warring world, so peaceful and unperturbed by human folly, excites me. Those strange people who were our ancestors in the long ago felt the wonder of these mountains and valleys and, with the unerring instinct of genius, yoked this sense of awe and life's daily toil and conflicts offered, something with the impress of the eternal upon it. And so for two thousand years or more, innumerable pilgrim souls have marched through these valleys and mountains to Badrinath and Kedarnath and Gangotri, from where the baby Ganga emerges, so tiny and frolicsome, but to grow and grow in her long wandering till she becomes the noble river that sweeps by Prayag and Kashi and beyond.
>
> Shall I ever go wandering again in these mountains, and pierce the forest and climb the snows and feel the thrill of the precipice and the deep gorge? And then lie in deep content on a thick carpet of mountain flowers and rays of the setting sun? Shall 1 sit by the side of the youthful and turbulent Ganga in her mountain home and watch her throw her head in a swirl of icy spray in pride and defiance, or creep round lovingly some favoured rock and take it into her embrace? And then rush down joyously over the boulders and hurt herself with a mighty shout over some great precipice? I have known her so long as a sedate lady, seemingly calm, but for all that, the fire is in her veins even then, the fiery vitality of youth and the spirit of adventure, and this breaks out from time to time when her peaceful waters seem angry and tumble over each other and spread out over vast areas.
>
> I love the rivers of India and I should like to explore them from end to end, and to go back into the dawn of history and watch the processions of men and women, of cultures and civilizations, going down the broad streams of these rivers, the Indus, the Brahmaputra, the Ganga and also that very lovable river of ours—the Jamuna.'

Nature shaped his vision. Within and without jail, as he watched the clouds from the windows of his closed rooms, he reflected on the flow of Indian history and discovered the dynamics of a culture with all its ups and downs. Often it was the clouds which made him ask questions about himself and about the world around both in the past and the future. Harmony with life was his theme, and what did this harmony represent: it was the ability to communicate with nature, plants, animals and of course human beings.

In another letter, written from Almora in 1935, he speaks of all this, always considering himself as a student. In his own words—

> I have always been a bit of a student, trying to learn to understand, but largely this effort was intellectual. There was also the emotional element in it, the learning from crowds, the appreciation of mass psychology. Latterly I have felt drawn more

> and more towards nature—to plants and animals. May be it is a relief and an escape from human folly, human cowardice and human knavery; I feel more in tune with nature. I notice little things that I had not noticed before. I sense the pulsating and throbbing life round about me. I notice the sensitive growing tip of a creeper plant, how full of life and energy it is. Animal-like, it seems and sometimes almost sinister looking; even the feel is hairy as that of a young animal. It stands up seeking for something to catch hold of. See, it looks just like a snake, with a snake's rounded nose and small eyes; or it coils up, catching something in its grasp. Fascinated, I watch it.
>
> I feel that this is a hopeful sign in me. I am growing still, getting more educated, more in harmony with life. If only human beings were not such spots of disharmony!

It was this insistence of harmony which made him speak of a well integrated personality; someone who would be always in harmony with life and nature and as he said, "the very reverse of the quarrelsome, dissatisfied, ever complaining type that we see so often today......"

Literature was his first love; both the shaper as also the vehicle of communicating his humanistic vision and what he concretised in a most remarkable manner in a programme of action as soon as he took over the reigns of power. Poetry, he said, has not only "attracted me and I go to it for relaxation but it has also inspired me for work." His early education had given him a taste for science and it was this scientific training which later made him insist on the Indians developing a scientific temper. His humanism was a juxtaposition of the scientific and the artistic of intense activity along with an ability to reflect, imagine and be silent.

Understandably he became the pioneer of many new initiatives in the field of what we today call as 'cultural activities'. The first of these was in 1947 when, on the occasion of Asian Relations Conference, he insisted that there be a music and dance performance in the Red Fort. It was not common in those days to organise what was known as cultural programmes. Short of choreographing the numbers, Panditji directed just about everything relating to the performance. Of greater significance was his decision to include in the Republic Day Parade, marches by a vast number of tribal communities of India and to hold a folk dance festival. Today considered as a routine affair, this decision was epoch-making for the urbanite Indian. This was an eye-opener of the vast diverse rich vibrating India. Indeed by making this one decision, he laid the foundations for another perception of Indian culture, so far only articulated in a few books, such as those of Kosambi.

An exhibition of Indian Art was held in UK, London at the Burlington House in 1948. This was the very first exhibition which had been compiled. It included the masterpieces of the Mauryan Bull capital, the famous Chola Rama and many others. The exhibition returned and was housed in Rashtrapati Bhavan. It was here that the incipient seeds of a National Museum of Art sprouted. In fact the National Museum was housed in Rashtrapati Bhavan for many years until it had its own building.

A museum movement in India was necessary, if museums had to be changed from store houses to institutions of art and scholarship. Under the leadership of Maulana Azad and Nehru, the first Central Advisory Committee on Museums was established. A policy on National Museums was evolved and impetus was given to the holding of exhibitions. Not unimportant amongst these was the exhibition in Hyderabad House based on the Salar Jung collection which was to be known later as the Salar Jung Museum. One could recount other instances.

The period of the early nineteen fifties—fifty two or fifty six—was one of great activity, dynamic action and the establishment of many new national institutions. The three Akademies and the ICCR were established during this period. Jawaharlal Nehru himself was the President of the Sahitya Akademi. He, along with Maulana Azad, was always anxious to uphold the autonomy of the Akademies and was equally anxious that the Akademies be the highest opinion making bodies rather than administrative institutions. This was also the period of the very first initiatives taken by Shri Jawaharlal Nehru to launch major programmes of International Cultural Programmes. Often he told us that so far India has known the world only through the English language and British eyes. It was important that we now know the world and the great civilizations of other lands directly. In 1954, he directed all arrangements that were to be made in order to receive the first major cultural delegation from China soon after the visit of Chou-en Lai. He personally talked to the officers how to receive, arrange welcomes and one saw in the Prime Minister of this country a man who was as keen and meticulous about protocol as he was of politics. Soon after followed the visit of major Indian delegations to China, to Southeast Asia, to the USSR and to West Asian countries. Would anyone have believed in the nineteen forties that Indian music and dance, traditional sarod and sitar, so far confined to the courts of Indian princes and at best close *mehfils*, would suddenly become a potent tool of establishing a cultural dialogue? While such large delegations were one part of the initiative, a concerted effort of making translations of Indian classics into foreign languages, such as Kalidasa's writings into Arabic and Persian, was the other sustained effort.

1955–56 was an important year for many reasons. The 2500th anniversary of the Buddha was celebrated where scholars and monks and savants came from all parts of the world. Again it was Jawaharlal Nehru who took the keenest interest in going through the organisational plans and programmes of holding of such a conference. His speeches at the conference and his meetings with leaders such as The Dalai Lama, The Panchan Lama and those others from Sri Lanka, Thailand, Mongolia were truly inspiring. It was as a result of this conference and some later developments that Panditji reflected one day on Indian history. He said in a note there was a time 'when Chinese pilgrim came to India to savour the message of Buddhism and to carry it to lands far and wide. A time has now come when we should receive in our land the fruits of their work. Towards this end, three institutions should be established—first the Huen Tsang Memorial, second the Central Institute of Higher Tibetan Studies in Varanasi and the third the Institute of Buddhist Studies at Leh'. But for this perspicacity, we may not have laid the foundations of a systematic study of Buddhism, especially in its Mahayana aspect.

Soon followed the first Conference of UNESCO held outside Paris. Memories of that Conference still reverberate after a lapse of three decades. It was during this period that the major programme of mutual understanding of the east and the west was launched by Dr. S. Radhakrishnan.

International Cultural Relations, global cultural dialogue, was a concern but an equal concern was the fostering of talent for the promotion of traditional learning in India and the strengthening of Sanskrit and Persian and Arabic institutions which had begun to languish for lack of State patronage. Although these institutions continue to fall outside the formal system of education, despite the commitment of both Jawaharlal Nehru and Maulana Azad to create linkages between the two systems, it was not possible to do so. Nevertheless, despite criticism, both the Sanskrit Banaras Visva Vidyalaya (then not a University) as also the Dairul-Marif were given grants and support. Of fundamental importance was the initiative taken to launch the project of a Dictionary of Sanskrit based on historical principles. This project continues.

Although the late fifties and early sixties brought in many different types of pressures, both from within and without, it was during this period that four Central Universities were nationalized. Bills were passed after heated debates and new initiatives taken to establish institutions of modern Indian languages. This was a concurrent action along with all that was being done in the field of science, especially the establishment of the CSIR and the chain of laboratories. This was also complementary to the initiatives of a change in policy regarding handicrafts, handlooms and all that is understood by the craft centres. By 1964, foundations of a network of institutions, fully or partially financed by Centre or States, in areas in disciplines hitherto untouched by Government had been established. Planned budgets were available even if meagre.

In January 1964, he addressed perhaps one of his last major international conferences, namely, the International Congress of Orientalists. Never before had Orientalists met east of the Suez. Orientalism was the intellectual pursuit in the heart of Europe. It required tremendous effort to persuade the international body to hold a Conference in a venue of the countries to which the study belongs. Jawaharlal Nehru addressed this Conference on 4th of January 1964. A galaxy of the world's most distinguished scholars belonging to the fields of Mesopotamian, Sumerian, Altaic, Hittite studies met. Jawaharlal Nehru addressed them in the following words:

> "Why is a person an orientalist? I suppose the very idea involves people from outside this oriental sphere, as it may be called, looking into the ancient lives and thoughts of those who were resident in this sphere. I have been resident, born and bred, here, and I cannot very well look at it from outside; of course, even looking at it from inside, if the mind be adapted to other things—one may look at it from the point of view of an outsider also."

And he went on to ask how a synthesis between the old and new could be achieved:

> "Because today all of us, wherever we live, especially in the older civilizations, have to find some method of arriving at some synthesis between the old and the new. We cannot discard the old and uproot ourselves, for we should think of the old as something of value which has come down to us. If we want to give it up, or circumstances force us to give it up, we become rootless. But we cannot live in the past. We have to live in the modern age and understand it, adapt it to our ways. How to bring about this synthesis between the old and the new is one of the problems before us.
>
> How can you bring about that connection between the two? It is a strange world we live in, with changing conditions and searching out new avenues. But with all the progress that we make, it is essentially knowledge of the external world and the forces that control it, and technology and science. It is not very much

concerned with knowledge of yourself or of ourselves. We go back to the ancient saying, the Greek saying, the Indian saying or that of any other country, where people always laid stress on a person knowing himself: "Know Thyself". The ancient way of thinking really concentrating itself on knowing oneself, and they forgot to learn about the external world in which they lived. Today we are concentrating our minds on the external world—it is very necessary that we do it—but perhaps we ignore the individual and what he is, and do not know much about it. The two approaches, the external approach and the internal approach, have to be, I suppose, combined in order to make us realise what we are now, how we are to face our problems. I am suggesting this to you, but I am not sure if it is not outside the scope of those who are here. But I do suggest to you that it is desirable for us to learn something of ourselves, apart from learning something of the outside world about us. Therefore, perhaps in this era of change that is so confusing today, it would be helpful if we thought quietly about ourselves, about the world at large, and not merely be concerned with the atom bomb and how to escape it. Of course, we want to escape the atom and hydrogen bombs; we all want to have peace, without which there can be no progress. But in addition to that, it may be necessary to go a little more deeply into what we are, what the world is and where it is taking us to."

His global vision as also his commitment to achieve a synthesis and balance between the old and new, the outer and inner, was deep. He spoke from intense experience. The man of universal vision stirred the assembly to a standing applause. Soon after in May he passed into history himself.

It was given to some of us to be charged with a task for establishing a memorial in his name. In October 1964, the President of India decided to dedicate the Teen Murti House to the nation and to build it into not only a museum but an institution for study of contemporary history. This was a befitting tribute to a man of contemporary vision who had miles to go and promises to keep. The President inaugurated the Nehru Memorial Museum and Library on 14th November. Since then it has stood for discovering the paths which Nehru had paved. In building these institutions and sustaining them with the vision of the man whose name they commemorate, we shall repay in some small measure the debt we owe him.

10.

Madan Mohan Malaviya

On the solemn occasion of the inauguration of the National Memorial of Mahamana Madan Mohan Malaviya, one remembers with a sense of gratitude the founding fathers of the Banaras Hindu University and a generation of Indians who symbolized all that was and is noble, altruistic and inclusive in the vision and values of this country. Concurrently there is a sense of failure because of a consciousness of not having been able to consolidate and concretize this vision and build upon the foundations laid by them. Has this generation, in its unquestioned strides of achievement to be a powerful player in the global world, somewhere lost the capacity to maintain the *meru dand* (the central spine) of a holistic tradition of India?

Mahamana Madan Mohan Malaviya, the man who gave up much to establish an institution of learning which would be all-encompassing for the eradication of caste barriers and any other social or economic barriers, unselfconsciously ensured that neither 'temples nor rivers' were the exclusive site for any particular group. Although the University he established was and is called the 'Banaras Hindu University', in his own words he declared unequivocally:

> 'India is not a country of the Hindus only. It is a country of the Muslims, the Christians and the Parsees too. The country can gain strength and develop itself only when the people of the different communities in India live in mutual goodwill and harmony. It is my earnest hope and prayer that this centre of life and light which is coming into existence, will produce students who will not only be intellectually equal to the best of their fellow students in other parts of the world, but will also live a noble life, love their country and be loyal to the Supreme ruler'.

It was this vision, this all-embracing capacity of India, that enabled Mahamana Malaviyaji to assemble people from all disciplines to share and reinforce his vision. These included Mrs. Annie Besant, who cooperated with him most positively to create one institution and not two. Scientists such as J.C. Bose, P.C. Ray, C.V. Raman, came naturally. There was Dr. Harold Mann and Professor Sam Higginbottom. This was an international gallery without an international conference! Above all, Mahatma Gandhi, who had just returned to India from South Africa, came to Banaras to attend the foundation stone-laying ceremony, and he addressed his first public lecture in India on 6 February 1916. This is a heritage that this University has a mandate to treasure, to preserve, to conserve and to take it to the future.

As for the founding father Pt. Madan Mohan Malaviya, what can be added beyond what Mahatma Gandhi had said about him? Paying a tribute, Mahatma Gandhi called himself a devotee (*Pujari*) of Malaviyaji, also saying that Malaviyaji was the soul of Kashi Hindu Vishvavidyalaya, later called Banaras Hindu University, and Kashi Hindu Vishvavidyalaya was the soul of Malaviyaji.

The dedication and idealism with which the University was started was taken forward with as much commitment by succeeding Chancellors and Vice-Chancellors, who took the University to many great heights. The Vice-Chancellors included amongst others Dr. S. Radhakrisnan, Dr. C.P. Ramaswamy Iyer and Acharya Narendra Dev. Maharaja Krishna Raja Wadiyar IV of Mysore, Chancellor, laid the foundation stone of the Engineering College and introduced a most innovative course for artisans. This was way back in 1919. Others followed by strengthening various disciplines, all too many to be mentioned. Can one forget the name of Govind Mohan Malaviya who brought together from different parts of India some of the greatest scholars to teach in the University, whether they had degrees or did not have degrees? They included people like Professor Hazari Prasad Dwivedi and doyens like T.V.R. Murthy, Vasudeva Saran Agrawala, Rajvali Pandey, the great musician Omkar Nath Thakur and the musicologist Alian Danielou. Ashi Naresh had not only donated 300 acres for the University but was also the motivating spirit behind establishment of the College of Indology.

In addition to the scholars who were members of the faculty, there was the most gracious, generous presence of the late Shri Rai Kishan Das. He donated his unique and unparalleled collection of art objects, paintings, coins, textiles as also the original manuscripts of some of India's great poets and novelists. I recall vividly the transfer of this great collection from Malaviya Bhawan to what is today the Bharat Kala Bhawan, an institution of international status and standing. Rai Kishan Das shared the vision of the nationalist leaders. He was at home with Shri Jawaharlal Nehru as with Malaviya family. His home, Sita Nivas, in the BHU was a magnetic situ for all to assemble. This was the dialogue of culture and civilization, languages and sensibility.

Elsewhere, in the field of medicine, there was a balance of attention to the domains of allopathy as also Ayurveda. The Banaras Hindu University thus became a confluence of the study of the parallel streams of traditional Indian knowledge as also modern, western disciplines.

Rarely such a confluence come together of scientists ranging from those in the field of pure science—physics, chemistry—to technology, to engineering, to music and, naturally, the humanities and the arts. That today it has 129 faculties of the several institutions speak of the advances that the University has made and the contributions of its faculties and its students to the study of different aspects of human knowledge. Little wonder that it has attracted scholars from all parts of the world and many eminent scholars, such as Raimon Panikkar, Andre Scrima, Bettina Bäumer, Alice Boner and others who had made Banaras and its University their second home.

With such a legacy of commitment and total dedication and selflessness and such achievements in the growth of knowledge, there are still many miles to go and many promises to keep.

This year's theme is 'A Blue-print for the Transformation of India into a Powerful Country'. The only comment one can make on this as a humble student of this University who has learnt at the feet of some of the greatest scholars and teachers, is that no blueprint can be made for the transformation of the country: the blueprint first and foremost has to be for transformation of the self, a self which is not self-centred. Once this attitudinal change takes place, which is the message of the country at the level of value, selfless action, prepared and inspired by *Lokahita,* then and then alone can this country become powerful in the real sense. No civilizations have lived without material progress, but no cultures have lasted long without a body of values which provide the motivation for detached action and which provides the *meru dand* for living. A powerful country has no other measure but the measure, first and foremost, of self-discipline, restraint and self-accountability at both the personal as also the collective levels.

This is a moment of reckoning for us because with all India's achievements in different spheres and in different domains and in different disciplines, when it can send out the Chandrayan I to the moon, India has also to remember the words of both Mahatma Gandhi as also Malaviyaji that India is a country for each and every one at every level. A blueprint for transformation can be made only when there is equalization in terms of recognition of knowledge of the literate and the illiterate, the culture of the rich and the poor, and the recognition of the unique capacity of each individual in the country to contribute. This is the inclusive society that we speak about and this is the message of the great leaders and visionaries who founded this University or supported it. India indeed has the potential to evolve an alternate model of development which would be more suited two-thirds of humanity. The vision of the founding fathers of the University of Banaras Hindu University lay in the principle of this *Samanavaya* and, one may add the word, to create *satbhavana* through *sambandh*.

11.

Kamaladevi Chattopadhyaya*

Kamaladevi Chattopadhyaya was a person who represented a historical moment of change in this country and was also an agent of change. The values she embodied she actualized throughout her life. It is not for me to recount her journey from childhood to adolescence to youth to adulthood and finally that mellowing ripeness and richness of experience, extending love and affection to all, young and old, the disempowered and the empowered. Not for a moment throughout her life did she flinch an inch to make compromises on values that she inherited from her mother and grandmother. With utmost ease she could take courageous action. In what words can I pay tribute to her, the little I, who since childhood received from her unbounded love and trust as also candid, sharp criticism!

Biographies of Kamaladevi Chattopadhyaya have been written, and she has contributed her own memoirs as well. Rich compliments have been paid to her by political leaders, specially her companions during the freedom struggle and particularly members of the Socialist Party—e.g., Narendra Dev, Jayaprakash Narain, Yusuf Meherally and others. She could argue with Mahatma Gandhi, interrogate Jawaharlal Nehru. She refused to be the President of India, because her calling was of a different kind and at a different level. Theatre and the arts, the fragrance of flowers, the sweet smell of jasmine which she wore on her hair from childhood to old age, the immaculate attention to dress and coiffure, was the natural feminine who could match effortlessly, with a smile, with humour and laughter, masculine power! She believed in making the ordinary, extraordinary. She was a person who gave dignity to the crafts and the craft persons. She made it fashionable to wear hand-spun, hand-woven *sarees* and adorn homes with the crafts. Today they have acquired a status of 'brand names' in the design market, domestic and international. Welcome as all this is, one wonders whether Kamaladevi Chattopadhyaya would have thought that this was the fruition of a plant or a seed she

* Extract from KV's first Kamaladevi Chattopadhyaya Lecture organised by CCRT in 2009.

sowed, or regretted the fact that while the creativity has been acknowledged, there has not been an equal acknowledgment of the craft persons. Her agenda here was to give economic sustainability, dignity and pride to the makers and of course bring about a sea-change in the sensitivity of the elite.

Since the moment of agreeing to deliver this lecture I have been filled with memories and this lecture could be a sharing of these memories, not just my memories but her memories of me! One episode would probably be relevant. We sat in a formal meeting. In my foolish manner I began to argue or disagree with her. She listened and then turned round and said to me, 'You shut up. You were too heavy to be carried when we were collecting salt at Chowpathi during the Salt Satyagraha. I had to hand you over to your mother and had to go to court arrest in the cause of the salt of freedom'. Naturally I was stunned, to say the least. Within a second, however, with her characteristic disarming smile, she said, 'Anyhow let us listen to her argument. There is something there'. Often, and more than often, I thought that Kamaladeviji was giving us this freedom salt, i.e., freedom salt of the spirit which permeates all dimensions of life.

On another occasion, my mother lay ill in hospital. Kamaladeviji came to see her. The two women held hands and there was exchange of emotions through eyes, no words were uttered. She came out of the hospital. As she was going to sit in the car I said to her, 'Kamaladeviji, thank you very much for coming; you know what it means to her'. She snapped back at me, 'What impertinence! I knew your mother before you were born'.

These two very personal recollections give an insight into her character at the most human level. However, as we all know, she was called in her days in Britain 'the uncrowned Queen of India'. Wherever she sat and whenever she spoke or initiated a programme, her presence and her words communicated her conviction and her dedication to the causes that she championed. I have watched her from near and far, first, when she went off without notice (with my mother) to Kashmir, when the first attack of the infiltrators took place, to bring relief and solace, specially to the women, and then her relentless work in the rehabilitation of refugees in Faridabad. There was the other Kamaladevi in her public persona as a key figure in the first Asian Relations Conference of 1947. The artist Kamaladevi was naturally involved in the establishment of many institutions and was consulted by the political leadership in the setting up of the national academies of India following independence.

In her book 'Inner Recesses, Outer Spaces', apart from many other important issues, she gives a vivid account of her conversations with Maulana Azad on the establishment of the Academies and also his views on what he considered the Academies to be, i.e., something in the nature of the Greek academies as envisaged by Plato, and not administrative institutions. He adapted the term as 'Akademi' to be in congruent with the Greek pronunciation and also to conform to the Hindi pronunciation. According to Maulana Azad, says Kamaladeviji, the role of the Akademies

> 'will be to canalize fruitfully the new cultural forces released after independence. While I believe that arts have to derive their sustenance only from the people, the Government must undertake their development and continuity as its primary duty. The Akademies will however be autonomous in their internal working and will include in their composition not only State representatives but equally representatives of important art organizations and distinguished individual artists. The Akademi of dance, drama and music will be the first to be set up. Because of your active interest in them, I wish to share my thoughts with you'.

She also gives an account of the genesis of the National School of Drama. It was my privilege to work with her in the early years of the formation of the Asian Theatre Institute, the incipient institution of what is today the National School of Drama. It was also my pleasure to work with her as a Vice-Chairperson of the Sangeet Natak Akademi and of course as Vice-Chairperson of this institution, the Centre for Cultural Resources and Training.

12.

Aruna Asaf Ali

Aruna Asaf Ali—the frail, fragile, almost evanescent figure—was part of my consciousness from the age of eight. I recall all too vividly the first encounter. I had accompanied mother to Arunaji's home. We had walked around in the lanes and bye-lanes of Delhi, behind Jama Masjid, until we paused against a big gate, a wooden gate. I can almost hear the screeching of the gate as it opened and then we stood to meet this sparkling, radiant, sharp but gentle soul. The occasion was the meeting of the Women and the Children Seva Dal of the Congress. There was also the unforgettable leader of volunteer Memobai. Whatever else happened relating to conducting processions, shouting slogans, the pitch of the slogans, the singing of the song, *Sare jahan se acchha....*, or *Jhanda ooncha rahe hamara...*, the first impression was one of strength in gentleness.

From that day to this, Arunaji has flitted, in and out, of the memories of the whole generation of Indians, both pre and post 1942 movement. In 1942, and later when she went underground, it was the excitement of idealism, of taking part in a great national adventure, not without the excitement of being a peripheral part of a detective drama to have Arunaji come home at night and leave in the morning before anyone knew. We were as if taking part in historic revolutions, even if it was somewhat confined to carrying secret letters between Connaught Place and Hailey Road where the Patnaiks lived. The shades of a variety of opinions, ideologies and methodologies of achieving freedom took hold of us. While some became Gandhians, committed to the path of non-violence and the slogan "Do or Die," others looked with admiration to the Socialist Acharya Narendra Dev, Bishamber Pande and others. A few were sharply divided between commitment to emerging Communism—the Soviet Block and the Royists and radical humanists, i.e., who expounded support for the Allies because the Allies were for democracy. Betting of life and taking of vows was normal, we lived intensely and passionately in causes we believed in, but those we understood only partially. Amongst those who absconded and believed in paths divergent from Gandhiji was Aruna

Asaf Ali but they were all, and especially she was, the recipient of abundant love and affection from Gandhiji. When she recounted several encounters with Bapu on the ethical issues of ends and means, it was the pristine sincerity of her being which illumined the experience and the message.

Reminiscences apart, this frail frame took up issues with leaders and Governments with the perseverance and strength of flint. The wiry frame contained as if a high tension wire which was energised by any calls which demand justice, equity and freedom. No slave follower of 'isms' despite her Leftist inclination, she had been quick to respond to any need and to take positions in the interest of India, not parties or narrow 'isms'. She comprehended the worlds with a very special flavour of global brotherhood which transcended political polarities. What lent stature to each of her utterances was the quality of self-effacement as also a complete innate unselfishness.

In a Nehru Memorial Lecture, I was as overwhelmed as I was surprised when she frankly admitted that perhaps it was wrong for the 'Progressives' to insist that religion should not be taught as part of the educational curricula. While bemoaning the situation in different parts of India, the conflicts and violence in the name of religion, caste, creed, she said that perhaps had religion been taught or religious studies been made part of the educational curricula, the younger generation would have had the opportunity to become acquainted with all forms of religion and have respect not only for one's own religion, but, also for other religions. Its elimination/absence in the curricula in a country with strong religious traditions, tantamount to so-called religious education coming only from narrow-minded sectarian interpretations, which naturally led to fundamentalism and confrontations. Coming from someone who has stood almost for atheism, this came as a surprise. But it should not have been a surprise because it was coming from one who was growing every minute and who was sensitive to all that happened and was happening in and around.

Arunaji's stature as political leader, woman, writer and editor was enhanced by the humility and grace of her presence. Wherever she was, she trod the earth lightly and the fragrance and the fresh purity of her 'being' was elevating. I was privileged to see and experience and receive the most precious gift of her love and affection.

13.

Behind the Stoic Figure of Courage and Candour—Madhu Dandavate

One may well ask: what is an a-political person like me doing here? Nevertheless, with utmost hesitation I speak. I am honoured to be invited to speak on this important occasion. Professor Madhu Dandavate sent me his book, *Dialogue with Life*, and wanted me to speak. I could hardly say 'no' to his ever-persuasive, warm and affectionate request, almost command. Understandably, I was hesitant, almost reluctant, conscious of my altogether too many inadequacies on many dimensions and spheres. As on a previous occasion, when he asked me to deliver the Yusuf Meherally Memorial Lecture, there was no way to persuade him to accept my 'no'.

Surely this man of 'stainless steel', literally and metaphorically, enabled me to have access to the many dimensions of his life and the life of our times. It was fortuitous and ironical that he should have been interviewed by Usha Prasad of the Nehru Memorial Museum and Library, an institution which may well have been closed down during the Janata Government regime. But that is another story, not to be told here.

I am glad that the institution survived to become a repository of the archives of many leaders and personalities who are the makers of modern India. I have no doubt that posterity will have much to 'learn' from the private papers and the records of the Oral History Division. Madhu Dandavate's interviews will constitute a most important testimony of an active participant and a keen observer and commentator on the dynamics and dialects of the making of a young parliamentary democracy.

For me, reading the book was the replay of the history of our times, from the perspective of a person who was nurtured through his grandfather and father, aunt and others, into literature, Western and Indian, the classics Bhasa's play and the *Arthasastra*, *Ramayana* and *Mahabharata*, and one who was fired with a zealous commitment to justice, social justice and moral values. It is the theme of social justice and moral values which runs through the work, no matter which situation the author finds himself or which personality he encounters, praises or is critical of.

This is evident from the formative years: when he prefers Sita to Rama, and is indignant at the injustice done to *Eklavya* in the *Mahabharata*. Once he plunges into politics, as a young man in the 'Quit India' movement in 1942, or during the Goa liberation movement, or during the agitation of Samyukta Maharashtra, and later as a parliamentarian, it is the sense of 'justice' and moral right which are the motivating forces of his long and arduous journey through many a moment of turbulence, suffering and pain, as also joy and jubilation.

As I read the book, it was not a cold, distant, analytical narration of history of contemporary India. Instead, it was a candid personal account of one who was concurrently a participant and an observer. Naturally the perspective and narration is based on personal experience, growth, involvement and critical insights into the dynamics of socio-political processes of the last eight decades. The book engaged me from the first to last, like a novel, where you keep expecting the unexpected to happen. What l have to place before you, therefore, is not a cold, objective, critical analysis of a book by a leading figure in Indian politics and his commitments to a particular political ideology, and the issues which engaged him in Parliament and the positions he took as a member of a political party. Instead, I thought it may perhaps be of interest and value to identify the unifying thread of this account, by pointing out the deep and unshakable values which motivated his journey in life, from the youngest days to today, where he is. For me the book revealed the sensitive and strong 'human' being who was ignited by, as he says, less with passion but more with compassion, with accountability to oneself in upholding moral values, and as one who does not consider his bitterest opponent an enemy. It is the firm belief in these human values which filters through the text, both implicitly and explicitly.

However, before l trace the trajectory of this dialogue with life, let me, as l did on the occasion of the Yusuf Meherally lecture, share with you my response at a personal level. For me this was a refreshing of many memories some of childhood, others of adolescence, and yet others of adulthood, as a receiver and partaker, but not at all as an active actor in the political process. This will be so also of others of my generation.

Among the personalities and characters which people the pages of this book are naturally the towering figures of Gandhi and Jawaharlal Nehru, whether you have known them personally or not, whether you have been in agreement or disagreement with their ideology and their views. They have been the principal shapers of a generation, specially those of us who were born in pre-independent India and have lived their lives in independent India. For me, as someone who had received the affection of both in small measure, poignant memories of 'meeting' and communication were brought back. Also, as I read through Madhu Dandavate's book, I could not but go back and compare this engagement with the two leaders with that of Kamaladevi, for me my second mother. In her book, *Inner Recesses, Outer Spaces*, she gives a vivid account of her many meaningful encounters with both, but particularly Gandhiji. The comparison is relevant, because both Kamaladevi and Madhu Dandavate were avowed socialists, and each describes vividly the establishment of the Socialist Party in 1934. The two, along with Jayaprakash Narayan and Acharya Narendra Deva, were deeply committed not only in words but in deed and conduct to the moral and ethical values upheld by Gandhiji. I recalled how at one time Acharya Narendra Deva had vehemently argued with Mahatma Gandhi on the use of the words 'truth' and 'non-violence' in his credo, but the same Narendra Deva had paid the most moving tribute to Gandhiji on his death, when he said 'our crown, our king, is gone. The man who was pride to mankind has left us sobbing and weeping.' Acharya Narendra Deva sobbed as did the audience.

Acharya Narendra Deva, whom I had known as a friend of my aunt and mother, had left an indelible impression on me. His erudition, his span of reading from Shakespeare to the *Adbhidharma Kosa*, to Bhaskar and Aryabhatta, was phenomenal. I recall vividly how he urged us as children to inculcate an insatiable desire for reading, reading and reading, and imbibing. Madhuji's book revived those memories and reminded me of Acharyaji's letter to his son (Ashok Nath Verma) from jail, urging him to send books after books to jail. I wondered how many political leaders today, whether in jail or outside, would pour over the tomes of ancient Pali texts and attempt to resolve mathematical equations of Bhaskar II and uncode *Lilavati's Mathematical Paradox*. As Professor Madhu Dandavate recalls in his book,

> I was present at a Press conference addressed by Jawaharlal Nehru after his release. He was asked a question, "You wrote *The Discovery of India* but you had no sources inside the jail for reference?" Jawaharlal Nehru said, "Of course, I had no references in the form of books, but I had two living encyclopaedias with me: Acharya Narendra Deva and Maulana Abul Kalam Azad".

Madhu Dandavate's life was undoubtedly influenced in a significant manner by men of the caliber and complexity of Acharya Narendra Deva. And of course there is the light-footed, sprightly figure of Achyut Patwardhan, years senior to Madhuji, but almost his friend. They shared the school and locality. I recalled the impish delight we got whenever Achyutji and Arunaji came to seek shelter during their period of absconding, the small chits we had to pass on to Biju Patnaik sitting in Hailey Road. It was not the political dimensions of the post-9th August 1942 movements of an Achyut Patwardhan, an Aruna Asaf Ali, a B.V. Keskar, a Bishamber Nath Pande which came to the forefront in my consciousness, rather the human dimensions of a mystery film which I had seen in real life under the safe roof of my father.

Reading Madhuji's account I was in giggles, not because of what he said, but because of what it triggered in me as memory. I could go on and on and on, for there are others in the book, whom I did not know personally so well, but well enough to distinguish a public persona from the human. The personality of Dr. Rammanohar Lohia comes to mind. One had heard him 'roar like a lion', as M.C. Chagla used to tell us at briefing meetings before Parliament questions, and yet here was a man at home, friend of my dear colleague Roma-di in Miranda House, who was full of poetry and humour, human to the core in those twilight meetings in the evening. Madhuji's references to the contributions of Rammanohar Lohia brought these memories back.

And lastly of Jayaprakashji. Dr. Madhu Dandavate's poignant references to JP as the leader of the socialists and as heralder of the call for Total Revolution, took me back to his days of the Sarvodaya and Gramdan movements in 1958, when both my dear friend Lakshmi Jain and later S.H. Vatsyayan, my husband, left all to join him. So as not to continue along the line of associative memory, let me say that Madhu's *Dialogue with Life* for me was the replay of many precious moments in the journey of my life personally and some others of my generation. I have watched and learnt from the journey of these men of courage who by volition then renounced active politics. Achyutji comes foremost to my mind, whose journey culminated as a disciple of J. Krishnamurthy, and also of Bishamber Nath Pande, who mellowed from his early fiery days to become Babaji, totally dedicated to Gandhi in order to re-establish communal harmony. It is not necessary to recount Kamaladeviji's self-conscious renunciation of the arena of active politics.

And now to return to the man of stainless steel, who has cultivated several surgeries and abundant jail terms and one who has searched his soul, while jailors have cracked the soles of his shoes. Behind and inside the stoic figure of courage and candour, there is the sensitive human being nurtured, as I said, from his childhood on literature, Indian and foreign. The influence of his grandfather, a littèrateur of renown, and translator of many Sanskrit works, is profound and enduring, as also of his father and equally of his aunt. Poetry and music were given as family inheritance, as was the aspiration to become a scientist, rather than follow his father's footsteps as an engineer. The pursuit of science, specially physics, the interest in poetry and music, and of course cricket, went hand in hand with the role of a political activist. The affirmation of social justice was a constant companion.

Professor Madhu's narration is replete with references to many incidents of his life where he and others demonstrated an unshakable commitment to social justice and acted in order to uphold moral values. One such instance comes to mind. It is Madhuji's account of Acharya Narendra Deva resigning from the UP Legislative Assembly as a consequence of the Nasik resolution of the Socialist Party in 1948. Acharya Narendra said, 'Sir, we were in the Congress. We have now left the Congress and have no moral right to continue in the Assembly.' Gobind Ballabh Pant, the Chief Minister, responded: *Ap ke bina yeh mehfil challenge nahi.* Acharya Narendra Deva replied, 'It will go on. That is the compulsion of political morality,' and added in response to further questions, 'I am not guided by the written law. I am guided more by the inner moral law of life. All of us are resigning.' I may add that the beginning of the speech was the memorable sentence: 'Parting is always painful and sad' etc. Recounting the incident, Madhu Dandavate's comment is of significance.

> When I think of that statement of Acharya Narendra Deva about the moral tone of politics and compare it with present day politics, we find that today politicians are selling their soul for patronage, wealth and power.

Another moving example of moral courage is Madhu Dandavate's and S.M. Joshi's conduct in the context of the Samyukta Maharashtra movement, when even a C.D. Deshmukh, whom we all remember as the founder of the India International Centre, also resigned, on moral grounds. Madhu Dandavate protected the studio of a Gujarati gentleman. When the proprietor of the studio thanked him, the reply was,

> You need not thank me. I have only followed the avowed policy of the Samyukta Maharashtra Samiti which believes in a peaceful movement without hatred against any linguistic group.

Equally educative is the unique experiment of S.M. Joshi (that thin fragile man, whom also I had the privilege to know) that members of the movement should stay with the Gujarati families in their chawls. S.M. Joshi was determined, Madhuji tells us, to use Gandhian methods to run the movement.

One could not but agree with Madhu Dandavate that party affiliations and ideological differences is one matter but at no time should there be the abandonment of moral values and human compassion and affection. Thus, one can only echo what he states in the Preface and at the end of the book, 'Future Course'.

> With hindsight, as I cast a glance at the evolution of my life from the formative stages to the present turbulent times, I realise that there is an imperative need to inculcate in our personal and social life, human values like freedom, equality, social justice, religious tolerance, secularism, environment friendliness, dignity and empowerment of women, and above all a scientific temper for ensuring social and economic reconstruction.

And no account would be complete without mentioning the special personal and intellectual bond between Madhuji and Pramilaji. She shared his values and visions of life, and gave him, as he says, 'unstinted support and inspiration'. And then in the penultimate para, 'in the evening of my life', in his words, 'my quest for truth, justice and freedom and equality will still continue. So will continue my search for aesthetic joy on the works of eminent thinkers and writers in the fields of knowledge, the arts and literature.'

Professor Madhu Dandavate's commitment to inculcating the scientific temper, and to apply his knowledge in practice, is amply borne out by the leadership he provided in technical matters as the Railway Minister. Only a sound grounding in Physics and a Physics Professor could argue in favour of double-headed engines, and many other intricate matters of science and technology.

As for his love and response to the arts and his involvement with the Prithvi Theatres and the INT, this is well known; I too had known Prithivirajji since my childhood and helped in a tiny manner in the presentation of those momentous plays after Partition—*Pathan* and *Dewar*. In the INT Madhuji's name was familiar. Kamaladevi and Damu

Bhai often spoke of him. There were other common friends—Usha Mehta, that fragile frame of sterling silver, Kumud Mehta and to an extent even Mrinal Gore, each with a different political affiliation but all friends. Indeed, before I knew him personally, it was through the circle of writers and theatre workers that I knew him and of his deep engagement with matters of the heart and spirit.

And to conclude this inadequate comprehension of his 'dialogue with life', multifaceted and multilayered, it would only be pertinent to point at that dimension of life which endures, which transcends all outer horizontal life of activity and action. Human values and human touch is what he has stressed throughout. Understandably, there is 'pain in the heart' as he looks back and compares and contrasts the spirit and heritage of India's freedom struggle against the present political and social atmosphere. In his words,

> I feel a deep pain somewhere in my heart. I am pained to see the divisive forces, which seek to wreck India's composite culture, plural society, the secularism and federalism of the Indian Constitution.

The most touching and moving amongst his many human encounters is with Mrs. Indira Gandhi, his political opponent. However, as he says: 'No political opponent is an enemy', and more, all are human subject to the one indisputable law that to be human, with compassion, is the quintessence of life. While being an ardent opponent of her policies, he acknowledges the artistic side of her personality. Madhu Dandavate describes these encounters with great warmth of feeling in his obituary speech in the Lok Sabha on January 17, 1985 after her assassination, now included in the volume compiled and edited by Dr. Subhash C Kashyap, entitled '100 Best Parliamentary Speeches: 1947–97.'

> Sir, in this House, I recollect so many instances. I do not want to take the time of the House. But permit me to quote two interesting experiences of mine. One was during the Bangladesh War. One day when we were all debating certain issues after the recess, we found Smt. Gandhi running to the House like a child with beaming smiles on her face. She came to the very same seat and with the permission of the Speaker she announced, "Sir, I have come here to announce that Dacca has become the free capital of free Bangladesh. " Sir, to that announcement a full-throated support was given by the entire House and there was some sort of an earthquake in the House. There was a joyous atmosphere. And I again remember on that occasion I just got up immediately, I remembered an old poem which the freedom-fighters and martyrs sang for them:
>
> Oh, liberty, can man resign thee?

> Once having felt thy generous flame
> Can dungeons, bolts or bars confine thee,
> Or whip thy noble spirit tame?

> I just said in the end that I did not remember who was the poet, and she immediately gave the name of the poet! I remember that experience.
>
> Sir, there was another experience of mine with a personal slant, when I was occupying the Treasury Benches in 1977 and I remember the day Mrs. Gandhi was elected from Chikmagalur constituency to this House. Unfortunately I was not present in the House. I was present in the Rajya Sabha answering questions about the Railways. I was not present when she took the oath in this House. After the recess, if I remember right, along with Mr. Vasant Sathe she was moving through the library corridors, and I found her and just said, "Indiraji, congratulations." She said, "You have brought distinction to your government." And then she said, "It was my misfortune that you were not in my Cabinet." And I said, in my humorous vein, "Madam, I was fortunate not to be there." She laughed and laughed and smiled. Those smiles I still remember. In the midst of tears and agony I cannot forget those shining smiles. Those smiles remain with us.

I conclude by quoting the most poignant part of his obituary speech, because it is only Madhu Dandavate's words that can convey the depth of his feelings:

> Many have lost many things in this country when Smt Gandhi died. The Congress-I lost its President. The nation lost its Prime Minister, Rajiv lost his beloved mother. The Congress-I could get back a new President, the nation could get back a new Prime Minister. But Rajiv has lost his mother forever. And, therefore, I pay my homage not only to the former Prime Minister; I am one among those who believe, what of the Prime Ministership, all the power of the world can never be a substitute for a mother's love and affection, and therefore, Sir, on behalf of the entire House let me give my heartfelt and sincere condolences to Rajiv Gandhi. Remember that whatever be your policies and perspectives, it is the indomitable will of your mother that should be the heritage that you should carry with you.

As important and equally moving was Shri Rajiv Gandhi's response:

> Professor Madhu Dandavate, I want to tell you that I was moved by your speech, as much as I was moved at the time of the death of my mother.

Yes, Rajiv Gandhi's words came from the heart, and I owe to Rajiv Gandhi a deep debt for the implicit trust he placed in me so as to enable me to articulate through the programmes of the institution, the Indira Gandhi National Centre for the Arts, a holistic vision of the Indian cultural and civilisational traditions. It was an attempt to understand India on its own terms so that the multilayered complexity of a great civilization which has endured could be comprehended. The search was for the evolution of an alternate paradigmical model for evaluating a holistic culture. It is a pity that this institution has suffered from the fall-out of mistrust, misjudgments and even misunderstanding propelled by political compulsion.

But to return to the *Dialogue with Life,* may this man of stainless steel with a tender human heart, sometimes in pain and agony and at others joy and ecstacy, and always with undying optimism, live long.

In his words,

The show must go on,
Time alone will pronounce....

(9 October 2005)

14.

Life and Time of Bhabesh C. Sanyal

While thanking the Lalit Kala Akademi and specially its Chairman, Shri Mirdha, on whose command and persuasion I am here despite my reservations, I feel both inappropriate and ill-chosen and inadequate for this great task. I accepted for two reasons. First, because as an undeserving receiver of Bhabesh Da's affection how could I say 'No'? Second, being a rootless Delhiwallah myself, I thought that it might be interesting to take this opportunity to recreate all the ins and outs of the highways and by-lanes of Delhi as miniscule of the national and international scene. Like Bhabesh Da, not certainly matching his stature, Keshav and I also are members of families who travelled each year from Calcutta, Santiniketan, Banaras, Lucknow, Delhi, Lahore, Rawalpindi to Kashmir. There is a significance of this annual journey in terms of shaping minds and inculcation of a pan-Indian sensibility. But of this, later. At the moment, allow me to thank you once again for having invited me to deliver the key-note address. I shall raise some issues which may twist and lock problems, more than open, with keys of perception.

In India when a man reaches the age of 60, a celebration is held, called 'Shashti Purti'. On this day, man enters another phase of life as absolute giver. In the ceremony, gifts are given by him who attains this age. Each decade thereafter is a gift, a gift to be gifted. In the West it is a Happy Birthday, each time from the childhood to old age. In making the statement today in the context of revered Bhabesh Da's 90th Birthday I only wish to underline that on this day one says *Pranam*, *Charanvandana*, seeks *Ashirvada* and prays that the gift of gifts of the art of living may continue to be his, to be gifted to us,

The formulation of the Symposium/Seminar suggests or implies a point of view and an approach in regard to the relationship of man, society and artistic experience, finally artistic expression. Extending the argument further, it would almost imply mildly the tension, even perhaps confrontation, first between man and his art and second, between the art and the artist vis-à-vis his 'times'. Presumably, the word 'times' is an indicator of not merely the physical linear flow of 9 decades or a century, but subsumes the spatial dimensions of socio-cultural, politico-economic milieu, regionally, nationally and internationally.

Without going into the finer nuances of the formulation and the diverse levels of intellectual discourse it can stimulate, it would be advisable in this Key-Note Address to raise or, at least, identify the issues relevant to a critical appraisal of the 'times', the 'art' and the 'man', in this case a particular, creative person of genius and stature.

The first lock to which we have to put a key is the complex network of socio-cultural and politico economic milieu in which an artist works. How is he affected by the milieu and how does he in turn, influence, change or transforms his 'times'? Perhaps, it would be advisable to begin backwards as if to identify the socio-cultural, economic-political milieu of the 'times' and then proceed to look at the art of those 'times' and then move to the man who is the artist. This is almost beginning from the absolute outside, the landscape, then defining the contours of a specific region/area and then the individual. One could begin with the centre of creativity, i.e., the 'man' and then move outwards rather than move from the outside to the inside. However, I have chosen to draw attention here to the contemporary situation not only in terms of the immediate Indian socio-economic backdrop but also to the larger scientific and intellectual developments which are relevant for an understanding what we have termed as 'times'.

First, the 'times'. In terms of calendar, this was the beginning of the century. But perhaps it would be useful to go back another five decades. The latter half of the 19th Century witnessed some momentous changes which irrevocably changed Man's comprehension of the cosmos, his life on earth and conditioned him to accept new space and time paradigms. As is well known, the renaissance in Western Europe had succeeded in convincing man of his centrality, almost supremacy. The 19th Century reinforced this world-view and went further in making him believe that he was not just one amongst all living matter; instead, he was the best, the most evolved and therefore, fittest to survive. The combination of a theory of evolution, a mechanistic science, a dualistic philosophy of Descartes brought about a deep internal change not only in the West, but for many other intellectual traditions, including our own, singly and together, they made man subscribe to a world-view and to comprehend both himself as also the world around him through a very different and alternative perspective. While Darwin has made man subscribe to only a one-way flow of linear progressive arrow time, Newton's mechanistic science along with Descartes' philosophy created a complete dichotomy between 'Mind' and 'Matter'. Freud divided the physio-psychical man as a fertile ground for the inner conflicts between impulses, I, ego and super-ego, etc. All three together asserted division, separateness, fragmentation and conflict. Man, Nature were in conflict; groups within society were in conflict; the psyche of Man was in conflict. The consequences of a tacit acceptance of this world-view had far-reaching implications in the sphere of the arts. Protagonists of these philosophies and sciences were almost more important in changing the psyche of 'man' than the socio-economic changes which took place as a result of the Industrial Revolution. While the Industrial Revolution only underlined the hiatus that had taken place between the 'man' and nature and culture, the theories of Darwin, Newton and Freud made impossible for most to think that 'man' was a whole one amongst all living beings, inter-related and interdependent. Disharmony, conflict replaced harmony and coherence. The last decade of the 19th Century or the beginning of the 20th Century was such that the 'thinking man' was already aware of a sense of loss of the 'whole' and the beginning of dichotomy between 'man' and 'nature', between the rural and the urban, between the physical, emotional and the spiritual dimensions of the inner landscape of Man. Obviously, the aware, educated Indian assimilated these notions, even if at a conscious level he may not have articulated his acceptance or rejection.

The second dimension of understanding the 'times' is not in terms of the changes which took place in the mind of man and his comprehension of the phenomenon of life and the nature of the universe but at a much more horizontal level which we recognise as the socio-political cultural movements in a given geographical area. Now India, specially in relation to the West on the one hand and South-East Asia and East-Asia at the end of the 19th Century and the earlier 20th century, becomes relevant. Obviously, India was not divorced from all that was happening in areas remote and adjacent. While at subterranean levels and at the highest ascensions of consciousness there was an internal dynamics, distinctively Indian, at the socio-cultural and intellectual plane, the influence of a world-view articulated by Darwin, Newton, Freud and Marx and the consequences of the overpowering spread of colonial rule at a socio-economic and cultural plane was in evidence. The history of India, regionally as also nationally, is all too well known to be recounted. Nevertheless, it would be useful to glance at the milestones and the socio-political changes which took place in India, which, in turn, affected the socio-cultural structures of the country which include the artistic. This section or the second key or the second lock, if you like, should therefore deal with politico-economic, socio-cultural dimensions of humanity, both in India and Europe. It would be well to remember that many parallel as also interpretative movements were taking place. Although India was subjugated and dominated by everything that we know as the imperialist power, there was also the inner dynamics of its own culture; besides, India was influencing the West and stimulating new forms of creativity.

In India, while continuity was maintained with a world-view which one could identify as the perennial flow of a unitary vision, there was also the phenomenon of multiple streams, commonly identified as the medieval phenomenon of regional identity. Both the unitary vision or the perennial stream as also the distinctively regional identities were parallel and not in a sequential flow, as often assessed by historians. A third factor now entered and this was both the effect of industrialisation in Europe and colonization in India. Resultantly, as at the level of the scientific, philosophic and intellectual discourse, alluded to briefly, so also at the socio-cultural level, there was a complex inter-webbing of an ancient vision, medieval diverse streams of socio-cultural identity and perceptions generated by the twin effects of European industrialisation and colonial rule. In India, two things become evident. While at one level, the artistic experience and multiplicity of expression continued within the periphery of life cycle and function, the village temple or mosque, at another, India began to share the European acceptance of dissociation of function and art. Art for art's sake took root.

It was ironical that while Europe was increasingly becoming conscious of the negative consequences of dissociation of life and art and was trying to reach out to Indian and Asian traditions, India was absorbing the Western vision of considering artistic expression as an autonomous activity. It may be remembered that it was against this dissociation that strong voices of dissent were raised. Most articulate amongst these were those of Coomaraswamy and Eric Gill. Allow me to quote in full some of their writings.

> "With the division of 'art' from 'work' and 'beauty' from 'use' in the modern world, art comes out of the artist and gets attached, so to say, to the work of art itself. The creator of 'art', now called an 'artist', personifies art and is given the sole prerogative of its production. Beauty too comes out of the thing made to be an aesthetic sensation desired for its own sake. No longer the property of a thing

that shows forth the fullness of integrity, harmony and intelligible clarity due to its being, no longer identified with goodness and truth, beauty is now associated with a select category of things made".

And again Eric Gill writes in the Holy Tradition of Working:

"The relation between the image in the mind of the maker and the executed work is one of more or less complete identity—more complete in the case of physically useful things, less complete in that of objects, whose usefulness is spiritual. The reason of this is that the final cause, the end of the work, in the case of the physically useful object is more defined and, being defined, its limits are easily recognised and can be perceived by one sweep of the mind. But in the case of paintings, sculptures, music and poetry the limits being spiritual are less easily discernible".

The second quotation is of great significance especially because many have commented on Bhabesh Da's concern with the image in the mind of the maker and the executed work. The question of a complete coherence between the image as conceived in the mind of the artist and the form which it takes through the hands of the artist, has been discussed over centuries. Is this coherence greater, better, more complete in objects which are useful or in those forms which have no utility? Further, can the two separately or even together, have another type of usefulness, usefulness of the mind and the soul therefore at a spiritual level, i.e., in other words, can this coherences be such as to transform both the maker and the made? Eric Gill and Coomaraswamy held a view-point on this which could perhaps be debated at length by this Seminar. The distinction between art (or craft) and fine arts continues to hold our attention. Both A.K. Coomaraswamy and Eric Gill brought up this issue time and again:

The distinction between art and 'fine art' is, in every sense but one, a superstition; many superstitions are wide-spread, so the mere popularity of the distinction need not concern us.

The idea that the distinction between art and fine art is that art is skill applied to the making of useful things and fine art is skill applied to the making of things of beauty, is clearly unreasonable, because there is no reason why useful things should not be beautiful, and there is no reason to suppose that beautiful things have no use. Are tables and chairs and houses and pottery necessarily ugly? Are portraits and statues and church paintings and wall decorations necessarily useless?

And the idea that the beauty of useful things is accidental whereas, in the fine arts, it is the usefulness that is accidental, is equally unreasonable, for you cannot have beauty by itself, any more than you can have art or culture by themselves".

The excerpts quoted require no elaboration. We are still debating these issues in art as a result of the changes in world-view as also societal structures.

I would only like to draw attention to the fact that these changes were not reflected only in the visual arts. Similar trends can be witnessed in the literary and the performing arts. The three have to be seen together, so also the European and Indian situation has to be seen in relation to each other and not in isolation.

Briefly stated, while India was being influenced by much of what was happening in Europe, India was also influencing and had influenced major artistic movements in Europe through a detour route, via both western Asia and the Far-East. Critics have now recognized the Indian and Asian influences in the evolution of major European movements, be it the Romantics or the Impressionists or even the pre-Raphelites.

It has also been recognised that exposure to African art triggered off new trends in European art. Of equal validity are developments in the fields of music, although this was not so evident in the formal aspect of classical Western music. New genres emerged.

Lastly, there was the movement in the West of establishing institutional frameworks and professional companies for dance, particularly ballet. The rigidity of the ballet was also questioned by the pioneers of the modern dance, whether Isodara Duncan or later Ruth St. Denis, and others. Contrarily, in India, while indigenous streams continued, there was an assertion of the individuality of the artist, the break-away from social cultural coherence, the establishment of institutional frameworks, such as schools and art academies. Like the West, there was an effort to rehabilitate the art of music and dance in a new institutional framework breaking away from the temple or the court context. To all this, one has to add the distinctive Indian feature that the arts were also a tool and a very important instrument for the search of a national identity, under a colonial rule.

It is important to take cognizance of this situation because the post-1948 developments in India cannot be fully understood without this pre-independence background, and amongst different layers of society.

This then brings us to historical period of the two decades preceding 1948. This coincides with the personal artistic journey of Bhabesh Da and his contemporaries.

The third lock to which a key has to be employed is this complex situation of a political subjugation, a heightened awareness of the Indian socio-cultural situation, and a self-conscious search for an identity, through the arts and more broadly speaking the heritage. In parenthesis, one must mention here the role of the discovery of Indian manuscripts and the work of the archaeologists in respect of monuments, whether a William Jones or a Princep or a Cunningham, the renewed attention to Kalidasa and Sanchi and Ajanta, and the understandable and natural influence on contemporary creativity in the arts, literary and visual.

Understandably, the question of What is the Art and What is the Indian Art occupied the minds of artists. Who could be a more authentic voice for describing the situation than Rabindranath Tagore? Speaking on Art and Tradition, he said in 1926:

> Our modern mind, a hasty tourist, in its rush over the miscellaneous, ransacks cheap markets of curios which mostly are delusions. This happens because its natural sensibility for a simple aspect of existence is dulled by constant preoccupations that divert it. The literature that it produces seems always to be poking her nose into out-of-way places for things and effects that are out of the common. She racks her resources in order to be striking. She elaborates inconstant changes in style, as in modern millinery; and the product suggests more the polish of steel than the bloom of life.
>
> What is Art?—Art is the response of man's creative soul to the call of the real.
>
> The individual mind according to its temperature and training has its own recognition of reality in some of its special aspects. We can see from the Gandhara figures of Buddha that the artistic influence of Greece put its emphasis on the scientific aspect, an anatomical accuracy, while the purely Indian mind dwelt on the symbolic aspect and tried to give expression to the soul of Buddha never acknowledging the limitations of realism. To the adventurous spirit of the great European sculptor, Rodin, the most significant aspect of reality is the uncasing struggle of the incomplete for its freedom from the fetters of imperfection, whereas before the naturally introspective mind of the Eastern artist the real appears in its ideal form of fulfillment.
>
> Therefore, when we talk of *Indian Art,* it indicates some truth based upon the Indian tradition and temperament. At the same time we must know that there is no such thing as absolute caste restriction in human cultures; they even have the power to combine and produce new variations, and such combinations have been going on for ages, proving the truth of the deep psychology.
>
> .... When in the name of Indian Art we cultivate with deliberate aggressiveness a certain bigotry born of the habit of a past generation, we smother our soul under idiosyncrasies unearthed from buried centuries. These are like masks with exaggerated grimaces that fail to respond to the ever changing play of life.

> Art is not a gorgeous sepulcher; immovable brooding over a lonely eternity of vanished years. It belongs to the procession of life, making constant adjustment with surprises, exploring unknown shrines of reality along its path of pilgrimage to a future which is as different from the past as the tree from the seed. Art represents the inexhaustible magnificence of our creative spirit; it is generous in its acceptance and generous in its bestowal; It is unique in its manner and universal in its appeal.

There was a second complementary movement, more assertive in its return to archetypes from Indian myth and legend. Bankim Chandra was easily the most outstanding protagonist. He re-invoked the image of the Mother Goddess in its new form of Mother India in chains and fetters. *Ananda Math* and *Vandemaataram* were the logical outcome.

The third stream which stimulated the first two and yet continued to be different was of those who saw the Indian social reality in its blinkered orthodoxy, economic disparities, caste and class hierarchies and its hide-bound male domination. Both literature and the visual arts reflected this reality and was determined to break these internal shackles through the medium of art.

This then brings us to a fourth lock of the Indian artistic situation and the endeavour to utilize many keys for resolution.

While individual creativity and voices of rebellion and reform, resurrection and reformulation continued, there was a concerted effort to consciously resituate the place of art in society and education. It is significant to remember that the initiatives to establish institutions for the arts came from great writers, painters and dancers and not from the patrons of art. This was as true of Rabindranath Tagore and Santiniketan as it was of poet Vallathol in Cheruthurathy and Rukmini Devi in Kalakshetra.

The establishment of these schools and institutions assumes significance when juxtaposed with the history of the establishment of the four Art Schools by the British notwithstanding the transition within these European academic models to the Indianization which took place at the hands of a Havell, Abinandranath, a Gaganendranath and of course, a Nandlal Bose.

My emphasis here is on the motivations as also the process of transition set into motion by these initiatives. It was an effort to legitimise, to re-form into a new whole fragments of the tradition which lay scattered and broken and to provide an institutional framework for transmission of skills and techniques.

In short a highly personalised system of transmission was being gradually transformed to an institutional framework which was part derived and part local specific. No assessment of the trends in paintings including the much debated Bengal School, the restructuring of Kathakali and the re-statement of Bharatanatyam or the popularisation of classical music by Vishnu Digambar, would be complete in the absence of an investigation into the socio-political, economic, cultural milieu and the image of India as conceived in the minds of the artists.

Discussions, debates have been confined to speaking of the content, the revivalist tendencies but have not in fact gone into the complex network of forces at work.

It is time now to arrive in our discussion on the fifth lock or phase in 1948. Political history is too well known to be recounted so also is the acquaintance with the euphoria of independence followed by disappointment and scepticism. Let me not speak with *my* voice here. Let me bring to you the concerns of those who were sensitive men and women deeply involved in issues which faced India on 1st January, 1948. My source is *Modern Review*; the principal organ of dissemination of the authentic voices.

The editorial of January 1948 draws attention to the situation in Kashmir, problems between India and Pakistan and the Kashmir issue in UNO.

> **The New Year**
> The Old Year has passed out amidst the trials and agony of millions and the acute nervous tension of the hundreds of millions inhabiting the Indian sub-continent. But despite the manifold horrors to which the people were subjected and the terrible ordeals through which the despoiled, dispossessed and ravished millions of innocents had to pass, the year that has passed would be marked forever in Indian history as the year of independence and the year of the parting of the ways of the two ideologically different peoples. 1947 was in all truth a year of black gloom and despair, lit only with freedom's solitary brilliant shaft of light, clearing through the darkness.
>
> **Kashmir Questions at UNO**
> The Government of India has placed the Kashmir issue before the Security Council of the United Nations Organisation. Pakistan Dominion and other Dominion representatives in Delhi have also been apprised of India's intention to raise the issue before the Security Council. The Indian Government have for some time past been in communication with the British Government who have been fully posted with India's case. This decision to approach the Security Council is

without prejudice to the military operations which are now in progress in Jammu and elsewhere. It is presumed that this reference is a prelude to a relentless and more vigorous drive against the raiders.

The United Nations legal counsellors at New York are of the opinion that India's decision to refer the Kashmir dispute to the Security Council is entirely proper and legal."

You will probably remark that, Kapilaji, is this 1948 or is it yesterday's paper? Let's go further. J.B. Kripalani was concerned with the rise of regionalism in India. The question of State boundaries and the establishment of zonal commissions, and the formation of Linguistic States was a central concern.

ALL-INDIA CONCRESS COMMITTEE
Camp: 6, Jantar Mantar Road, New Delhi

22nd August 1946

My dear Kali Babu,

"I had personally talked to you about the formation of the Zonal Committees. Now that the Boundary Commission has given its award there should be no delay"... "I have already told you as to how the Zonal Committees are to be formed." "The matter must be expedited."

J.B. Kripalani

This is even more contemporary an issue. Let us now turn to subsequent issues of this seminal magazine. I shall pass over those that carried obituaries and tributes to the Father of the Nation. They are important because they give us a clue to the responses which Gandhi's life and death evoked in the mind of the thinking Indian. Nevertheless let me take you to the writing of O.C. Gangoly on the position of the arts and crafts in India.

"Many people believe that our precious heritage of beauty and of craftsmanship inherent in our handicrafts could be saved by the generous patronage of the wealthy and by the sentiments and sacrifices of our patriots with a vow to pay more and to use the hand-made products in preference to the machine-made ones. It is by raising the tariff-wall of love and patriotism that we could save our heritage of beauty and of skillful and creative craftsmanship. I do not know if this is a sound economic doctrine and if craftsmanship can be helped to survive its struggle with competitive industries. But 1 believe that craftsmanship and the cultivation of beauty stands for a spiritual communication between man and man and can invest our life with spiritual and divine values. The weaver who handles the warp and the woof of the silken threads with the skill and mystery of a magician to fabricate a piece of dhoti and sari caters not only for the needs of our body but also for the needs of our mind and soul. For he very often weaves with his threads as symbols of his good wishes for us auspicious decorations and patterns intended to work as charms to chide away all evil thoughts and to inspire the leading of a clean, chaste, a spotless life. This personal human appeal, this piece of good wish conveyed by the maker of the cloth to the user of the cloth, this sense of spiritual communication between man and man can never come through the products of dead machines."

I would like to underline the fact that this is not A.K. Coomaraswamy, the fierce critic of Industrialization speaking, nor is it an Aurobindo championing the cause of Indian art against its vehement Western critics but it is O.C. Gangoly who does not take on a defensive position, who is the author and art historian. He goes on,

'Those of us who are concerned for the existence of beauty in the world are often accused by so called practical men of business of a lack of disinterestedness and selfish motives. It is supposed that we desire beauty because we are artists and lovers of Art, and that were we not artists and connoisseurs of Beauty, we would be as indifferent to the matter as they are.

Roughly speaking, a work of art, a creation of an artist, is simply "a thing well made"; ultimately it is the sensible expression of man's love of God, and in every work beauty is its essential perfection. Beauty is, therefore, a thing of religious significance, ineffable, independent of fashion or custom, time, or place, and so to be judged by the material criteria of a commercial civilization or by the threadbare culture of job hunters and place-hunters."

There is one further excerpt which could very easily become the subject of a full seminar. Here O.C. Gangoly warns us against commercialism and art through the case in the sale of art and asserts, "we are artists because we believe in beauty and not that we believe in beauty because we are professional artists".

From O.C. Gangoly, let me turn to Rev. Kamaladevi Chattopadhyay. Here was a political worker, a social activist and an unceasing upholder of lost causes. How did she see 1948? Her concern was for a breakdown of moral fiber. She cries out in anguish:

The present moment is fraught with unprecedented confusion. The human mind has been completely terrifying aftermath. The old landmarks have been eroded

> out, moral standards thrown into utter confusion, rating in humanity an utter frustration. History is after all as much of a biological process as an individual and the symptoms of historical pathology according to psychiatrists are almost identical with those of the individual. For the historical process is only that of collective individuals reacting together to a given option. In the last three decades humanity has probably lived through experiences as new and as widely flung from each other as events separated by centuries. Humanity has obviously failed to adapt itself to these staggering changes and come to bear the stigma of imbalance.

Quoting Martin Gumpert, a well-known American physician as also another physician, Dr. Mackey, says: the fog of mental and emotional disturbances affects almost every public function and can be felt in United Nations, in the Congress, in our schools and on our streets". There can be no doubt that the misdiagnosis and mismanagement of the so-called functionally ill patient is the medical scandal of the day". Kamaladevi then remarks, "The greater tragedy is that this is much more than a medical scandal; it is a fateful social tragedy. For the malady of imbalance is confined not to just army of patients but almost our entire society and citizens on whom rests the responsibility for raising the state and deciding the destiny of millions. So man still continues to dream, hope and strive for a more humane world from which exploitation and expression, poverty and disease will have disappeared and the state become the suppression of this noble life. For moral standards become meaningful only in translating these codes in terms of everyday life or, as someone has said, transform morals into politics. In this lies the salvaging of humanity from the present moral morass".

In the same article, she spells out her ideas on education. These are as relevant in the field of art, education as science-education;

> "If the aim of education is to create wholesome attitudes towards life in order to establish harmonious and happy social relationships, it is necessary to make the child assimilate the more abiding values, ideologies, thoughts and actions which make for a larger and fuller individual life, and a richer and finely adjusted social organism, impart a philosophy of life, a spiritual foundation on which to build, a rod with which to measure, for in proportion to its adherence to this, will its purpose and function in life be evaluated".

Does one need to make any further comments on issues which faced responsible citizens, sensitive artists at the threshold of freedom and independence? Are these issues not with us even today, be it political or social or nearer our concerns of the place of art in society, institution building and the role of artists in society?

Finally then we arrive at our last lock and the key required to open up the many rooms and crevices of the creative mind, the maker of images as ideas and as visual form. Our locale is Delhi and how this capital is transformed and in turn influences others outside its periphery. The centre of our attention no doubt is the creative genius, the man and artist Bhabesh Da whom we are honouring. In his personality, his life and art he has held the key of perception. My distinguished colleagues, Mr. Farooqi or Mr. Mago and Mr. Keshav Malik, have delineated the developments in the world of the visual arts through decades. Repetition of this or anticipation of the material which will be presented is not necessary. I would only like to comment on the journey of this artist and man and citizen as a process of reflecting his times. Here is a person who consciously or unconsciously inherits and absorbs ideas generated on the phenomenon of life on earth as a result of scientific discourses, shares the changes of perceptions brought about by the thinkers, philosophers, psychologists, is part and parcel of the national movement of freedom, has a width of experience of regions as far flung as Assam and Punjab, is deeply committed to the establishment of an institutional framework (as Founder of Schools especially the Silipi Cakra), he goes through the phase of the idealism generated by independence but also partakes of the pain and anguish of partition, witnesses the erosion of values and yet is whole and rooted. This ability to absorb and assimilate, churn within ones own psyche, life experience at different levels and to express it with a sincerity of purpose distinguishes authenticity in art, from the endeavour to adopt or emulate latest trends or movements of style in art.

This brings up once again the question of what constitutes the experience of a person who is both a member of society, is participator and watcher, and yet one who has the gleanings of an inner life-call it transcendence or spiritual. This man who has been given the tools of artistic expression, how does he transform the experience to the artistic expression and in turn how does this art influence others and finally how does this art transform him to be friend, guide, philosopher, in life? As he has said, but as I would say again and again, the crucial test is that the creator of images within the mind and subsequently through the medium of clay, line, brush or colour, sound, music, movement and dance, in the final reckoning becomes a towering human being only when the art transforms him to make life the greatest artistic experience and expression. Bhabesh da has arrived because he knows the art of arts, the art of living. *Pranam* to him. May, as I said in the beginning, this gift of gifts of the art of living be his to give for many more years and may we have the humility and generosity to receive.

15.

Remembering Mohit Sen: An Unfettered Soul

To pay an explicit tribute to friends through words is not easy, indeed very difficult. It is more so, when your own life, in one way or the other, has been intertwined with theirs, private and public. Vanaja and Mohit, their lives, separately and together, is a playback of the trajectories of some if not many of my generation, some slightly older, some younger, but all children of pre-independent India whose adulthood coincided with political freedom and active engagement in the domains of education and political and social movements. As important a distinguishing feature, we all went abroad for higher studies at the crucial transitional moment and returned to dig our feet into the ground of the reality of India.

Vanaja and Mohit—the two were part of the Cambridge groups, comprising Lotika Mitra (Monu didi bhai) and Sita Chari and K.N. Raj whom I had known longer. Didi bhai (Monu—Lotika Sarkar) continues to be mentor and guide, Sita an inseparable kindred soul wherever she may be, and K.N. Raj's brilliant, sometime wry wit, brings silent giggles in solitude. I watch the photograph of Mohit, Monu, Vanaja, I.G. Patel and Mohit in the souvenir dedicated to Vanaja, and am in a state of nostalgic reverie, and do not wish to be awakened into the thunderous fracturing of our lives today. The companionship and bonding respectful of the wide differences and range of our respective intellectual pursuits has persisted over these decades, wherever we are. Once physically together, there is once again the fresh breeze of the boundless or unclawing bonding.

Vanaja I knew more, both in her graceful physical self as also her kind and resolute professional identity as outstanding teacher and scholar. Mohit walked in and out, as he did in Didi bhai's flat in South Avenue, and I stayed almost opposite. Also he walked in and out of the political circle, because the lines were not so sharply drawn between political ideologues.

The Communists met the Congress people, even the Royists, and there were animated and passionate discussions for hours without a tinge of personal rancour. A little later, though frequently but as precious, were brief meetings when Mohit was in Delhi, meeting those in the power.

He said little, but we shared much silently. There was immediate rapport, whether in personal meetings but more frequently telephone conversations. Recounting them would diminish the value they held.

As I read and re-read the autobiography 'A Traveller and the Road'—the Journey of an Indian Communist, much comes back, as I said, as a playback of a long familiar reel of his life, lives, our lives, and the lives of a generation before, i.e., his parents. The descriptions of his childhood and growing up have very special meaning for me, who grew up in Calcutta, in and out of the elite of the Brahmo Samaj, but also imbibing every scent and aroma, sensuous and spiritual of Shantiniketan, receiving the boundless affection of Gurudeva, while Mohit turned a Communist through the seminal influence of his brother and of course others.

Others like me considered Ramanand Chatterjee (Editor, Review) as the light-giver and pathfinder. Every page of Modern Review, Pravasi and Vishal Bharata, was avidly read, discussed and churned. It was the literature which attracted us. Tolstoy, Gorky and Turgener and later Dostovesky. Although much has been written on the nationalist discourse vs. the Communist ideology etc., it will demand a more analytical study on the making of a 'generation' of Indians of the 40s and 50s.

I have been tempted to go off on a tangent, on other familiar and concurrent journeys on the road—some intersecting, others meeting at crossroads, to be separated again, but all in the avowed sincere faith of being first and foremost accountable to 'self'. Mohit's autobiography brings home this unshakable and the consequent travails, as also fulfilment. In that sense he will always remain a comrade, not of the party affiliation but of the unfettered soul. An apology and inadequate as tribute, but a deeply felt tribute nevertheless.

16.

J.C. Kapur: The Futurologist

Shri J.C. Kapur, Scientist, engineer, futurologist, the world citizen—all this has been not only recognized but the two eminent speakers here have made his presence felt.

Personal contact for nearly 30 years, sharing his vast reading, was the greatest both delight and fulfilment, because yourself was filled with information, perception, critical insights. Whether in his house in Maharani Bagh or in the graceful luscious farm which Urmilaji so gently but efficiently organized, it was a pilgrimage for many. His embrace was large and generous; his international persona was evident in all that he undertook. He participated actively in the dialogue and civilizations. His home and house was a centre where persons of all walks of life walked with grace, gently, but in dialogue incisive. Concurrent with his international persona and his several books, was an Indian absolutely situated, firmly grounded in the civilization and cultural trajectory of the many streams of Indian thought. He could not be identified with a single stream and he looked on all streams and in his own perception. This comes through in all his writing, as also his dialogues. Here I only want to remember the most animated dialogue in the Surya Foundation, especially with his friend and with whom he communicated so easily—the late P.N. Haksar. The sharpness of those debates was as valuable as the fraternity of love and affection.

Amongst the many, many occasions that one learnt, I want to draw attention in this brief presentation to a special volume of the World Affairs 'Eternal India—Resounding voices of silence—emerging images of the future.' This was published in 2002. I had the privilege of working very closely with him in both identifying contributors as also trying to weave a web of inter-relationship between and amongst the several authors. I looked at the volume again last week. I was struck by the face that what J.C. Kapur had to say in his editorial in regard to 'Eternal India—Resounding voices of silence—emerging images of the future' still holds good. Indeed, as in many other spheres, J.C. Kapur was a futurologist. His theme of Juxtaposing an integral culture with technological and mechanistic views runs through much of his writing. Let me quote only one paragraph:

> The present human state is therefore becoming both dangerous and elusive at the same time and has very little chance for transformation because civilised life is increasingly coming under the spell of this new barbarism in diverse ways. The processes for the preservation of the status quo, by power systems on one side and the compulsions for change on the other, are giving a commercial veneer to religion, philosophy, science and aesthetics, leading to a struggle with nature and a ransacking of civilisations. True civilisation is another process, which is the search for higher levels of consciousness and the meaning and purpose of life.....
>
> India is the inheritor of a highly endowed civilization going back many millennia. The continued recovery and renovation of traditional knowledge systems, literature, aesthetic and philosophical traditions, myths and legends is the responsibility of all civilised people. The pluralistic psyche of India should encourage, search and accept every segment of its history including the most recent Islamic and the British centuries. It is the sacred task of the archaeologist of knowledge to repair the tears and reconnect India to its deepest frontiers of history and knowledge. The faster we connect with our past continuity, the stronger the foundation on which the structure of our future can be constructed. The lessons of history are that all his rise civilization structures built on shallow foundations of violence, greed and lust for power invariable collapse.'

In the same volume it was J.C. Kapur's desire to include two documents of great relevance, one by Swami Vivekananda—'Why India Still Lives'—and the other by Rabindranath Tagore, as extract from his work 'Sadhana: The Realisation of Life.'

17.

Sri Ramakrishna Paramahamsa Thakur

On this auspicious occasion of the 175th birth anniversary of the great seer and saint of our times, Sri Ramakrishna Paramahamsa Thakur, what kind of tribute can one pay him? His gaze was comprehensive. From the earth to the sky, from the flowing waters of the Ganga to the Shakti of Shakti, Kali Durgamma, he saw in all creations God. For him, as he said often and more than often in conversations and in dialogues, God permeates the animate and the inanimate. He stressed that one could not identify a part for the whole. In one seminal illuminative moment he said,

> God who has become all this. Then you see that God, *maya*, living beings, and the universe form one whole. God includes the universe and its living beings (pp.327–28 of the Gospel).
>
> Suppose you have separated the shell, flesh, and seeds of a bel-fruit and someone asks you the weight of the fruit, will you leave aside the shell and the seeds and weigh only the flesh? Not at all. To know the real weight of the fruit, you must weigh the whole of it—the shell, the flesh, and the seeds. He must accept the whole thing: seeds and flesh. Seeds and shell and flesh belong to one and the same fruit.

Then he explains this metaphor:

> The shell may be likened to the universe, and the seeds to living beings. While one is engaged in discrimination one says to oneself that the universe and the living beings are non-self and unsubstantial. At that time one thinks of the flesh alone as the substance, and the shell and seeds as unsubstantial. But after discrimination is over, one feels that all three parts of the fruit together form a unity. Then one further realizes that the stuff that has produced the flesh of the fruit has also produced the shell and seeds. To know the real nature of the bel-fruit one must know all three.

What Thakur said is a seminal truth of the many manifestations of Indian art. Neither Indian architecture nor Indian sculptures nor the images of the Śiva, Vishnu, Devi, can be broken up into categories or understood in terms of only their formal elements, pose, hand gestures. They have to be absorbed as a whole.

The Indian arts are a spiritual experience although through a different trajectory. The Indian art also, particularly Indian architecture, is akin to taking a pilgrimage. A pilgrimage is taken so that you ascend from the mundane to the spiritual in ever striving for refinement, elevation and merging with a divinity, which transcends not only the mundane but symbolizes the whole, as Thakur said.

In this brief and inadequate tribute to the Great Master I have only put down some thoughts on how gateways—whether they are the *thorans* of the *stupa* or the *gopurams* of the South Indian temples—are gateways not only of a physical journey but also spiritual journey from the outside to the inside, through outer sunshine to the inner darkness, but in fact from outer ignorance to inner enlightenment.

18.

Swami Ranganathananda

Reminiscences about evolved beings is a difficult task. One is always conscious of the limited self who has had the privilege of being in touch with an infinitely high and deeper person. Swami Ranganathananda was one such personality who combined in himself the dimensions of Karma, Gyan and Bhakti.

The opportunity to meet him in flesh and blood was a blessing no doubt, but more, one knew him as a holder of that knowledge which has had a long history of Indian civilization and culture, and an equally distinguished history of the legacy that he had received in the long chain of disciples of Ramakrishna and Vivekananda.

For many amongst us in India the search of knowledge and the search of wisdom of our own roots has come through a detour journey. Often enough this journey has been as if a turning point after immersing oneself in the riches of the civilization and culture of Greece, Europe, etc. Like many Indians and for many overseas Indians, the world of Ramakrishna and Vivekananda has opened to us not through a direct communication but through the writing of Romain Rolland. It was through the volumes of Romain Rolland on the lives of Ramakrishna and Vivekananda that many childhood memories were re-evoked, of visiting Belur Math and visiting the places where Thakur was seen in Calcutta. Those visits were meaningful but not meaningful enough in terms of the intellectual curiosity in regard the extraordinary lives of both Ramakrishna and Vivekananda. One had to return to the life and work and message of the two through the writings of Romain Rolland.

Even so, nothing much happened except to read through the pages of the gospel. The desire to re-read the life of Vivekananda arose after hearing Swami Ranganathananda when he was in charge of the Ramakrishna Mission in Delhi. He delivered his weekly lectures on Gita—these were special. We thronged to listen to him, because rarely had the meaning and message of the verses penetrated into our beings. Of course, as a generation brought up sometimes in repeating the verses of chapters 2, 3 and 12, one paid no great attention to the import of these verses on one's own life. It was Swami Ranganathananda's exposition of these chapters and his explanations of the verses and his repeated emphasis of relating the message to life here and now which made the experience so meaningful. I believe that the lives of many may not have been transformed but certainly changed in terms of values after seeing and hearing Swami Ranganathananda.

At a more personal level, it was customary to sit on the dais and be near his feet, receive *prasad* from him and wait for that all-embracing smile which would wash off any tensions. In the mornings he gave expositions on *Isavasyam* and some portions of *Kathopanishad*. Each of these were openings for further exploration and investigation. He was accessible, full of humour, had information about everyone, caring, a guide to all those who came for their immediate mundane problems.

It was my fortune that I was so placed in life that there were opportunities to be in close contact with Swamiji—or Maharaj, as he was called—as a member of the Indian National Commission, where every word he said was listened to with attention. It was as a result of his observations that India took the initiative of suggesting many meaningful programmes for UNESCO. One of these was in regard to promotion of international understanding for evolving a global civilization. This advocacy was long before the word of 'globalization' or 'international understanding' became current. Maharaj undertook extensive tours abroad to different parts of the world—Europe, America, Latin America, and other places. One played a very small part in facilitating these tours. The gift was to hear him speak about some of his experiences when he returned. There was always some very special message in the easy narration of episodes or anecdotes of his trips. Maharaj held together learning, scholarship and a deep understanding of the human predicament. Naturally he advocated a socio-political policy of inclusiveness which he called 'Samanvaya of religions'. To quote him:

> 'India has succeeded in cultural and religious fields, but not so in social fields; that is the challenge before modern India. Our leaders took up the challenge and our constitution contained the vision for an egalitarian social order. The universal vision of 'SAMANVAYA' is necessary for India's progress in socio-economic policies. Swami Vivekananda has said this. We have to provide a healthy body politic, wherein freedom, dignity and equality of all men and women are realized. Whenever these were denied in India great men came to uphold dharma. After

> Upanishad period, this great vision came in the form of Krishna and Buddha. Krishna was an outstanding personality. Krishna is a truly universal personality and 'SAMANVAYA' of religions. Diversity is a centrifugal force and unity is a centripetal force. Srikrishna speaks of unity in diversity'.

Again years rolled by. Swamiji was now the head of the Hyderabad Centre. One heard of the extraordinary programmes he was conducting. Of and on when he came to Delhi there were occasions to meet him. Also a cousin of mine who was very close to him was constantly sending me messages from Maharaj. I was touched that he should remember. But of course Mahàraj had a phenomenal memory.

Once again there were occasions a few years later to know him in yet another dynamic role as Secretary of the Institute of Culture, Calcutta. This time he succeeded in establishing an institute which was undoubtedly an extension of the Ramakrishna Mission, but it had an even more extensive agenda of international understanding. He laid the foundations of a most impressive library, an institutional framework of holding frequent seminars and lectures on a wide variety of subjects, the facility of teaching nearly 14 foreign languages and of course a most imaginative children's library. All this supplemented with a international guest house. The foundations laid by Swami Ranganathananda were to be followed up by his other successors, viz., Swami Lokeshwarananda and finally by Swami Prabhananda. For me it has been a great privilege to know of them both in their work of the Institute as also in their international work, specially of Swami Lokeshwarananda and the deep impact that he left in the Soviet Union.

Swamiji was always at pains to bring home that spirituality was not a matter of being a recluse; instead it was a matter of working with intensity but dispassionately. In his own words, he described Dynamic Spirituality as follows:

> 'Vivekananda said millions and millions of Indian people live like neighbours to brutes. A social change for development comes only out of character efficiency and retention of the youthful zest and joy in life and work. There is no point in going here and there for spirituality. It is here, and now. It is not cheap magic or mystery cultivated in one's life and work. Swamiji exhorts us that it is better to live for an ideal for an instant, than to lead life for years like a jellyfish, as Vidura in Mahabaratha said to her son King Sanjaya (Udyogaparva 120–15). This is to say that it is better to live intensely for an ideal vision than to vegetate for long years. This will drive away clouds of cynicism and frustration from the skies of

> India. Each one will be responsible for the nation's well-being. Bernard Shaw refers to the precept of self-motivation thus: 'This is the joy in my life to be used for a purpose you consider mighty, to be a force of nature and not a clod of ailments and grievances always complaining that the world does not devote itself to making me happy'.

I was naturally also impressed by the fact of his assertion and his advocacy of the place of women in society. He said: 'Among the modern leaders who stood for the complete equality of men and women, the most outstanding was Swami Vivekananda. He has spoken in the clearest terms that no society can progress with men alone getting education and opportunities and women being neglected. Indian society bears that mark of arrested development, because its women were neglected for centuries, they were denied economic and social opportunities for education and for development. Swamiji said that a bird cannot fly on one wing, it needs both the wings. So to make Indian society dynamic, we need to educate women as much as men'.

No more needs to be added. However, I would like to recall two instances which have been precious gifts to me. One morning Swamiji, whose affection I had received in abundant measure for many decades, rang me up. He said to me, 'Kapila, you have to do some *sewa*. I was puzzled, naturally diffident and apprehensive of what kind of *sewa* could I do to the Mission or the Ramakrishna Order. I was no ritualistic follower. Swami Ranganathananda was sharp, as always. "Don't worry, I am not asking you to come to Belur Math! There is a piece of work to be done. You know the Cultural Heritage of India volume VII. These articles have been lying unattended for over a decade. As it has happened, all previous scholars who had shouldered the responsibility of editing the volume—including S.K. Saraswati, K.K. Dasgupta and K.K. Ganguly—had been snatched away before they could complete their task. I am suggesting that you should complete this volume'. Naturally I took up the task. The volume was to be released at the hands of the Prime Minister of India in March 2007.

To recall another instance: Swamiji's concerns were not only of the spirit hereafter, he was a man of the world here and now. His concern for India and the future of this country was immense. I had the privilege to communicate with him during his last days. In one such meeting at the Institute of Culture when he lay in bed with his blood counts being counted, he called me and said, 'Kapila, there is a task, there is something I want you to do, I have this book on 'Enlightened Citizenship and our Democracy'. I have raised some fundamental questions about civil society's citizenship and the nature of our democracy comparing it with the original idea of Greek democracy. I am anxious that you personally hand over this book on my behalf to the Prime Minister of India.' This, he held my hand and repeated. I went down to my room, he called me again and told, 'do not forget'. This was the best blessing I received from him. The task he had given to me was accomplished at the March 2007 function of the release of the Cultural Heritage of India volume.

19.

Tribute to Swami Lakshman Joo

It is indeed very gracious of Bettina Baumer to ask me to write a few lines as tribute to the sage of Kashmir, Swami Lakshman Joo. I was neither a pupil, nor devotee, nor fortunate enough to sit at his feet for the many discourses he gave or participate in *yajnas*. Nevertheless, I knew of him, and his teachings through many in Srinagar, and of his teachings through Thakur Jaidev Singh, whom I knew both as a musicologist and an ardent admirer and devout *sisya* of Swami Lakshman Joo.

Nishat was no strange place for me. My grandmother had lived there far away from the family city house in Srinagar to recoup from her illness. My mother knew the garden and the upper terraces of Nishat like the palm of her hand. To each companion, she spoke with the intimacy of filial love and affection.

Long after, when visits to Kashmir were less frequent, although regular, a visit to Nishat, specially the area beyond the formal garden and its vicinity was a must, almost a pilgrimage. It was on one such visit, when she herself (mother) was no longer physically active to stride across hills and mountains, that she and I hesitatingly without notice or prior appointment arrived at the door-step of Swamiji's *asram* and while she sat in the car, I went in, to be greeted warmly by Swamiji's sister. I introduced not so much myself but told her about my mother, and, my long term desire to have *darsana* of Swamiji. Not only was the rapport instant, but more she eagerly accompanied me to bring mother in. We walked steadily and in silence to sit in the porch waiting for his arrival.

Yes, he arrived, clad in white, with the clear luminosity of one who had experienced. His slight frame radiated *tejas* and *ojas*. No words were necessary and none exchanged for nearly twenty minutes. This was communication perfect at another other level and dimension.

With trepidation I broke the silence and spoke of Thakur Jaidev Singh. He responded warmly and affectionately. However, it was evident that my mother and he were speaking to each other without words and any external signs.

I was all too conscious of my ignorance about Kashmir Saivism, dared ask no questions, but I had filled myself with the essence of Kashmir Saivism, in the human embodiment in whose presence I found myself. No more was desired or asked for.

Over decades I have known Swami Lakshman Joo through his writings and the writings of others, particularly Thakur Jaidev Singh, Janakinath Kamal and of course Bettinaji who has imbibed so deeply and sensitively his teachings.

This is neither occasion nor am I competent to speak about the profundity of his experience and the depths of his comprehension about Kashmir Saivism. Each time I have picked up his short simply written book on Kashmir Saivism I have been struck by the fact that his depth of experience and vastness of knowledge is matched by a direct simple articulation in words: Who else could communicate through simple similes and analogues the complexity of the Theory of the Alphabet (*Matrikacakra*) and the Theory of Reflection (*Pratibimbavadah*). Only two excerpts from his writing in his words give a glimpse of this ability to communicate complexity through simplicity and depth.

The first in the context of the Theory of the Alphabet, where he employs the motif of the cup shaped mirror, and the second in the context of the Theory of Reflection. In the first case, he says:

> "The reflection of the universe, which has been explained earlier as being in the form of a cup shaped mirror, is represented by the sixteenth letter of the Sanskrit alphabet, *visarga*, the letter "h". In Devanagari script the letter "h" takes the form of the two points of the colon ":". And these two points of the *visarga* (:), represent the two cups in which the reflection of the universe takes place. These two points are known as *Siva Bindu* and *Sakti Bindu*."

In the second, explaining *svatantrya*

> "In the ordinary worldly course sound is reflected outwardly in ether and inwardly in the ear. Touch is reflected outwardly in air and inwardly in the skin. Form is reflected outwardly in fire and in a mirror and inwardly in the eye. Taste is reflected outwardly in water and inwardly in the tongue. Smell is reflected outwardly in the earth and inwardly in the nose. These reflections, however, are just like the reflection in a mirror. They only take place individually. All five reflections are not available at once, only one thing is reflected in each. In a mirror form is reflected. Touch cannot be reflected in a mirror nor can taste, smell, or sound. A mirror will only reflect form. It is only in Supreme God Consciousness that you find all five reflected at once. In fact, although these reflections are experienced individually in all of the organs, sight in the eye,

sound in the ear, etc., these reflections could not even be observed if consciousness were not there. Awareness is needed and this is found in consciousness and not in the organs.

"The universe, therefore, is reflected in the mirror of consciousness, not in the organs nor in the five gross elements. These are merely *tattvas* and cannot reflect anything. The real reflector is consciousness. In consciousness, however, you see only the reflected thing and not anything that is reflected. That which is reflected (*bimba*) is in fact *svatantrya*. This whole universe is the reflection in God Consciousness of *svatantrya*. There is no additional class of similar objects existing outside of this world that He reflects in His nature. The outside element, that which is reflected, is only *svatantrya*. The infinite variety which is created is only the expansion of *svatantrya*.

"You can understand this by taking the example of cause and effect. When a potter makes a pot he takes clay and gives form to that clay with his potter's instruments such as a stick, string, and potter's wheel. Within the potter's creative activity two kinds of causes can be distinguished. There is the material cause which in Sanskrit is called *upadana karana*. This is that cause that travels with the effect. It cannot and does not become separated from the effect. Secondly, there is the formal cause which in Sanskrit is called *nimittakarana*. The formal cause does not travel with the effect. The material cause is the potter's clay and the formal cause is the potter himself and his stick, string, and wheel. In the ordinary worldly course the reflected object (*bimba*) seems to be the cause of the reflection (*pratibimba*) because the reflected object cannot exist without that which is reflected. We have seen, however, that all reflection is really a reflection in God Consciousness. If the reflected object is really the cause of the reflection then what kind of cause is it? Is it the material cause, which travels with the effect, or is it the formal cause, which does not travel with the effect? It cannot be the material cause because that would mean that there is something outside of God Consciousness which travels to become part of the effect which is the reflection. Yet, it is our theory in Saivism that nothing can exist outside of God Consciousness.

« xxx xxxxxx xxxxxx » xxxxx

"This universe, therefore, is found in the reflector of God Consciousness, not through the agency of anything of which it is a reflection (*bimba*) but through His *svatantrya* where the universe is contained in a seed form. *Svatantrya* is the seed of everything. Everything exists in the mirror of God Consciousness with *svatantrya* as its cause."

What else can one add as tribute? The master's words are the most precious as they emerge from deep experience and reflection.

Swami Lakshman Joo was indeed the carrier of the long and profoundly important stream of Kashmir Saivism. Here was a contemporary embodiment of the sage tradition of a Abhinavagupta Utpaldeva, Kshemraia, and others.

It is gratifying to note that his legacy of both experience and scholarship is being fostered by another generation of Indian and foreign scholars.

I once again thank Bettinaji for having asked me to pay my tribute through inadequate words.

20.

Message on the Occasion of the 80th Birthday of H.H. The Dalai Lama

Incredible that His Holiness will be 80 on 6th July 2015! Why incredible, because this human frame embodies eons of the ancient wisdom and the introspective and the meditative experience. We as smaller beings can only acknowledge that we have been cleansed through the cataracts of compassion, innocence and a generosity universal—universal for all life of earth, sentient beings. It is we who acknowledge this precious and incomparable gift of being receivers of this messenger of ancient wisdom and introspective and meditative experience, and one who has beckoned us to recognize and live by a faith in universal responsibility.

His Holiness had come to India in 1956 as if someone who had come from *devalok*. In 1959 he had to come to India, after a most arduous physical journey, to be in exile, but this is no exile, as he has himself said, there was freedom in that exile. What was a momentous and incomparable tragedy of a region and a people has, over these decades, become a boon to humanity. For now, the message of compassion and peace, the message of interconnectedness of life, and the message that each living form can vibrate with the recognition of sacredness, has permeated the world. Centuries ago, the teachings of Nagarjuna were, in a manner of speaking, exiled, but now the wisdom of Nagarjuna has returned to India in another incarnation. His Holiness has often said that 'India is the guru and Tibet is the chela' and has added, with that enigmatic smile which can only be his, 'now the chela has perhaps become the guru'!

It is to this guru of gurus that one bows, prays, that may his radiance radiate the world! One is too small to wish him on his 80th birthday, but even in that consciousness of inadequacy one can pray that the *parampavan* may walk on this earth for many, many more years, as the world seeks, so do I, his blessings.

21.

Swami Dayanand Saraswati

It is kind and generous of respected Swami Agnivesh to invite me to participate in this important meeting on the life and work and contribution of Swami Dayanand Saraswati.

The distinguished speakers at this forum have thrown invaluable light on Swami Dayanand Saraswati's intellectual and social encounter with other religions and faiths, especially Islam, Christianity and Sikhism. There is little that I can add to their presentation, except to underline the fact that here was a seeker of truth who investigated, interrogated and, thus, also endeavoured to establish a candid dialogue across diverse schools of thought, religious precepts and, more, practices. He examined the tenets of all faiths, including Buddhism and Jainism. The basis of these comparisons is a vast subject unto itself.

Instead, let me take this opportunity to say something at a more personal level about the deep impact of Swami Dayanand Saraswati's relentless and unceasing emphasis on returning to essence of the foundations of all that we understand by the general appellation 'Hindu'. Logical was his emphasis on not only returning to the Vedas as essence, but on translating the essence through action. The instrumentalities for this to him were education, first and last. Rigorous discipline and training were the key. Conduct, honest, moral and ethical action were the ultimate test. Thus, hypocrisy and double-talk were an anathema. Fearlessly and tirelessly he exposed 'hypocrisy' and outward form caged in outward 'dogma' and sectarian narrowness. He spared no one in asserting that hypocrisy of any form was the root of many social evils.

His journey from the first moment of departure from the home after the incident of the mice on the Sivalingam to the last in persuading Maharaja of Jodhpur, was of a zealous seeker and reformer. He had traversed the mountains, ascended the peaks of Badrinath, Kedarnath and Tunganath, had lived and conversed with all those who were considered the repositories of wisdom and all those others who considered themselves the custodians of the innumerable sects and cults. He interacted with the

Brahmo Samaj leaders, Maharshi Debendranath Tagore and Keshab Chandra, met Ramakrishna Paramahansa, but he held his own to stress and declare that the perennial source was the Vedas in their pristine purity. The countless debates he held with the priests and pundits of several denominations in the face of fierce opposition and hostility, speak of the indefatigable courage and conviction and unshakable commitment of purpose. Re-reading the details of those debates (*Sastrartha*), one is struck by the fact that there was an incredible open space to publicly and openly debate differences of comprehension, and understanding, and thus practices of this broad and immeasurably diverse ocean, which is called 'Hinduism'.

His concern was to separate the chaff from the wheat, to extract from the textual sources a philosophy of life which would guide conduct and action.

As pointed out before, education and training were the principal agencies of this endeavour to reform the society of his times, and to nurture a new generation of Indians who would eschew 'caste' and sect and who would be intellectually empowered to reform.

The chapters in the *Satyartha Prakasha* (translated as Light of Truth) on education are as revealing as they are meaningful. Long before the Indian nation state spoke of free and compulsory education, Swamiji advocated the primacy of education. He advised that all children (girls and boys alike, and without distinction) must be sent to school and given physical, mental and moral education.

Appropriately, he begins the chapter 'The upbringing of children' with a famous quotation from the *Satapatha Brahamana*, i.e.,

> 'Matrimanam Pitriman Acharyavan Ptu°usho Veda'
>
> 'Verily that man alone can become a great scholar who has had the advantage of three good teachers, viz., mother, father and preceptor'.

Swamiji's emphasis on the care of the mother is as important as her role as the first teacher of the child in the matter of correct pronunciation, proper accent. While he lays emphasis on the learning of Sanskrit, he also recommends the learning of other languages. Throughout the two chapters dealing with the upbringing of children and education, Swamiji adopts a rational and broad-minded approach. He wants people to know the physical body and the working of the metabolism of the body and not be swept away by blind superstition, astrology and the rest. This advice coming at a time as it did, was a radical step to eradicate ignorance about physical health and primary education. For him 'parents' who neglect the education of their child are his 'veritable enemies'. The highest duty of parents is to educate their children. Acquisition of knowledge and pursuant of truth and moral conduct are the goals of the education. For him, all should be educated, sons and daughters of princes or beggars or those less affluent. He advocated an egalitarian school system. These were the nascent beginnings of what we understand by the term neighbourhood schools.

We know to our cost that unlike these goals, there is a wide gap between educational opportunities open to the rich and those for the poor. Translated in our terms, Swamiji was advocating the establishment of a system of neighbourhood schools, where all—from different socio-economic strata—would be given the same education. Alas, despite the success of the Gurukula system and that of the DAV schools, there is a wide disparity between the so-called elite schools and others, both in the public as also private sector. Swamiji repeatedly reiterated that all 'should be treated alike, the rich and the poor'. We are far from achieving this 'goal' despite six decades of independence.

Swamiji further elucidates on the content of education and dwells at some length on the content, curricula and pedagogy of teaching and learning. He elaborates upon the system with great lucidity. He stresses the fact that education should develop the physical and mental abilities. Imbibing moral values based on the essential core of the Vedas was crucial.

In the end, in his characteristic manner, he admonishes all those who wish to prevent any section of society from acquiring knowledge. He unequivocally states: All men and women, i.e., the whole of mankind, have right to study and acquire knowledge, Kshatriyas, Shudras, women. With great confidence he draws attention to the Vedas, particularly the Yajur Veda, to underscore the point that 'Brahmans, Kshatriyas, Vaishyas, Shudras, women, servants, can learn and preach the Vedas'.

> 'Let all therefore acquire knowledge, practice virtue, shun vices . . . '

Knowledge was not the privilege of any particular section of society, nor of gender.

He takes his argument to its logical conclusion. In answer to a question, he replies, if knowledge was not meant for all, then why did God create the organs of speech and hearing in their (Shudras and women) bodies? In short, Swamiji is both interpreting the Vedas but is also strongly advocating 'non-discrimination' on the basis of Varna, caste or gender.

In order to impart a well-rounded education of the body and mind, he recommends that women/girls be given a sound physical education. Besides physical exercise and the skills of defence and attack (*gataka*), Swamiji is of the opinion that women must acquire accounting, and skills of trade, and knowledge of basic medicine. Besides, both mathematics and the arts should be given an equal weightage. Of course, the system must inculcate moral and ethical values. For him 'knowledge alone is the inexhaustible treasure, the more you spend on it, the more it grows'. Education alone would transform the individual and reform society.

These assertions in the *Satyartha Prakasha* were the inspiration for the system of the Gurukulas and the DAV school system. While the former established by Swami Shraddhananda provided a vertical education of one kind, specially Gurukul Kangri, the DAV school system was broad-based, open to all castes and classes and gave an equal emphasis to the knowledge system of the Indian tradition as also acquaintance and command over English language and modern subjects. A balance was sought to be achieved. The role of the education systems inspired by the ideals of Swamiji and the institution started by him, Arya Samaj, played important role in reforming Indian society. Many broke away from the shackles of narrow sectarianism, as also blind superstition and belief in mindless ritual for resolving problems of material life.

The spread of the message and the establishment of the institutions was swift, almost meteoric, specially in Northern India. In distant Kashmir and throughout Punjab emerged, as if overnight, schools for girls without pardah. There was no discrimination on account of caste, social status. Indeed, many followers of Arya Samaj gave up using their last names so as not to reveal their 'caste' affiliation. Generic endings, such as 'Kumar', etc. began to be used. Today we have to re-evaluate this movement when 'caste' and religious sectarian affiliations are entering the entrails of our political systems.

Has there then been an increase in re-establishing non-productive social hierarchy on the basis of birth or caste? This has certainly weakened the social fabric, and has impacted negatively on the efficient working of a democratic system of governance.

Gender is understandably a much discussed, debated issue, is also the cause of distress and disturbance. Swamiji not only wanted girls to be educated and given equal opportunities, but he went further, and rightly so, in denouncing child marriage. He was the first also to challenge the taboo of widow remarriage. In short, he wanted women to have the same rights, privileges as men.

Thus the issues which Swamiji brought to the fore and fought for are still with us, despite the many changes that have taken place in the century and quarter after he passed away. We are nowhere near achieving the goal of 'free and compulsory education,' at the primary and elementary level, 'caste' in its negative incarnation as a basis of mobilizing votes in a democracy has become visible, and gender inequalities in forms uglier than before are before us. Can we restore balance and health again? The intellectuals, spiritual leaders of India were social reformers, their thoughts and actions were in accord. Can we emulate them to shape the India which will be as deeply rooted, as broadly 'inclusive' and as firm in its foundational core values, as open to discussion and debate with the precepts and values of others?

22.

Sri Mata Amritanandamayi Devi

It is a great privilege for me to be invited to participate in the celebrations of Her Holiness Mata Amritanandamayi Devi's fiftieth birthday. This is undoubtedly an auspicious occasion for her as also for all those who have been enveloped and embraced by her love, affection, graciousness and generosity. Mata Amritanandamayi represents a long line of women seers, saints, social reformers who have transformed the collective psyche of India by their sheer presence. Their experience of the inner life of reflection and introspection, of *tapas* and *Sadhana*, has, as it had to, manifest itself in diverse ways of public action for the good of humanity. India's history reverberates with the aura and aroma of towering mother figures, be they the mythical goddesses, Usas, Saraswati, Uma, Parvati, Lakshmi, Durga, or the human saints, Andal, Lalleshwari, Mirabai, Sharada Ma, Anandamai or now Mata Amritanandamayi. I pay my respectful *pranams* to her. May she continue to bestow her blessings on this large multitude of humanity in the all-loving embrace which is hers. *Sat sat pranams* again.

Many ancient civilizations in all parts of the world separately but simultaneously conceived of the creative benign energies in the form of a mother goddess. These include the earliest depiction of 'woman' as sustainer and nurturer of humanity—the Venus figures of Europe and the mother goddess figure of the Near East, Mesopotamia and of course India. The mother goddess was a symbol of fertility and fecundity of the 'Earth', the primal mother.

In India, apart from the mother goddess figures of Harappa, Vedic mythologies are replete with references to the creative energies of the female. Sometimes the descriptions allude to natural phenomenon, such as *Usas* or *Ratt. Usas* is called *cira nutan* and *cita psfani* (ever new and ever ancient). She arrives each morning to distribute her glow and *jyoti* to the world. At other times, they are visualized as the ever-flowing waters of the rivers as in the case of Saraswati. She epitomizes the perennial sap of life, fluid and liquid. In time to come Saraswati is equated to the faculty of speech, *Vak*, that one faculty which distinguishes the human from other forms of life. The sacred articulated word is revered as a goddess.

There are then the women who are the essential life of the plants, the vegetative world. They are associated with the trees and forest. The hymns to Aryani invoke the beauty and purity of the vegetative world. And yet at other times they reside in the celestial worlds of the heavens. They descend to earth for a limited period to return to the heavens. Such is the case of *Urvasi*, and the famous dialogue between *Pururuva* and *Urvasi* in the Rg Veda encaptures this relationship.

Gradually but surely these early goddesses and heroines assume the form of goddesses or deities. Before long there develops an elaborate mythological world where the women holds a central position in the cosmology. Lakshmi, or Sri, is supreme. She belongs to the oceans, accompanies Visnu as he slumbers over the everlasting and eternal *Seshasayee*. But she holds her own as the centre of terrestrial happiness and harmony. She is auspiciousness and fulfillment combined.

The daughter of the mountain, Parvati, is Uma, Sati, Parvati, who is as austere as beautiful, as young as powerful. All these then merge into the great pantheon of the goddess in her manifold forms—Saraswati, Lakshmi, Durga, Mahishasuramardini, Chandi, Kali and Bhagavati. The grand conception views the Saraswati as the morning dew, fresh and evanescent, the white of purity, the embodiment of music, learning (*vidya*) and the arts. She is the spring of life and seasons and is thus associated with Brahma, the originator. Lakshmi is the centre of domesticity, the noontime, giver of food, the *annapurna*, and the indispensable companion and consort of Visnu. She is beauty, material prosperity and contentment. The evening of the day the seasons brings autumnal ripeness and power. Now she is Durga, the wielder of weapons, the destroyer of evil, and the *shakti*—Supreme. The circle is complete with Kali, the symbol of Time, as cosmic time, Mahakali, in its ever recurring circle of birth, death and re-birth. These mythical figures and goddesses of the imagination, have been invoked and revered in their innumerable forms and names, in all parts of India, from the North to the South; East to the West. The annual calendar is punctuated by their 'presence' through the regular and diverse festivals of spring, summer, rains, autumn and winter. In short, it is the female energy which is power and empowering, worthy of reverence and admiration.

The characters of the epics are remembered day in and day out in the equally significant and symbolic conception of the *pancha kanyas*,

Ahalya, Sita, Draupadi, Tara and Mandodari. Each embodies a value and virtue which has been an ideal to be emulated. They are invoked in rituals, their stories are narrated by the *Harikathas* and *Kathavacakas* and they come live in song, dance and drama. Together they reflect the deep sense of reverence. They are the role models for living.

This picture of goddesses and women has to be complemented and even contrasted with the picture of 'woman' and in some if not all 'social' and legal texts. This includes some portions of the epics and treatises such as *Manusmrti* and the *Arthasastra*. "Woman" here is unequal, subordinate in many respects, and is often mentioned in derogatory terms. It is not possible to overlook this aspect of the historical legacy. Understandably some scholars and critics have spoken of the inherent inconsistency or certainly ambiguity within the Indian tradition, Hindu, Buddhism and Jaina alike. We have to juxtapose the exalted, empowered image of the goddess with the almost perennially subordinated and economically disempowered 'female' of the social order. Undoubtedly Manu declares that 'where a woman is respected, the Gods dwell'.

Over these centuries with all the ups and downs of history and political invasions and changes, there have been the concurrent movements of the exalted status of women, as also their subordination and deprivation. Powerful voices of dissent, of the need for an equilibrium, a balance and restoration of order have been raised. The saint-poets of medieval India, Andal, Mahadevi Akka, Mira Bai and others like Lalleshwari, articulated the free spirit, boundless and untethered, and spoke of the union of the human and the divine. The women of the seventeenth, eighteenth and nineteenth centuries, a Ramabai, Iravati Karve, Margaret Cousins, Annie Besant and in our times a Kasturba Gandhi, Kamaladevi Chattopadhyaya, Durgabai Deshmukh, amongst others, have been role models of our generation, my generation.

Today there is a new generation of active and enlightened women leaders and writers throughout the country. They have raised their voices, and they have also done stupendous admirable work for the upliftment of the depressed and deprived sections. More, the women's movements are most effective when they are ground movements, such as those of 'Chipko' in the Kumaon hills. Countless other examples could be added. It is not necessary to recount here the admirable role of women in different domains of life, ranging from public, political, social and professional, scientific, legal and artistic.

In sheer contrast to this positive and optimistic picture, full of light and hope, there is also a dark and dismal and disturbing reality of both the changing attitudes to the woman and the perpetuation of the atrocities committed against women, not to speak of the continuation of unequal 'legal' and social rights. We cannot close our eyes to the pernicious evil of dowry and dowry deaths, where a woman has been reduced to commodity: nor can we overlook the fact that despite *Panchayati* reforms, there is resistance to the bill on reservation in the electoral process. More disturbing is the phenomenon of rape and violence at both rural and urban levels. These are signs of social and moral disorder. The imbalances and inequities have to be addressed at many levels, not the least of them being the collective effort of community and civil society. No 'legal' or legislative measures can be enforceable if the social fabric does not itself bring about a gender balance and restore the original sense of dignity and honour accorded to 'women' in Indian philosophic and intellectual streams.

Amongst the many other causes of these increasingly social disorders is the image and representation of the women in the electronic media. Decades ago, the woman was represented in literature, poetry and the media as the embodiment of 'Mother'. This included the writings of a Bankim Chandra, the poetry of Subramania Bharati, and the sensitively portrayed women characters in the dramas and novels of Rabindranath—*Chandalika*, *Ghare Bhaire*, and others. The screen and film followed with the portrayals of *Mira* where M.S. Subbalakshmi acted and *Mother India* where Nargis gave the powerful portrayal of Radha as the symbol of indomitable courage of the woman. There were others in the films of Bimal Roy. Gradually the emphasis shifted to portraying of the ever-suffering mother and wife, submissive, suffering and supplicant. Stock images of burly aggressive men and praying women with folded hands waiting for justice and love were not infrequent. A socially aware cinema came into being, with the evocative and sensitive work of directors like Satyajit Ray, to be followed by others, not to mention Adoor Gopalakrishnan and others from Kerala. Juxtaposed with this highly socially and morally aware cinema was the commercial cinema, where there were and, alas, continue to be the two poles—one of the one-dimensional portrayal of women of mythology, much bejewelled but unconvincing and exaggerated, and the other of incessant and uninterrupted through constant interruptions of the advertisements. Day in and day out, from morning to night, with the regularity of clock time, the women's body, her physical form, is made a consumer commodity of titillation, attraction, allurement at the grossest level of human sensibility. She is the vehicle of selling all goods from soap to cars, to much else. She intrudes and enters into homes at regular intervals, whether it is news of war and rape, hunger or poverty, conflicts or disasters. Resultantly the media is indeed the message, and the message of the 90 per cent of the advertisements is woman, body clothes, the 'thing', the object of attraction and allurement at the level of physical wants and desires. This image of the woman is universal from the airports to the homes, from lobbies of international five star hotels to the humblest of hamlets in hill sides and village sheds. It permeates the video parlours, the VCR mandirs as they are called. It acts on the undiscerning and unsuspecting mind as a drug more potent than drugs and self-administered syringes. It deadens sensibilities and arouses passions for an unreal world of desires and acquisitions. It becomes a mental attitudinal impediment for self-discretion and even rejection. Ultimately, indirectly it affects attitudes and human action, in the unsuspecting, susceptible, unformed minds.

I could go on to narrate and analyze with my very limited and altogether too imperfect a knowledge of both the traditions and long continuation of the 'exalted' and the desecrated image of the women—Goddess, pure and shining, *Jyotirmaya*, and the dark, polluted, invaded object of desire. But no more. I have said enough, only to return to my initial sense of admiration and awe for those who symbolize the purity and love which gives them power to uplift and elevate. Mata Amritanandamayi is that symbol, and let her light of love and action enlighten and purify and take us from the gross to the subtle in the sea of universal love which is hers.

23.

Kaviraj Gopinath

To speak about Mahamahopadhyaya Kaviraj Gopinath is no easy task. How does one so small and little dare to pay a tribute to a doyen, a colossus, more a 'rishi' of our times? I had the great privilege of coming in contact with him during my stay in Varanasi as a student/disciple of that other great, frail in frame, Dr. Vasudeva Saran Agrawala.

I did not reside in the campus. It was instead in Godhulia, in the home of the late Sri Prem Chand. Sigiriya was close by and of course one had heard about the Mahamahopadhyaya. But who would ever have the courage to go to the home of this great savant and *Sadhaka*? Also at the University, Banaras Hindu University, where I silently imbibed the pearls of knowledge, not unmixed with wit, humour and bantar, there was an urbane atmosphere of intellectual discourse which kept one thoroughly engaged. Coupled with it, was the reputation of Kaviraj Gopinath, that he had little or no use for mere intellectual pursuits and for degrees. Yet deep within was a strong urge to at least have *darsana* of this living legend. So close and so distant.

Then one day, from a most unexpected direction, the opportunity arrived unasked: the great philosopher and scholar Dr. Dharmendranath Shastri arrived in Varanasi. He came to visit his niece in her make-believe little home in a sprawling four storey near empty building. He was both uncle and guru. He could ask incisive difficult questions. Affection and austerity and strict discipline went together. He represented a different stream of Indian scholarship than all that I was encountering in the campus.

In my dreams I could not associate him with Mahamahopadhyaya Kaviraj Gopinath. Shastriji was a rationalist, a trifle left-inclined and had no use for all that he called the hocus-pocus of the later Sanskrit and Indian traditions. Emerging out of a disciplinarian education of Vrindavan *gurukula*, he had travelled far and wide to investigate other paths, specially in the schools of philosophy of Nagarjuna and Dignag. Mahamahopadhyaya was known as a *Sadhaka*—a *Siddha Purusa*—with a

Saivite and as also the *Shakteen*. In my ignorance and part knowledge, I could not conceive of an association between the two. With these assumptions, I was dumbfounded when Shastriji turned around and said to me one afternoon; 'I am going to visit a great scholar who is my guru, Mahamahopadhyaya Kaviraj Gopinath. Would you like to come with me? I am not very sure if he will see you, but he may. Come.'

It was an incredible manna from heaven, more so because it was so unexpected. Of course, I accompanied him. As soon as we entered, from a distance I saw a man seated on his *asana*. He was centred and yet at ease with grand-children playing around him, one climbing his shoulder, the other on his lap, yet there was a presence which was both distant and radiant. From the first moment I knew I was in the presence of an extraordinary being. Before I could gather my wits together to walk in, I saw an incredible happening. Shastriji had rejected all ritual and formalities. Suddenly I found him doing *Sastang Pranama* prostrate before guru Gopinath. I could not believe my eyes. Throughout childhood Shastriji had taught us children to question, to argue and never to bow down. For me he was a radical amongst Sanskrit scholars and formal obeisance of any kind was the last thing I associated with him. To see him thus, in *Sastang Pranama* spontaneously and with deep reverence, was a revelation on several dimensions at the same time.

What I could not learn from several tomes of books and all intellectual discourse became clear and lucid in an instant. Indian thought and its several branches of knowledge were neither sectarian nor insular. It was my education and conditioning that had made me stereotype disciplines and scholars. We had been conditioned to view each stream and layer of the Indian tradition in insulation within a framework of confrontation and mutual opposition: in fact each was a distinctive, clearly distinguishable layer, within a well-conceived framework and structure of over-layering. Each was an integral part of a whole. It was for me to experience and discern the invisible but real thread of vision which bound all parts together.

It was this experience of an instant, momentary and ephemeral in physical time which like lightening made me see in a flash that the tradition and its true human repositories were a whole organic integrated system.

So began my journey of seeing the parts and the whole, the refined distinctions of each layer and to make connections and interconnections in seemingly disparate and unconnected streams of Indian thought, philosophic schools, intellectual discourse, artistic expressions, and the primacy of the experience which was the beginning and the end.

Nevertheless, Kaviraj Gopinath was a human of the world and in our time of the late nineteenth and twentieth century. He lived in chronological historical time and yet, as he progressed through his life, he belonged to another dimension of time and space of a perennial flow of the Indian ethos. In being so, he was the epitome of trans-time and trans-physical space. The man who was seated on a simple *asana* with grand-children playing around was a reality on one level; the intellectual giant who could converse and debate on practically all branches of knowledge with piercing incisiveness was another, and there was the third which transcended the intellects and moved beyond as a *Sadhaka* and mystic.

The body, mind, intellect and soul, *sarira indiriya manas buddhi* and *cetana* continuum has been much spoken of in Indian thought, from the *Rig Veda* to the *Katha Upanishad.* Mahamahopadhyaya appears to have through discipline harnessed the energies of the physical, the intellectual, the emotive and the experiential into one integrated whole. This is borne out from the writings of all those who have written about him in *Kaviraj Gopinath Abinandan Granth.* Since my own first hand acquaintance with him was short but powerful, I can only recreate the personality of the man and his work through the many tributes of the people who knew him. Some have written chronological life sketches. Others have spoken of him as teacher-guru in their specialized disciplines, and yet others have thrown light and illumination (*prakasa*) on the *Sadhaka* and mystic.

What is the picture that emerges from all this writing and the reminiscences?

First, at the purely physical level of chronology, the physical life, the landmarks, are well known indeed, all too well known. Despite this, perhaps after the lapse of a few decades, it would be pertinently educative to remember these again.

Kaviraj Gopinath belonged to a distinguished lineage of Brahmanical scholarship. The genealogy can be traced back to the great Bhatta Narayana (nearly nine generations). However from the moment of his physical birth, the child and the boy only had to face a series of misfortunes and vicissitudes. Dr. Bhagwati Prasad Singh of Gorakhpur University presents a graphic account of his great-great-grandfather ancestor Kamal Kant's economic wealth and social status, in Maimensingh, now in Bangladesh. However, Gopinathji's father Pt. Vaikuntha Nath was left alone and helpless at the tender age of six years. A series of providential misfortunes had brought this about. Fortunately he was taken in the care of Pt. Kalachanda. Pt. Kalachanda looked after Pt. Vaikuntha Nath like his own son. He had him married soon to Subhda Sundari in AD 1876. She was the daughter of Harishchandra Moulick. She had lost her mother at a very young age and was brought up by a foster mother. Pt. Vaikuntha Nath received his elementary education in Kothalia. He completed his higher studies in Presidency College, Calcutta. He graduated in 1885 with a first in English, Philosophy and Sanskrit. Amongst his college fellows were Naredranath (Swami Vivekananda), Sir Bajendranath Seal, Satish Chandra Mukerjee and Rajendra Prasad, the first President of India. He entered Sanskrit College to pursue his MA in Sanskrit. However, before long he suddenly fell ill and passed away in 1887.

Gopinath Kaviraj was the posthumous child of Pt. Vaikuntha Nath and Subhda Sundari. Born in December 1887 the baby was looked after by the mother who alternated between the maternal and paternal family. His primary education began in Kothalia. By 1898 he had received training in Bangla, Sanskrit and English. Soon after, he joined the new English school in Phamran. Two years later in 1900 he was married at the age of thirteen to Kusum Kumari who also came from a Pandit Kuleen Brahman family. However, on account of another series of misfortunes and frequent illnesses, Gopinath had to leave Bengal and take asylum in Jaipur. During the journey to Jaipur he was apprehensive and doubtful. Fortunately he found yet another benefactor. Through another series of events he reached Queens College, Varanasi. It was here that he received a thorough training in the then modern research methodologies under Dr. Arthur Venis, the then Principal of the Queens College. From this point onwards the life of Pt. Gopinath is well known. He was first employed in this college as Librarian of Saraswati Bhawan in 1914 and he became the Principal of the College in 1924. He worked in this capacity until 1937. In these capacities he was both a seeker as well as a giver of knowledge. In 1937 the British government conferred the title of Mahamahopadhyaya; the University of Allahabad and BHU a *Honoris Causa* D. Litt. He was appointed the first honorary fellow of the University of Burdwan. He later received the Padma Vibhushan, finally the Bharat Ratna in 1976.

Mahamahopadhyaya Kaviraj Gopinath edited seventy-two texts in the series 'Prince of Wales Saraswati Bhavan' texts. He wrote on *Sakta* philosophy in the volume *Philosophy Eastern and Western* (1950). His book on 'Aspects of Indian Thought' (University of Burdwan) was a landmark. The essays in the book (1) Doctrine of Patibha, (2) Theism in Ancient India, (3) Nyaya Vaisesika Philosophy, (4) The Problems of Causality, (5) Stages in Yoga, (6) Kaivalya in Dualistic Cultures, (7) Nirmana Kaya, (8) Vrna Sarva Philosophy, (9) Pasupate Philosophy, (10) Sakta Philosophy, (11) Philosophy of Tripura Tantra, (12) The systems of *cakra* according to Goraknath, (13) Virgin Worship—are all illuminative expositions on drawing obscure aspects of the Indian traditions.

His bibliography of Nyaya Vaisesika Literature is a guiding star for many researchers of this branch of Indian philosophy.

Besides these essays, he wrote in Bengali and gave oral discourses by the thousand, which have left an indelible mark on all those who heard him. His mastery of *Pali* and *Prakrit* is well known. He had mastered French and German under Dr. Norrman. However, along with these intellectual pursuits of being a librarian, a principal of the Sanskrit College and a writer and author, there was that inner core in him. He took initiation from Swami Visuddanand Saraswati in 1938 and pursued that path till the end. Ultimately he was the preceptor and propounder of *Akhanda Maha yoga*.

What does this simple narration of his life signify?

To me this epitomizes a journey of life which was seeking and then asserting integration at all levels. The landmarks of his life in the time span from his birth to passing away is only the outer layer. Here he fulfilled his duty as a child, boy, student, librarian, principal, husband and all else. However, he lived in this world, but was not of it, from the moment he began his inner meditation and *sadhana* which illumined all else.

As the Librarian of the Queens College he did a stupendous job of preserving and conserving the countless unpublished manuscripts of the Queens College, today the Sampoornananda Varanasiya Sanskrit Visvavidyalaya. A complete list is yet to be made of his tireless effort to collect and catalogue the collection. Today it is the richest single collection of manuscripts in all branches of knowledge. The seventy-two volumes he edited brought forth rare material hitherto totally unknown. The publications of these works changed the course of Indic studies in many ways. It was clear from the publication of these manuscripts (I do not have to recount the list) that there lay a vast body of primary material which was awaiting the attention of scholars. From my point of view the valuable work remained incomplete in the absence of a conceived programme of the continuation of the work, collecting and editing the material. He had retired from the college as its principal in 1937, the pace of work slowed and in between even stopped. When I was asked to draw up the conceptual plan of the Indira Gandhi National Centre for the Arts, the first task I identified was that of conserving this heritage. The microfilming programme of the IGNCA in twelve centres of India was a continuation of the work of pioneers like Mahamahopadhyaya Kaviraj Gopinath. It is clear that in this field we need many more researchers, scholars and editors. Most deductions on the branches of knowledge of the Indian tradition are based on the perusal of very important but, alas, partial material. I believe that Mahamahopadhyaya's work needs to be continued with fresh enthusiasm and mobilisation of human resources which are fast depleting.

But the second dimension of his work relates to the many vistas he opened up for intellectual discourse. His command over languages, Sanskrit, Pali, Prakrit, French, German, Bengali, Hindi, and his deep study of the streams of Buddhist, Jaina, Shakta, Virasarvism, Kashmir Saivism and Vaishnavism and the different schools of *darsanas* to specially Nyaya Visesika, made him a towering philosopher of his time. Scholars from different disciplines came to him for illumination. He guided each at their own level and stage of preparedness as recipients. It is not surprising therefore that his students, direct and indirect, should range from a Dr. Dharmendranath Sastri, a rationalist and scholar of Nagarjuna and Dignag to Kalidas Bhattacharya. He could speak to Navajyoti Rastogi on Trika, as to Debabrata Sen or to Gounda Gopal Mukhopadhyaya. From Baldeva Mishra, to Baldadeva Upadhyaya to Dr. Adityanath Jha to Gopalchandra Sinha—all revered him.

It is therefore not surprising that the many, many tributes paid by a galaxy of scholars reflect different facets of the one single illuminated self. He did know the subtle shades of difference between each school of thought and philosophy the *darsanas*, *tanta agma, sakta* and much else and yet he held them together with a rare integrity. Somewhere and with a keen flash of illumination he saw the unifying vision and the underlying invisible golden thread behind the diversity of intellectual approaches, school of thought and even different systems of *Sadhana*.

This was the level of mind (*manas* and *buddhi*): undoubtedly then he stood as his writing will stand for identifying the core, the unitary vision, rather than intellectual niceties of differentiation, and technical divergences.

I am too small a person to comment on his contributions in these fields and these branches of knowledge. However, from amongst his own writing I have chosen some excerpts which speak of his philosophy of life, and thus his very special contribution to the study of Indian philosophy or philosophic schools. As we all know the *darsanas* have been compared to different schools of philosophy in the western tradition. The interpreters and writers of the nineteenth and twentieth century, including Dasgupta and Dr. Radhakrishnan, and even TRV Murti, have tried to relate the *darsana* with the schools of philosophy and the sub-disciplines of logic, ethics, etc. etc. In contra distinction, Mahamahopadhyaya Kaviraj Gopinath reminds us repeatedly that the fundamental approach is different. He said the goals of Indian philosophy were:

> "In India, philosophy, especially in its earlier and truer form, was intended to serve a practical purpose. Bare speculation is invariably condemned as waste of energy, in as much as it leads nowhere; speculation is deemed blind without the guiding light which revelation or Higher Perception alone can furnish. Thus the premises from which Reason has to draw its inferences are naturally beyond its own reach and stand outside of itself."

As for reason he said,

> "Reason is, by nature, impotent and cannot in any way overstep its data. It is not creative nor intuitive; its function is interpretation of facts. Its ultimate resort is, therefore, nothing short of direct experience.
>
> But as human experience is limited in its scope and is liable to error, the experience on which our reasoning is based must be conceived as infinite and free from all the defects incidental to erring humanity. This infinite experience is embodied in the revealed scriptures. Philosophy, if rightly understood, is then only a step in the cultivation of a man's life. To be at all fruitful it must work in subordination to data supplied by Revelation. Else it is apt to run astray."

This implies that the ultimate source of true knowledge is revelation, but the facts of revelation cannot be accepted without any questioning in the present state of our life. We have to study them with the help of our reason. As soon as it is brought home to us that these facts are quite possible and not irrational, the function of reason as a factor of our culture is fulfilled.

For this function is simply to beget a notion of possibility (*sambhavanibuddhi*) in regard to a certain proposition, and not of its certainty. Certitude can never be reached by the intellectual faculties (cf. *tarkapratisthanat*). It has, therefore, a limited role, viz. removing 'the disturbing factors of doubt (*asambhivani*) and perversion (*viparitabhivani*)' in order to make the mind fit to 'receive the truth'.

As for truth, he said,

> 'it is easy to understand how different systems of philosophy, apparently conflicting with and subversive of one another, originate. The Highest Truth, which lends itself to the light of supra-mental Intuition, is indeed one and invisible but it appears in diverse forms when looked at from diverse points of view corresponding to the capacities and tastes of the individual Sadhakas.'

The differences in the formulation of the same single Truth are unavoidable because, he points out unerringly once again,

> 'so long as the individualised consciousness asserts itself—so long as we are unable to dispense with "mind" as an organ of knowledge—it is vain to hope for the attainment of the Absolute Truth. Relative or partial truth is all that can be reached by human reason. And these relative or fragmentary truths or aspects of the Absolute Truth, are held to be the immediate ends of the different systems of philosophy.'

The few excerpts I have quoted will make it clear that he was a man of vision, not a mere intellectual who finds arguments for taking particular positions and standpoints. Some have called him a synthesiser, others an eclectic, but he was none of this. He was instead the person who had experienced the one single luminosity of the Indian experience and could see the different colours of the rainbow as if in a spectrum. He could and did dwell on each of these colours, be it *Saivism* or *shaktism*, *Nyaya* or *Krishna tattva* but throughout he was filled and enveloped with that one single luminosity seen in different ways through different prism.

I am not competent to comment on his most outstanding work on the *tantras* and *agmas*. Much has been written on it. Nor do I dare to tread on the path of Kashmir Saivism. I am even less competent to open my mouth on Gopinath Kaviraj as a *Sadhaka* who knew and propagated *Akhanda Mahayoga*.

Here also I can do no more than place before you, second hand, some thoughts of his disciple Sri Manoranjan Basu's narration of Mahamahopadhyaya's meeting with Swami Yogatrayananda, alias Sashi Bhushan Sanyal, and Swami Vishuddhvananda:

> The third and final phase of his life commences with his meeting Yogiraja Sri Visuddhvananda Paramahansa Maharaja from whose mouth, he first heard of *Jnana Ganja* and *Surya-Vijnana*. He was simply astonished to find his supernormal yogic power and he had serious discussion with him about the principles and mechanism of yoga. He was so much charmed by his luminous

personality that he decided to be his disciple. Accordingly he got spiritually initiated by him on January 21, 1928 at his hermitage (*asrama*) at Hanuman Ghat, Kasi. Thus, we find that three great personalities, Dr. Arthur Venis, Yogivara Sri Sivaramkinkara Yagotrayananda and Swami Visuddhvananada Paramahansa Maharaja exerted great influence, though in different spheres, in moulding the life of the great Savant.

There was then the whole world of *tattvas* which Mahamahopadhyaya explored both on Sarva Sakti concepts as also Krishna or Vaisnava:

> The Universe of experience according to the Tantras consists of a number of Bhuvanas or planes of life and consciousness made up of *Tattvas*. In the *Saiva-Sakta agamas* thirty-six *tattvas* are recognized, out of which twenty-four counted from below are considered as impure, the next seven are mixed and the remaining five as pure. In this scheme Prakriti (24) marks the end of impure, maya (31) that of mixed and siva (36) that of pure *tattvas*. They may otherwise be called *atma tattva*, *vidya tattva* and *siva tattva*. Each *tattva* has a series of *bhuvanas* affiliated to it. The *bhuvanas* are the abodes of living beings and endowed with bodies and organs made up of the substance, materiality of which corresponds to the nature of their *Karmas* of *Jnana* and the degree of their perfection. The *bhuvanas* of the *Prithvitattva* represent its sphere known as *brahmanda*, the *Bhuvanas* of Prakriti form the *Prakrityananda*, those of the *Tattvas* up to *maya* represent the mayanada and the bhuvanas of the tattvas upto sakti beyond maya constitutes the *saktyanda* which is the widest sphere. Beyond *sakti tattva* there is no limitation and consequently no sphere, though *bhuvanas* are said to exist even in *Siva Tattva* which is identified with *Bindu* and *Santyatita Kala*. The *bhutakasa*, *cittakasa* and *cidakasa* are the supports under which the aforesaid worlds constituting the entire universe belong.

And finally what about Khanda and Akhanda Mahayoga. In Mahamahopadhyaya's word

> As soon as the artificial barrier raised between the higher and the lower self is demolished the pure self emerges as a radiant and eternally self-aware existence of Joy in which the two aspects of its being appear as united in an eternal embrace and ineffable sweetness. This is Yoga in the truest sense of the term".

He further says,

> "Yoga is really the paramount power which leads us not only to a knowledge of the higher life, which is spiritual, but also to its practical realisation by the self.......". It is exclusively Yoga that one can find the key to the solution of all the problems of life and mind as well as to the realisation of the supreme end of Existence."

From the point of objective, Yogis are divided into two broad classes, such as Khanda and Akhanda. Khanda Yogis are of two types: Khanda Yogi and Mahakhanda Yogi. First, the objective of Khanda Yogi is not limited within the realm of achieving *Cidakas*, he goes far beyond it. The seed of competency is given by the spiritual preceptor in the form of initiation and the spiritual adepts by his individual efforts makes such seed germinate in the form of a tree, full of flowers and fruits. The Yogis are always alert, they are never indifferent to their duties and obligations. The Yogi preceptor at the time of initiating his spiritual adepts in the line of Yoga gives them *asana*s (seats) which give them protection. This *asana* giving affair is something very mysterious.

It is best not to elaborate Khanda and Akhanda in this.

24.

Acharya Vasudevaji

In the plot of land where stands the House of the Arts, known as Rabindra Bhavan, there lay, not long ago, a series of barracks built for the US troops during World War II.

In these lived two scholars, who epitomise for me different facets of the Indian tradition: one revealed for me the beauties and great depths of English literature while planting seeds for looking at the world of Buddhism: the other was the guide and guru for showing the path for unravelling some of the complexities of this dense and fertile wood of the Indian artistic tradition.

The first came from Bengal. Dr. S. Dutt, a world renowned scholar of Coleridge and Buddhism: the other was Dr. Vasudeva Saran Agrawala. It is to the second that I pay my tribute in inadequate words, made more inadequate through the English language, in which some aspects of his work and personality cannot be expressed.

Scholars, savants, art critics and politicians have assessed his monumental contributions: many have spoken of his versatility, his wide range and his phenomenal intellectual growth. It is not necessary for me to add to it. I can only speak of the gifts I received from him of vision, of discipline and of knowledge: the subjectivity of the approach may be pardoned on account of the limitations of my own capacity for receiving and not on account of the rich cascade of knowledge which flowed from this man and scholar who could explore hills and valleys, all manner of growth from the smallest hidden violets to the Banyan trees of the Indian tradition.

I remember distinctly the day I was taken by my mother to see the exhibition of Indian Art held in the building which houses the National Archives. We had walked up the stairs: she was greeted warmly by a thin austere looking man, who took us around; off and on, he would ask me a date of a particular king or hold forth on the great moment of discovery of the terracottas or sculptures on display. There was also a coin-collection where we paused considerably, and while he talked about the collections and with staggering facility reeled off dates and peculiarities of punch-marked and Dramma and Kusāna coins and the symbolism of the Silver, Māsaka coins, I was dumbfounded and wondered to myself, how anyone could remember so much. The first impression he made was of a man with a fund of information and knowledge: of his responses on the level of feeling or enthusiasm I got little indication. I went back to the exhibition and this time it was another man who held forth overjoyed with the beauty of the Pārvati head from Ahichchatra, the woman with a stylus and mother and child. It was this and a third visit which sparked off a peculiar communication. Then came another visit to the barracks where he lived: he sat on an unpolished Indian style 'takhat' (diwan) surrounded by volumes and volumes of books, which seemed too heavy to be opened, some dusted, others not. The conversation moved from simple queries about my reading and interest in poetry, to sculpture and dance. Dance, because I had been practising it under Gurus like Achchan Maharaj. He asked me if I had seen figures of dancing in Indian stone; of course, I had not, only the examples of Bhubaneswar in the exhibition had seemed like dancing figures to me. Two or three questions, affectionately put with negative answers, put me in my place, aware of my colossal ignorance. One less tolerant and proud would have forgotten about the English literature trained lady who had taken to some Indian dancing. Not he, for somewhere in him was the "teacher" who was spotting potential research students, grinding and moulding any material he got. In later years I had occasion to watch him closely in Banaras when he showed the direction of research to his student—Me, he armed with one or two books, one of them by Coomaraswamy and other by Havell. He also wanted to know if I had read the *Nātyasāstra*, was aware of Coomaraswamy's book, *Mirror of Gestures*, translation of the *Abhinayadarpana*. Of course I had not, but the very questions made me aware that there was more to dance than hours of practice. The two books were gone through, returned and seeds of an insatiable curiosity about what constituted the Heritage had been sown.

The two years following were spent in USA being trained further in English language and literature and European art history and methodologies of art education. As an Indian one was often called upon to speak about Indian religion, philosophy, literature and of course give dance-demonstration. Each time, the hidden reservoirs of the tradition had to be tapped: the fund was limited and an acute consciousness of inadequacy arose in my mind. The pictures of the Pārvati from Ahichchatra, the mother and child and the woman with a stylus I had carried with me, more with an idea of giving away as gifts, rather than something to be meditated upon. But soon, they grew upon one, each time revealing new facets, until one day while pursuing English literature and writing about aesthetics and new criticism, the intellectual year had taken another turn. The few remarks made by Vasudevaji on the need to know one's country better before one travelled abroad, the dates and the enthusiasm of Havell on the many armed images of the Hindu-sculpture, all acquired new meaning. The journey had begun homeward, unquestionably and irrevocably. The writings of Coomaraswamy were available easily and the bulletins of Boston Museum one could find. On one level, I was learning more about the West, not only English literature, Art history and education, on another, thanks to the encounters with Vasudevaji, I was returning "Home" to India.

I returned on the surface still back to English literature, but underneath to something else. Once again, l went back to Vasudevaji for guidance before taking a journey to the South. He gave me letters of introduction to Dr. V. Raghavan whose writings I had seen in the magazine *Triveni* and to the late Sri K.V. Ramachandran. City to city, village to village and temple to temple I travelled, exploring, imbibing and finding my roots: the reliefs of Chidambaram, the *pūjā* of Madurai, the sea-shore of Kanyakumari, the 10-day long wait at Cheruthurathy before I could see Kathakali, the staggering richness of the collections of the Saraswati Mahal Tanjore Library, the old issues of the Kuppuswami and Music Academy journal, all combined together to turn irrevocably from English literature and its beauties to other paths. Vasudevaji had been in no small measure responsible for this. The home-coming to disciplines of Indology was neither easy nor welcome by academicians: even Vasudevaji himself was somewhat sceptical of the capacities of one whose first disciplines were so remote.

Anyway, with this gurgling new-found enthusiasm I even wrote a book; it was perhaps full of small insights but little history and doubtful methodology of research. The transference from one field to another could not happen automatically: thinking, speaking English, one was analytical, critical, chronological. In the sphere of Indian art dates and chronology seems such a difficult matter that one gave up. This latter fault I have found with other Indian students who have travelled this indirect route, if they have not had the good fortune of being corrected and guided by one as austere, stern and painstaking like Vasudevaji. He read the manuscript, with some amusement perhaps; returned it with the remarks that while I had perception and insights, it was necessary to traverse the range of Sanskrit literature, sculpture, painting and the Śāstras before establishing inter-connections. Another set of books was handed over and I was introduced to the library of the Archaeological Survey of India and the photo-section. Soon after, he moved to Banaras and I was left to dig deep into Archaeological Reports and volumes and volumes of photographs by myself.

It was only after some basic spade work had been accomplished that I took courage to write and ask him whether I could enroll under him as a Ph.D. student, with Inter-relationship of Indian art forms as a subject. The reply came promptly in his bold Devanagari long-hand, welcoming the idea, but warning me sternly of all my inadequacies and how it was essential to have a thorough grounding in Sanskrit, to be acquainted with the whole field of Indian history and Art to be able to tap primary source material etc. He also wanted me to send him a summary by further defining and delimiting my subject. In reply to my revised synopsis and renewed request he asked me to see him in Banaras. Life seemed more hopeful, but I was still scared. He approved the synopsis, promised to place it before the Academic Council but gave me no hope since this matter of switching disciplines was no easy matter in the rigid university system, made more difficult both by the suspicious scepticism of many in the field of Indological Studies. But with a stroke of luck and Vasudevaji's indulgence it was accomplished.

I arrived in Banaras, to sit at his feet, not literally at his feet but certainly at his door. For hours, he was inaccessible. After many hours on stone steps, he wanted you to read aloud every line written while he lay as in deep slumber on the same unpolished *takhat* of Delhi surrounded by books. Often, I was convinced that I was reading aloud in a vacuum and suddenly like a tiger he would leap practically on the paper you were holding and say "Read that line again: what did you say? How have you got that? Go upstairs, on the third shelf the fourth book is such and such. Will you bring that?" And up I would travel, trembling that this was the last stroke, now I was finished. I remember many such incidents in the context of the references to the Vedas and the Brāhmanas. He had to satisfy himself about every grammatical rendering, footnoting, referencing, before you proceeded. Before long I realized that the stance of the sleeping Visnu was a picture of concentration and not of slumber. Then came the section on Sculpture: I was seeing too much into poses, all Indian sculpture was the dancing figure to me, I remember three days of heated discussion on the Sālabhañjikās where I have disagreed with Smith, Havell, even Coomaraswamy and Vasudevaji. Coomaraswamy's book on Yaksas was rare, but I had found a copy. I had quoted from it copiously and then came to different conclusions. He examined every line—brought forth pictures, made me analyse posture, feet positions of many many examples. It was only after he had gone through every line and word along with the reproductions that he was convinced. Then the eyes twinkled, smiles broke forth and out would come the comment *vibhor kar diya*.

There would be other occasions, when he would show a total disinterest in what you were doing or had brought to show. He was pre-occupied far away. As a concession to your presence, he would ask you to pick up pen and paper and order you to begin taking dictation. While he was dictating to you on Indian sculpture or *Harsacarita*, there would arrive another student whose field would be grammar or Pānini or Patāñjali. Without a moment's hesitation, there would be a second series of dictation going on. I have been witness to his dictating in one session on Indian Art, on Vedas, Pānini and words of the Janapada tradition to three different people: the group of research scholars or pandits working in the adjoining room on some aspects of *Pādmavata* was an addition, and off and on he would go and tell them something and return. This phenomenal erudition, with an unmistakable mask of deep intellectual organization, was as bewildering as it was impressive.

This pre-occupation with two or three subjects revealed the man and scholar in many significant ways. There was nothing static or stereotyped about these interests: the seemingly unrelated subjects or fields he attacked at a given moment showed an inner cohesiveness and was indicative of the intellectual journey he was taking. His early work of the thirties was devoted in the main to problems of identification, dating, on linguistics and numismatics. But very soon he moved from cataloguing, documentation (e.g. Catalogue of the Curzon Museum of Archaeology in Mathura; Identification of Nāgadvīpa JBORS 1937; Mathura Terracottas, JUP Historical Society 1937; A Sanskrit inscription of the Reign of Sikandar Shah), to interpretation and broader cultural studies. His own D.Litt. thesis on 'India as known to Pānini' had equipped him to bring the approach of reconstructing a particular era through literary and linguistic evidence: but unlike his predecessors, he did not confine himself far too long on the narrow field of dating or identification or for that matter on a pure grammarian's approach to analysing word, language, structuring.

Also not many scholars have the easy facility of moving from one intensive study in depth to the other: the scholars of his generation could, because the fundamental approach to the "tradition" was not limited to a scholar's ambition at finding something new, but at redefining, reconstructing the tradition by looking at different fragments of a whole. The joy of revelation accompanied every scholastic effort.

From Pānini he moved to the cultural scene of Bana's *Harsacarita* and to *Padmāvata*; in each of these works, the life and culture of the periods is reconstructed on the basis of internal evidence. But soon he moved even from reconstruction to a deeper interpretation of the tradition on two distinct levels. One the Vedas and the other Janapada. Vedic symbolism and cosmology preoccupied him completely for a period: Dr. Moti Chandra's mild scepticism did not deter him from exploring the riches of a new treasure he had found. He was immersed in it fully, reading, discussing and perusing every clue he could obtain. Alongside the joy of the artistic tradition, the study of Indian Art had not been abandoned. For me as a silent and close watcher it was interesting to see how his intellectual preoccupations had alternated between Pānini and Gupta literature and art for a while, until it took him to the writing of the *Thousand syllabled speech* (a study in cosmic symbolism in its Vedic versions). For me it was also an education to see how the Snātaka of Gurukula with an Āryasamāja background moved with ease, to that body of literature which was practically taboo to his upbringing, namely, the Purānas. The call of *jñāna* was so great that he was willing, ready to traverse any path, carve any route, to understand the tradition. His later work speaks of the withdrawn, speculative nature of his personality and of his inner growth as man and scholar. In departing from the beaten track of pure intellectual scholarship, he lost many friends and colleagues, but he persevered.

But to go back to Banaras and the evening gatherings in his study, the atmosphere was more relaxed then: Rai Sahib, Dr. Moti Chandra were often there: sometimes Hazari Prasadji joined: it was an intellectual repartee jam session: I had been witness to music/dance sessions of the great masters of the *oral-tradition* of the Sanpradāyas: this was the living śāstric tradition. Every sentence was punctuated with quotations, verses, grammatical mistakes, or idiocyncracies not unmixed with remarks of irony and humour on specimens of spurious scholarship, anecdotes of plagiarism and of the many subterfuges of museum curators or collectors.

Sometimes scholars came from outside: Sri C. Sivaramamurti I met at one such gatherings: so also Sri Adris Banerjee and many others. With them the conversation was of a different order revolving generally around the interest of the visitor. It was part of the training of a teacher to have students around, sharing and imbibing the message of these exchanges and discussions. Indeed, one learnt as much, sometimes more, from them than from pouring over volumes of printed material. And yet how different was all this from the atmosphere of a super-imposed 'seminar' or discussion of today which smack of artificiality, at the very moment of asserting commitment. And for that matter how different from the personal conversation of others, who talk of success achieved, conferences attended and promotions awaited.

It was clear that this group was looking at the tradition, the great and little; the Vedic or Janapada—the high classical or folk popular from inside with a tactile touch and not analysing it from the outside. This was an education, both intellectually and otherwise. For me, it provided the necessary foil to the *oral-tradition* of India and the Western tradition of objective analysis I had known. This open-minded generosity of allowing students to participate, share and the listeners and spectators was an essential feature: totality of the experience was the gift thus cooking for scholars or for the *Veda pādthīs* who came to recite was an additional training.

Gradually things fell into place, living and scholarship, abstraction and concretization, *śāstra* and *prayoga*, so called classical, and folk, great and little traditions, literature and the arts. Idol worship and abstract concepts did not stand in opposition. They were complementary, the term interdisciplinary and multi-disciplinary approach came much later; these scholars and Vasudevaji in particular had already practiced this and inculcated it in his students. No wonder the story of *Visnudharmottara* was repeated at every juncture.

For this, others and I are beholden to him: the gift we received was the training and ability to see single expressions, as parts of a whole: to establish inter-connections and to delineate the exact routes of inter-relationships between the different branches of the tree and the different plants of the multiple-specie forest of the Indian tradition. And himself, the man and scholar, grew in stature, as he moved from the world of fact, evidence and data collection, reconstruction, to a world of the pursuit of symbolism and finally a dedication to the 'Devi' contained in his

Devi Māhātmya. Here was a perfect example of personality which had travelled from the realm of pure intellect to that of feeling—verging on faith.

In personal behaviour and conduct one hardly ever got a glimpse of any feeling, far less of demonstrative affection. But one occasion I remember.

My work was interrupted, the last draft done under pressure and after a few severe admonitions from him. I travelled to Banaras, with trembling fear handed over the four sets of three volumes each. He had one look and said 'So at last this donkey load on a rickshaw has arrived.' My heart sank. I was sure I would be travelling back with the 'donkey load' and there would be No Guide's O.K. for final submission. I was staying with Pt. Hazari Prasadji and the latter's affectionate teasing that the Guru was hard to please was enough to keep me awake all night.

But the Guru had sat up all afternoon and night, gone through the manuscript, had marked one copy at several places and was already waiting for me outside Hazari Prasadji's house in the morning. I greeted him, still afraid: he came forward, embraced me affectionately and with tears in his eyes said, "Whether the examiners liked it or not is no further concern, I am satisfied". For one who was hard to please and harder to express his feelings, I was gratified that he had spoken.

25.

Vasudeva Saran Agrawala

The late Dr. Vasudeva Saran Agrawala, the thin, fragile, human frame, contained within his mind oceans, mountains, rivers and pools of scholarship, rare and precious, insights which facilitated looking deep into the ocean of tradition, ascend peaks of thought, follow the contours of the flow of rivers, pause to look at pools of local cultures. His journey was slow, steady, inspired by an unflinching commitment to investigating each and everything along the path: the 'word' and grammar were the constant walking sticks. Through them he could uncover the hidden meanings of all material manifestation, stones (architecture or sculpture), coins, texts, as also unravel the hidden symbolism of any form. He was a pilgrim in search of perennial value.

Today after a hundred years, it is time to assess the unique contribution of this giant among scholars of his generation. An outstanding grammarian, he was at the same time an archaeologist, an epigraphist, and numismatist. His command of Sanskrit—Vedic and classical—was not restricted to grammar. Through philosophy and etymology, he delved deep into the essence of meaning. Hindi, Avadhi and Braj were his inheritance. Thus he explored and navigated freely with ease in the texts of Sanskrit as also Avadhi and Braj. The corpus of vocabulary of oral literature engaged him. His interests extended far and wide without ever becoming superficial. The width of his span was matched by a depth of understanding and sudden insights of illumination.

His education in a manner of speaking was normal and ordinary. But he made the normal and ordinary into the extraordinary. In two seminal letters, written to the late Pt. Banarasidasa Chaturvedi on 1.6.1966 and 9.6.1966, he gives a straightforward account of his family, his upbringing and education. He acknowledged his deep debt to his grandfather, an ordinary villager and farmer who was known for his commitment to truth and justice. The grandfather instilled in the young Vasudeva a 'value system' which was to guide the grand-child for ever. If the grandfather was the shaper of character and giver of values, the grandmother who nurtured the young Vasudeva (after his mother's death when he was only six) was the fund of knowledge and wisdom in the oral traditions. The interest in Janapadiya vocabulary, proverbs and narratives was her gift. She embraced him with love and affection. With her love she planted the seeds of everlasting quest for the riches of the oral traditions.

From the village *madrasa* the young Vasudeva moved to Lucknow with his father. The subsequent education was all completed there, until the final D.Litt. However, along with formal schooling he also received training in the oral narration of the epics, particularly the *Mahabharata*. It was this training, he acknowledges, which ignited in him the desire to explore the rich and varied world of 'orality' at another level in the Indian intellectual tradition. His essays in *Madhukar* and *Lokavarta* bear testimony to his interest, and the fruits of the investigation are evident in his monumental commentary on the Mahabharat, called 'Bharata-Savitri'. He mentions in his letter to Pt. Banarasidasa Chaturvedi that he has commented on 24,000 *shlokas*.

Fairly early in his life (i.e. 1915) his father met Pt. Jagannath and requested him to teach his son Vasudeva. Pt. Jagannath accepted him as his disciple and trained him thoroughly in Sanskrit grammar. It was Pt. Jagannath who introduced young Vasudeva to Panini's Astadhyayi and taught him the text through the traditional methodology of 'memorisation', analysis and interpretation. This gave Vasudeva Saran Agrawala solid as rock foundation for his entire life.

Thus very early in Vasudeva's life three streams co-mingled: the oral and local through the grandmother; the epic tradition in narration; and the formal education in school and the traditional method of learning the text through Pt. Jagannath.

These influences and training in Vasudeva's formative years give us a very valuable insight into the very special point of view which informs much of Dr. Vasudeva Saran's writing. From a reading of his writing from the first to the last it is clear that he is neither textual scholar, e.g. P.V. Kane, arguing his case, nor an archaeologist in the tradition of a Madho Sarup Vats or Adris Banerjee, interested only in the material evidence, nor a Vedic scholar like Lakshman Shastri Joshi (another extraordinary giant), nor a conventional reader of the Kavyas, nor a historian even after his teacher Radha Kumud Mukerjee, or an art historian who was concerned only with stylistic issues or a folklorist doing field work in the anthropological mode. He is a class by himself, setting forth a new methodology without asserting that he is a path finder or an articulator of new theoretical models comprehending the Indian tradition.

However, despite the modesty and reticence, he does make explicit his intent and method. As mentioned at the outset, his primary tools of investigation continued to be 'words', meaning, context and symbolism. Indeed, he admits that he has endeavoured to bring together Sanskrit vidya and Indian art. He asserts, 'I have restored countless words and terminology pertinent to Indian archaeology and art through a study of Sanskrit literature. I have tried to narrate the story of Indian art through Indian concepts and words.... I firmly believe that the efficiency and appropriateness of this methodology will be acknowledged in decades to come'.

In other words, Dr. Agrawala is arguing for a distinctive methodology for evaluating the visual culture of India. He advocates applying 'criterion' which emerges from the literary and visual data. Further, he pleads for the application of technical terminology from within the tradition. These statements assume importance today because his successors have either followed the purely linear chronological path based on archaeological data, or have analysed the forms of Indian Art on the basis of what are called universal categories. Today he would be happy to find that there is acceptance of his particular approach. For his vision, scholarship and method we owe a sense of gratitude, almost a debt, to him for laying the foundations for a distinctive approach to the study of Indian traditions as exemplified in literature, architecture, sculpture and much else.

It would be impossible to cover all aspects of his scholarship in a single essay. Different people, both his contemporaries as also his students, have paid rich tributes, from the point of view of the particular discipline, as also their personal interaction with him.

The book 'Jnanamurti Acarya Vasudeva Saran', edited by Krishna Vallabha Tripathi (Vasudev Jnanpath, Lucknow), gives a glimpse of the multifaceted personality of Dr. Vasudeva Saran Agrawala. It also traces the principal milestones of long and arduous journey of Dr. Vasudeva Agrawala. The scholars present here are all his students, either direct or those who consider him as their Vidya Guru. Each one of them will deal with his contribution in specific fields and disciplines. It is therefore not necessary for me to anticipate their critical evaluation of Dr. Vasudeva Saran's contribution in specific disciplines.

Let me confine myself to the overarching *drishti* (vision and approach) of Dr. Vasudeva Saran Agrawala and illustrate this through his writing in different domains. Naturally this can only be highly selective, almost sketchy.

We are all aware that he began his career as the Curator/Director of the Mathura Museum. He is acknowledged as a cataloguer par excellence. He improved upon Dr. Vogel's catalogue, after examining thousands of images which lay uncatalogued and unidentified. So far archaeologists had understandably confined themselves to dating and establishment of chronologies. Dr. Vasudeva Saran painstakingly does that, but goes further. He attempts not only to see the image in its linear chronology, instead he goes behind and around the image by identifying textual sources which illumine the image. In so doing he enables the spectator to appreciate the cultural context of the image. Besides, his catalogues were based on solid research from a variety of primary sources. He placed 'terracottas' centre stage, in contrast to his predecessors. Terracottas as we know became a life long interest.

As far as Mathura art is concerned, he loved it, and brought out its essence in several essays. His masterly essay on the *Salabhanjikas*, in which he classifies the several pillar figures, will remain a watershed in Indian art history. His elucidation of the *Asoka dohad* motif was an eye-opener for many. He also followed A.K. Coomaraswamy and U.P. Shah by concentrating attention to *Yaksa* and *Yaksi* figures. Also, long before the terracottas of Sishupalgarh had attained international fame, he drew attention to them. His work on *Ahhichatra* is of course universally acknowledged. He goes into ecstasies over the Parvati and Siva head and, of course, Ganga and Yamuna figures.

Gupta art held his special attention. His monograph on Gupta art is truly an inspired piece of writing. Between 1933 and 1951 he wrote many essays, short and long, which exhibit his capacity to look at the image, and to relate it at the level of content to Sanskrit literature and at the level of form to Indian aesthetic theories.

His monograph on the evolution of temple forms is important for more than one reason. Like A.K. Coomaraswamy and Stella Kramrisch, he elucidates on the essentials of the *Vastu purusa mandala*. However, the value of his work lies in his meticulously tracing the history of the evolution of the temple structure. He forcefully argues that there is a direct connection between the Vedic ritual, the *vedi* and *vedika* and the establishment of the cella (*garbhagriha*). Almost like A.K.

Coomaraswamy, he moves from the concrete image and its literary source and cultural context to theory and *sastra*.

From 1951 onwards begins a period of great creative activity and phenomenal productivity. Vasudeva Saran Agrawala addresses himself concurrently to many theoretical issues. In each case he proceeds from an examination of words—terminology—and moves to context and from context to the perennial Vedic sources. His concern is with the beauty of the word and meaning (*sabda saundarya* and *artha saundarya*). Naturally he is drawn to exploring the relationship between the manifest and unmanifest (the *murta* and *amurta*), or deeper still, *vyakta* and *avyakta* of Upanisadic thought.

In his words,

> ''शब्द-सौन्दर्य और अर्थ-सौन्दर्य दोनों एक दूसरे के साथ जहाँ समन्वित रहते हैं, उसी श्रेष्ठ स्थिति को कवि ने वागर्थ से संपृक्त काव्य का आदर्श कहा है। जैसे काव्य में वैसे कला में भी आभ्यन्तर अर्थ और ब्राह्म रूप दोनों का जहाँ एक समान रमणीय विधान हो, वहीं श्रेष्ठ कला की अभिव्यक्ति होती है। गुप्त कला इसका उदाहरण है। उसमें बाह्य रूप की पुर्ण मात्रा को अनुप्राणित करने वाला जो अर्थ-सौन्दर्य है, वह शब्द का अद्‌भुत या विलक्षण रूप प्रस्तुत करता है।
>
> शिल्पी या चित्राचार्य अलंकरण संभार से संनतांगी कलाकृतियों का निर्माण करके ही परितृप्त नहीं हुए। उनकी कृतियाँ उस सविशेष अर्थ से प्राणवन्त हैं, जो बुद्ध के अनुत्तर ज्ञान एवं शिव की समाधि से अथवा लोकसंरक्षण में परमेष्ठी विष्णु के अहर्निश संवेदनशील स्वरूप से भावापन्न या ओजस्विनी बनी है। उन कलाकृतियों में कितनी रमणीयता, कितनी सजीवता और कितना अनन्त अक्षुण्ण आकर्षण है, इसे किस प्रकार कहा जाए। उनके सान्निध्य में स्थूल सीमा-भाव विगलित हो जाता है और मन दिव्य भावों के लोक में विलक्षण आनन्द, शान्ति और प्रकाश का अनुभव करता है। इस अमृत आनन्द या रस तक जो पहुँचा सके, वही चिरन्तन काव्य और कला है।''

Vasudeva's journey in a manner of speaking had just begun or perhaps reached halfway. So far he was exploring the oceans and retrieving different facets of Indian art through architecture, sculpture, coins and inscriptions. Now he begins to ascend Vedic heights. Again, his walking stick is words, words, and their multiple meanings and significance. For the journey he found a pathfinder in the person of Pt. Madhusudan Ojha. Dr. Vasudeva Saran Agrawala considered the Pandit his Guru, and the Guru felt that he had found a disciple, as Ramakrishna had found Vivekananda. It was Pt. Madhusudan Ojha and Sir Motilal Shastri who opened Dr. Agrawala's perceptive eye to the symbolic meaning of the Veda-s. As a consequence of revisiting the

Veda-s, Vasudeva wrote two seminal works, *Sparks from the Vedic Fire* and *A vision of the Long Darkness*. Each of these books is a conglomeration of Himalayan rocks. In his characteristic fashion, he takes up each word and phrase, or a mantra, as in the *Sparks from the Vedic Fire*, and then unpeels layers upon layers of meaning and significance. His elucidation of 'Gauri' and tracing it to the root *Gau* (Cow) is as convincing as it is unconventional. 'Agni' of course is central to his concern. No paraphrasing or quotations from these works can do justice to the insights of this genius. R.V.l.164 draws his particular attention. Each verse is explained in terms of its intrinsic 'symbolism'.

This examination enables Vasudeva Saran to then address himself to the issue of Vedic cosmology. Although Dr. A.K. Coomaraswamy had written essays on the subject, now collected together under the title of Vedic Exegesis (IGNCA publication), Dr. Agrawala's exposition stands on its own. Dr. A.K. Coomaraswamy also began with words, but his probe took him to comparison with Greek-Latin roots. Vasudeva Saran Agrawala restricts himself to the Indic tradition, and reconstructs the entire structure of cosmology, which he calls *Sristi Vijnana*.

A detailed examination of the Vedas, particularly some hymns from the *Rg Veda* and *Yajaurveda*, enables him to expound brilliantly on seminal concepts, Prajapati, Agni, Hiranyagarbha, Suparna. In each case he penetrates deeply into the Symbolism inherent in these concepts. He analyses the Nasadiya Sutra (R.V.l.129) in detail, both as a hymn of cosmology, as also the system of establishing correspondences. *Manas* is the individuating principle of the Mind, *Kama* the seed of the Mind. He comments brilliantly on the kinship of *sat* and *asat*. He decodes the riddles, specially of Rishi Vasukra (R.V.X27 and X28). Most illuminating is his explanation of the allegory of the blind daughter. Once again his explanation is based on the exploration of the unmanifest and manifest. In his words,

> 'The mutual relationship of the preceding stages of Formless Manifestation (Varuna's Dark Deep) and the subsequent stage of Formed Manifestation (Indra or Surya), is further brought out in bold relief by the allegory of the Blind Daughter. He, whose daughter is blind since birth, does not become wroth with her on this account. Which of the two will loose on him his anger—the man who leads her home or he who woos her (X.27.11)? The Blind Daughter (*anaksha duhita*) is the unmanifested Prakriti concealed within the womb of *Mahat* or *Parameshthi* (Universal). *Aksha, Chakshu, Jagarna, Kshobha, Srishti Ahah, Sukla Rajas, Jhoti* stand for creation or manifestation. As opposed to these are *Achakshu, Tamas,*

Ratri, Nidra, Krishna Rajas symbolising the unmanifested universal, *ab intra*. Cosmic consciousness, unless descended to the manifest material level, is conceived of as a blind girl.'

Sparks from the Vedic Fire, (A New Approach to Vedic Symbolism), Banaras Hindu University, 1962, pp.82–83.

Further he traces the origin of the *Ashtamurti Siva* mentioned by Kalidasa in the prologue to *Abhijnana Sakuntala* as also the first verse of *Malavikaquimitra* to the Vedic principles of the eight *Vasus*. Phrase by phrase he analyses Kalidasa's verse and relates it to the Vedic source. Finally, he asks the question, why was Agni called Rudra? His answer is

'The reason lies in the etymology of 'Rudra'—*yadrodit tasmathruth*,'

i.e. Agni becomes afflicted with hunger (*ashnaya*) for Soma which is its food, and this is comparable to the crying of the child for food (*Satapatha*, VI.1.3.10). Both become quiet when satiated, but that is only temporary, and the need for food returns again and again so long as life lasts. Agni is *annad* and Soma is *Ann*; deprived of *soma* Agni becomes *ghor* whereas provided with *soma* it becomes *shiva*

Sparks from the Vedic Fire, (A New Approach to Vedic Symbolism), Banaras Hindu University, 1962, p.119).

He extends his investigation to the Brahmanas, specially the Satapath, to show that Agni has eight names. He concludes his exposition by smoothly moving to the Puranas, and quotes from the *Markandeya Purana* (page 120). It is this kernel of perception which later flowers into the inspired book *Shiva Mahadeva, the Great God*.

A Vision in Long Darkness is a masterly study in cosmic symbolism as expounded in the verses of the famous *Asya-Vamiya Sukta* of Rishi Dirghatamas (R.V.l1641–52). Dr. V.S. Agrawala lucidly explains in the introduction the intent of Rishi Dirghatamas. The Rishi was grappling with the perennial question of the Mystery of Creation, 'Where is the teacher knowing the solution? Where is the pupil coming to the teacher for revelation of the Mystery? Who has seen the first cause from which emanated the primeval creation?' Dr. V.S. Agrawala comments: The Rishi 'takes quick snaps of the cosmos itself pointing to many symbols that carry the tale of its secret. The seer seems to take the confident view that the imprisoned divine splendour, although a veritable mystery, is present in every manifest form and is open to understanding' (Introduction to *A Vision in Long Darkness*).

Thereupon Dr. Agrawala investigates with remarkable insight and sharpness to decode this language of symbols. The language of symbols, he tells us, the ancients called *Nidana Vidya*. The method identifies objects, or phenomenon of Nature, and invests each with many layers of significance. He points out that, for example, the ancients conceived of the generative potencies of Mother Nature and of the cow and identified the two through a symbolic meaning, creating the picture of the thousand-fold universal cow who is the same as the *Thousand Syllabled speech*. From their point of view each created object, both natural and human, or activity or a thought, becomes a typical symbol pregnant with meaning. Dr. V.S. Agrawala concludes: 'A complete analysis of the Rig Veda and other Vedic texts places in our hands a comprehensive dictionary of symbolic language'. Pertinently he points out, 'the dictionary meanings are quite all right as found in the scholars of the East and the West, but the recovery of the consistent metaphysical ideas of the Vedic thinkers has to be accomplished if a full justice is to be done to the authors of these hymns' (p.11 of Introduction).

Addressing himself to the question, why Vedic thinkers selected the method of symbolism which appears obscure to us today, Dr. Agrawala's answer is that this was a deliberate choice. Perhaps it is best to recall his explanation in Dr. Agrawala's words:

> 'In order to explain the problem regarding the creation of the Cosmos and of the three primeval entities of which it is constituted, viz. Mind, Life and Matter, the Vedic thinkers seized upon the working of the Cosmos itself as manifested in the several categories and objects of creation. The Ocean, Sky, Earth, Air, Water, Fire, Sun, Moon, Mountains, Rivers, Forests, Trees, Animals, Men, Clouds, Rain, each one of these and many more are objects in Nature which stand out as the alphabets of world language robed in silence, yet eloquent with exploding meaning that can be deciphered according to the intellectual attainment of each thinker. The human body, eyes, ears, hands, feet, in-breath, out-breath, light, sound, movement —all these introduce us to a rich world of symbolical significance.

There are several advantages with respect to this method of conveying the cosmogonical ideas: firstly, this language is lasting through time and space. It is for man everywhere, already within his comprehension. He understands its meaning as a matter of course, being familiar with the concrete aspect of symbols in life, e.g., the significance of the cow is well known as the reproductive mother giving milk. Once the mind begins to think on this pattern, it enters an expanded orbit of meaning and recovers several isolated strands which build up a rich picture of the truth apprehended by each symbol.

The language of symbols is elastic and susceptible to decoding its multiple meaning. This is an advantage for it is possible to present a comprehensive world of thought through simple and minimum use of the words, e.g., the identity of the Earth with the Mother confers rich ideas of wide application at several levels relating to plants, animals, and men. Universal Nature or Infinity is archetypal of the principle of Motherhood. For the penetrating vision of the Seers the real objective is the deep meaning inherent in the cosmic creation which was termed as Veda, Rishi or Chhandas principle. Words are mere symbols of ideas like the manifest dependent on the unmanifest substratum. According to the Seer of this Hymn, Spoken Speech is only one-fourth in relation to the inspirational world of ideas which is three-fourths. Thus the Vedas are couched in a terminology which is invested with meaning that is universal, elastic and concretised in the natural objects ever present before us. The divine Brahman has identified himself with creation, called *Vak*, and Man is tackling *Vak* with his mind for the meaning behind it. The ordinary meaning of *Vak* is human Speech but it is the highest manifest faculty in Man and is accepted as the concretised symbol of the mystery of the Mind. The problem of the meaning of the Rig Veda thus lies in the hands of a unique language deriving in the fullest measure from the divine creation itself. The ancient belief in the divinity of the Vedas rationally signifies that the meaning behind words is drawn from the cosmic source. Whereas words belong to the level of Matter (*martya*), the meaning is ever radiating and coming from a transcendent source that is immortal. The two concepts of *Devam Manah*, God as Mind, and *Sahasrakshara Vak*, Speech of Thousand Syllables, are the highest contribution of Rishi Dirghatamas to the world of metaphysics. It is hardly possible to make a bolder or more eloquent statement about the nature of human Mind and human Speech, both flashing as unknown Mysteries.

From Preface to 'A Vision in Long Darkness', Dr. V.S. Agrawala, Vedaranyaka Ashram, Varanasi, 1963, pp.iii–iv.

With this explanation V.S. Agrawala proceeds to unravel the several layers of meaning and significance of the verses of the hymn. His concern is with the identification of the esoteric meaning (*paroksha*). He does so by breaking up each word into its semantic etymologies in order to arrive at the inner core meaning. For example, *Akshara* is derived from *Akashya*, the inexhaustible one. Later in the book Dr. V.S. Agrawala elucidates brilliantly on the relationship of *kshara* and *akshara* and opens up a whole cosmology from the two words.

Of special interest to him is the word *Vak*. Dr. V.S. Agrawala offers multiple explanations, quoting chapter and verse. The symbolism of the cow engages Dr. V.S. Agrawala in much of his writing. Here he offers a wide spectrum of meaning and the many layers of the significance of the 'Cow' as a symbol.

An examination of the words, the verses and the metres, enables Dr. V.S. Agrawala to interpret the integral vision of the hymn.

In the book 'Spark of the Vedic Fire' he had taken particular words; here he takes each verse (RV.164 1–52) and then deftly uncodes the meaning behind the principal symbol.

Dr. V.S. Agrawala's explanation of each verse exemplifies the piercing perspicacity of his own vision and skill. Mantra 2 which centres around the metaphor of the chariot, wheel, the three naves, and the seven horses, is explained with unparalleled lucidity to convincingly argue the relationship of the macro- and micro-dimensions; the one source and the three dimensions of Matter, Life and Mind, the seven horses. Together the incessant dynamic movement of Time (*Kala*) is the essence. It is clear from V.S. Agrawala's commentary that he has been able to uncode the 'symbol' at multiple levels of meaning. Again, it is the extension of this interpretation which leads him to write the important and oft-quoted monograph called the *Cakradhvaja*.

Most revealing is his explanation of Mantra 42 where he explains the significance of hair and locks, Kesh, Keshav, Keshi, etc. One is tempted to give the full text of his explanation, because V.S. Agrawala's ability to make uncanny connections through an analysis of the semantic etymologies is itself an integrated warp and woof of the fabric he reconstructs.

Symbolism occupied him with intensity. In the short monograph on the solar symbolism of the Boar Varaha, he continues with his very special method. This time his textual base is principally the *Matsya Purana*. He examines the various versions in the *Vishnu Purana* and the *Bhagavata* and other texts. After a textual analysis and comparison, he expounds on the symbolic meaning. In V.S. Agrawala's characteristic fashion, he traces the first references to Varaha to the Rig Vedic *Emusha*, *Varaha*, and to legend in the *Atharvaveda* (XII, 1.48). For V.S. Agrawala the legend has a definite cosmological significance:

> 'There are two stages in the conception, firstly that the Goddess Earth was concealed in the depth of the Primeval Ocean, and secondly that She was rescued from there by the 'Divine power of Vishnu in his Boar incarnation'.'
>
> From the preface to the volume 'Solar Symbolism of the Boar', Banaras Hindu University, 1963.

It is in the detailed analysis of the verses in the Puranas—Vayu, Matsya, Bhagavata and other texts, that V.S. Agrawala offers his comments on the symbolism of the legend and the significance of Yajna, *Varaha* and Varaha. As always, V.S. Agrawala begins with 'words' and etymologies (e.g., *vara* and *ahaha*) and appellations used. Each word is analysed in detail to reveal the hidden meaning. A number of questions are asked, and then interconnections are made, before reconstructing the import of the whole. This is not textual criticism. It is the penetration into the ocean of meaning and allusions. Everyone is familiar with the legend of the Boar and his rescuing the Earth. However, it required the keen insight of a V.S. Agrawala to make the connection with the first principle of turmoil as *Vayu* and *Varaha* and secondly of *Varaha* and *Agni*, and finally as Sun. The slim volume is an excellent example of a very distinctive methodology, hard to emulate, because it requires the command of language, words and a critical eye of the visual representation, and the intuitive insights of one immersed in texts ranging from the Vedas to Puranas. Of great importance is the fact that through this analysis and interpretation Dr. Agrawala clearly demolishes the view of some scholars that the Puranas were narratives, half historical, half mythological, without any conceptual continuity with the Vedas. He convincingly makes the connections between concepts and mythology and the visual image.

Indeed, at this point I might permit myself the liberty of being personal. I recall vividly Dr. Agrawala, my Guru's ecstasy as one day he exclaimed to me in sheer joy. 'Oh, Kapila, wonders have happened today. I have just discovered that the Purana-s are not just narratives of mythology, meaningful no doubt, but are in fact restating and re-articulating Vedic cosmology and symbolism in a narrative form; further they are as if coded icons of philosophic principles'. He was then immersed in the *Garuda Purana*, and set forth to explain the symbolism of

Garuda and Garuda as the *Vahana* of Visnu in terms of philosophic schools. Patiently he explained to me the significance of Garuda as *vahana* in terms of Sankhya philosophy. Had he been a modern scholar, he would have begun by asserting a new theoretical position, but Dr. Agrawala was himself: it was the text and the intuitive insights that came to him which were his fulfillment.

It is these insights which illumine his *Critical Studies of the Puranas*, specially the Matsya and Markandeya Purana. Unlike some other scholars, he does not concentrate on the Puranas as socio-historical documents to draw conclusions on state formations and social structure. He is instead engaged in penetrating deep into the symbolism of the countless myths and legends. Naturally, as an archaeologist and art historian he extends his investigation into the visual representation of the myths in sculpture and painting.

However, socio-economic aspects were of deep interest. This is evident from his magnum opus, *India as known to Panini*. Here his analysis focuses on these dimensions. As culling out cultural history from a text, the work remains unsurpassed over these five decades.

This dimension of life continued to interest him, even when he was totally engrossed in the Vedas and the Puranas. In fact Dr. Agrawala's interests were not sequential, but concurrent. As has been remarked by many, such as respected Ram Krishnadasa, and as witnessed by his students, he undertook to pursue several subjects concurrently. If the Vedas were of interest and the Brahmanas, concurrently he worked assiduously on *Jayasi Padmavat*, to produce another magnum opus. Earlier he had displayed his capacity for reconstructing cultural histories from *Harshacharita* and *Kadambari*, *Meghadoot* and others.

But no assessment of Dr. Agrawala's work would be complete, even in a cursory manner such as this, without a mention of Dr. Agrawala as a scholar of numismatics, and above all as an explorer and elucidator of the vast and varied world of the vocabulary of the *Janapada*-s. As mentioned in the very beginning, the influence of his grandmother was abiding. She had opened him to the world of oral literature and oral narratives and terminology. He made that into a rigorous discipline. In so doing he could once again make connections between the high and the popular, the textual and the oral. This was also another implicit new theoretical position.

In that jewel of a book, *Ancient Indian Folk Cults*, he vividly describes *Giri Maha* (Festival of the Mountain), *Nidi Maha* (Festival of the River

Goddess), *Sagar Maha* (Festival of the Ocean) and others. Here through textual references he recreates popular practice. The ecological significance of the festivals is made explicit.

Little need be added in regard to his competence and skill as Curator of the Central Asian Antiquities in the Archaeological Survey and as the selector with an impeccable eye of that Indian Art exhibition held in London in 1948. As is well known, the objects of that exhibition constituted the first core of the present National Museum.

Understandably and almost logically, Vasudev Saran Agrawala became the guru and guide for scholars in different fields. Fortunately we have amongst us many present here who are today acknowledged as specialists in their particular fields. Singly and together let us pay a tribute to this extraordinary scholar of our times. In acknowledging our debt and expressing our deep gratitude, we also have a solemn responsibility. While there are many welcome fresh developments in the study of the Indian literary and artistic traditions, there continues to be a need for re-inforcing a multi-disciplinary and inter-disciplinary approach, which was to the vision and methodology of a Vasudeva Saran Agrawala. Equally important is the need for greater insistence on a rigorous training in methodologies and skills of research. As teacher, Vasudeva Saran Agrawala was a hard and strict task-master, an austere though loving disciplinarian to the core. Can we aspire to measure upto him!

26.

C. Sivaramamurti

Sri C. Sivaramamurti was perhaps the last of the great doyens of Indian art who carried their monumental scholarship lightly and easily. Deeply immersed in textual sources, inheritor of a long cultural tradition, he was archaeologist, art historian, iconographer and musicologist combined. I recall closely guarding the slim volumes of the catalogue of Amaravati's sculptures of the Madras Museum and his innumerable other guides. His descriptions were clear and lucid, line drawings evocative. The Chola Temples Tanjavur—Gangaikonda cholapuram and Darasuram opened a new chapter, as did his book 'South Indian Bronzes' published by the Lalit Kala Akademi. He will long be remembered for his magnum opus "Nataraja in Art, Thought and Literature". Sanskrit poetry and verse were on his lips as was Tamil poetry. Any piece of sculpture would evoke from him a relevant verse; naturally Kalidasa was his favourite and "Sculpture inspired by Kalidasa" was a logical outcome.

I had occasion to meet him first in the house of my Guru, the late Dr. V.S. Agrawala. I was witness to many a stimulating dialogue between these two, and the other two, namely, the late Sri Rai Krishnadasa and Dr. Moti Chandra. Each complemented the other. The austerity of Sri Vasudeva Saran Agrawala, the strict grammarian and later metaphysician, was a foil to the rich enthusiastic exuberance of a C. Sivaramamurti. The connoisseurship of Rai Krishnadasa and the sharp secular urbane viewpoints of Dr. Moti Chandra provided a contrast and supplement. The last three also sat on the art purchase committee meetings of the National Museum handling objects and materials. It was a great learning experience for our generation to watch the watchful eye of them on. It was at one of these meetings, clasping a South Indian Bronze in hand, that C. Sivaramamurti passed away. It is to this devout man of great learning and exemplary humility that I dedicate this lecture.

The theme of the Nataraja has gripped historians, literary critics, sculptors, painters and musicians alike for over a hundred years now.

Historians of Indian art devoted considerable attention to the subject in the early years of the twentieth century. Some were attracted by its symbolic significance, others by the innumerable iconographical forms of the dancing Shiva and yet others by its historical development as a key theme in Indian Art. Aurobindo, Coomaraswamy, Zimmer, Stella Kramrisch, Gopinath Rao, Vasudeva Saran Agrawala, and Alice Boner are amongst the few eminent art historians who have given serious thought to Shiva as Nataraja and each has interpreted the significance of the concept through his or her particular view-point.

C. Sivaramamurti has been attracted to the theme since the days of his early writing; it was but natural that his long and distinguished contribution as an art historian should culminate in his encyclopaedic and monumental work.

C. Sivaramamurti, in characteristic fashion, draws freely upon sources ranging from the Vedas, Puranas, Kavyas and Agamas to sculpture, painting, music and dance; the mass of information is as impressive as it is staggering. He does not confine himself to India materials but extends his study to South-East Asia. Those already acquainted with the ease with which Sivaramamurti deals with diverse source material are not surprised; few living Indian scholars share his ability to draw upon primary source material which lies scattered all over India and abroad.

The narrative of the present work moves speedily through fifteen chapters covering twenty centuries and the large spatial area of India and South-East Asia. The text is supported by 22 coloured plates, 374 monochromes and 20 line-drawings.

The first three chapters include considerations on the symbolism of Nataraja, the Lord of Dance, the purpose of *Natya*, its antiquity and the significance of Shiva's dance. In the next two, the reliefs of Brihadishvara and Chidambaram based on the Fourth Chapter of the *Natyashastra* are examined. These are followed by chapters on the origins of the concept of Nataraja. In these chapters Sivaramamurti traces its origins to Vedic and Hymnal literature and its historical development through epigraphical evidence. The *Shilpa* texts are also examined in another chapter. This is followed by a chronological presentation of evidence relating to the Nataraja image in sculpture and painting. The whole span of Indian art, ranging from the pre-Gupta figures to late medieval painting, is covered. These are followed by a narration of the emergence and popularity of the theme in South-East Asia. The work concludes with a chapter on sites especially associated with Nataraja in India.

This massive array of informative material is matched by an equal empathy for the subject expressed in a style which is enthusiastic, if not effusive. The author's commitment to his theme and his dedication to the concept is unmistakable, almost infectious. Again, those familiar with Sivaramamurti's work expect this characteristic treatment of themes, which lie so close to his heart.

The chapters relating to the appearance and development of the image in sculpture and painting are the richest and most systematic. Painstakingly he presents evidence of nearly nineteen centuries in a chronological order. The two hundred and forty-two supporting illustrations present a visual panorama of the preoccupation of the Indian artist with this theme from the Satavahana and Shunga periods to the nineteenth century paintings of Chamba and Kangra. Sivaramamurti identifies three pre-Gupta examples from stone terracotta and coins as Shiva figures. Of these, the Gudimalam Shiva as Agnirudra (2nd century BC) is well known, but the other two—one a Shunga terracotta (2nd century BC) and the other a copper seal from 1st century BC Taxila—are welcome additions to our knowledge. The stylistic features of the terracotta are quite different from scenes of music and dance found in the Bharhut railings. The vertical treatment of the two lower figures, and the musician identified as a Shiva figure have little in common with their stone counterparts. A detailed comparison of this representation with the Bharhut apsara scene would have been pertinent. The copper seal from Taxila identified as an *alidha* is somewhat less convincing although the trident-like weapon may well be a *trishula* of later iconographical images. Both these important pieces could have been analysed more thoroughly from the point of view of content and form. They throw up many questions which the author chooses to skip over. It is easier to follow the logic of the narrative from the Gupta period onwards; here the earliest example of the Gupta Shiva from Nachna is illustrated for the first time. This is indeed a remarkable sculpture where we have a clear suggestion of the *Kari-hasta* for the first time. The author rightly draws attention to reference in contemporary Gupta literature to the dance of Shiva. It would have been, nevertheless, interesting to learn about the exact lines of development of the iconographical form with the characteristic *Kari-hasta* and *bhujangatrasita* movement. While the *Natyashastra* certainly mentions these in the context of the hundred and eight *karana*-s, it remains an enigma as to why and how the sculptor chose to select these particular movements for depicting Shiva's dance. A correlation of textual, literary and sculptural material might have unravelled these mysteries. As it is, Sivaramamurti confines himself to a listing of all sculptures which can be identified as the image of Shiva dancing and to an identification of the pose in terms of Bharata's *karana*-s and *sthana*-s.

The subject of Vakataka sculpture from Ellora has been examined at great length by Gopinath Rao in his *Elements of Hindu Iconography*; its principles of composition have been commented upon by Alice Boner in her work, *Principles of Composition*. Sivaramamurti describes these sculptures in great detail, drawing our attention to the various constituents of the sculptural relief. His method is the same, as that followed by Gopinath Rao, and he does not identify those purely formal elements, which deal with volume and line and which give these sculptures their unique rhythm and dynamism. The compositional armature of these reliefs is obvious to any discerning observer, and the value of Sivaramamurti's delineation would have been greatly enhanced had he analysed the abstract geometrical form which governs these concrete images. The proportions of Gauri Parvati and of the *gana*-s watching the dance are as important as the *lalita* or *chatura* pose of Shiva. Some comment on the sculptor's awareness of these aspects of artistic technique would have been welcome. Also, these and other examples of the medieval period, some published here for the first time, could have been correlated to the *Shilpa* texts which the author has so ably listed in chapter Eleven. Which an identification of each of these images from all parts of India to Bharata's *karana*-s convinces one of the pervasive use of the Natya terminology and of the evolution of a few stylised poses for Shiva's *tandava*, it does not throw light on the sculptor's autonomous vision, either conceptually or in its methods of concretisation. It would have been interesting to learn about the adherence and departures by the sculptor from the *Shilpa* texts where the subject of *nrittamurti*-s is repeatedly discussed. The variations achieved within the framework of the same movement, along with a distinctive regional flavour of each school, is also a fascinating and puzzling subject. This rich mass of material could also have been analysed from this point of view, and specially on account of the author's unparalleled facility in dealing with material of the Southern, Northern, Western and Eastern schools.

What is true of the sculptural reliefs and images in stones and bronze, is truer of the diverse schools of painting. Here, too, Sivaramamurti presents fabulous material, much of it hitherto unpublished and, therefore, most welcome and valuable, but the narrative, alas, confines itself to a description of the pictorial representation and identification of the pose but does not extend to an examination of the development of regional style. There is a world of difference between the Shiva paintings of Elura and those of Brihadishvara, even if it is similar poses that are being delineated; a greater contrast is seen between the Shiva painting of the Tanjavur of the Nayak period (17th century) and those belonging to the Mysore schools of a slightly different period in the eighth century. What is this difference which communicates a totally different sense of movement through line and colour? This and other questions remain unanswered inspite of the author's comprehensive and thorough descriptions. The visual impression of some of the later paintings is one of a static form as opposed to the dynamic rhythm of seventeenth century painting in spite of its ornate crowdedness and the rotundity of the human figures. We would have welcomed Sivaramamurti's comment on the causes which underlie these differences and changes. The theme of continuity and change in Indian art is manifested unequivocally in these artistic expressions; some light on this was called for.

Two earlier chapters are valuable for these analyses of the sculptural reliefs of Brihadishvara and Chidambaram; an examination of the reliefs of Vishnu dancing in the Sarangapani temple is also illuminating. The late Sri T.N. Ramachandran had analysed the Brihadishvara reliefs in terms of Bharata's *karanas*-s: it is a pity that this work has remained unpublished. Sivaramamurti has done invaluable service by now publishing these and others from the Sarangapani temple. It was only correct to devote an independent chapter to this important topic, which is of great interest to both art historians and students, by now publishing these and others from the Sarangapani temple. Perhaps a comparative study of the reliefs of particular movements in the three sites would have enriched the present study. As in the case of the sculptural and pictorial representation of movement in the general dance scenes, so also here, the sculptors of the three sites of Brihadishvara, Chidambaram and Sarangapani interpret the same verse of Bharata, often very differently. Also, the *karana* of Bharata is not a static pose, it is instead a cadence of movement and the sculptor can arrest only a single moment in a whole sequence of the earlier notion of scholars that the *karana* is a static pose. The few instances where a comparative analysis is attempted are welcome. The Sarangapani temple quite obviously represents a different flowering, and many movements of the sculptural reliefs of this temple are not seen either in Brihadishvara or the Chidambaram temple; while Sivaramamurti comments on a few variations, he restricts himself to an identification of the pose in terms of Bharata's *karana*-s. The material in those chapters (Four and Five), nevertheless, provides sufficient data for a detailed analytical study of this important subject of the depiction of dance movement in sculpture, and it is hoped that other scholars will further develop the subject with this material and that provided by Dr. V. Raghavan in his introduction to *Nrittaratnavali*.

In the chapters dealing with literary, epigraphical and iconographical literature, Sivaramamurti proceeds swiftly from association to association, reference to reference, not necessarily in any chronological order. These chapters are valuable for the fund of information they contain and also as expressions of the author's empathy for his subject. Sivaramamurti traces the origins of the concept of Shiva dancing to *Rg Vedic* descriptions of Indra's dancing. He believes that this was the natural result of the "continuous process of fusion of ideas concerning both at different stages." The author establishes a connection between Indra, Rudra, Pashupati and Shiva through the identical epithets which are used for these in *Rg Vedic*, *Yejurvedic* and classical Sanskrit literature. While this is plausible, and other scholars have also commented upon this, it would have been interesting to underline the specific contours of this development, transformation and over-layering. The concept of Shiva dancing emerges as a fully developed theme in classical Sanskrit literature, but the transitional stages between descriptions in Vedic literature, and nascent ideas in Upanishadic thought and the ritual of the Brahmanas remain unidentified. Bharata could not have given such predominant importance to the concept had it not been accepted in the literature and ritual of the period immediately preceding the writing of the *Natyashastra*. This closed book of the transference of the abstract concept into the concretisation of the image through the medium of the plastic and the performing arts has still to be opened. It is obvious that a correspondence between the idea and the image is established at all levels of thought in the Indian world-view, but the identification of the system through which this was accomplished and later sustained has not yet been touched upon by any art historian or philosopher. The dance of Shiva is one amongst many themes which could be taken as a touchstone to reconstruct the system which is implicit, but for which no texts have hitherto been discovered. Thorough and concrete manifestation in different media alone can attempt this. Perhaps Sivaramamurti himself will follow up this study by another in which this important aspect of

Indian art will be given serious attention. In short, what were the elements in early speculative thought and Brahmanical ritual which gave rise to a system of establishing correspondences and over layering?

The chapters dealing with *Natya*, its origin and antiquity, are equally informative. Sivaramamurti again moves freely between the text of the *Natya-shastra* and much later texts like the *Nrittaratnavali* (of Jaya Senapati) to analyse the different constituents of the Art. Although this is justified, we would have expected a closer examination of the vital changes which were taking place in different regions during a period of one thousand years or more within the key principles of *nritta*, *nritya* and *natya*. The inclusion of a whole class of movement called *deshi* also throws significant light on the sculptural depiction of the same movement in medieval times. The *nrittamurti*-s of Shiva could not have remained unaffected by the concept of the *deshi*.

Coomaraswamy devoted considerable attention to the symbolism of Shiva's dance by drawing upon Tamil sources. Sivaramamurti adds to these sources and quotes many more, including the important texts like *Tila-Kamanjari* and *Saduktikarnamrita*. All these sources tell us of the great significance attached to the dance of Shiva and its valuable supporting evidence. Nevertheless, we would have welcomed a more rounded and fuller interpretation of the dance from Sivaramamurti, as he is one who has reflected upon this theme for many years.

It will perhaps be obvious from the above that Sivaramamurti's task was none too easy and the putting together of material itself is a contribution for which we are beholden to him. The fact that further studies are still called for only underpins the gigantic nature of the theme, its massive content, pervasive sway and its endless complexities of form and technique. Some of these Sivaramamurti has touched upon and has given us food for thought; others we hope he and those who follow him will undertake. His work will remain a landmark in the history of the treatment of the Nataraja theme for decades to come, but it must not be considered as the last word beyond which nothing can be said. He has opened up vistas for further exploration.

27.

Niharranjan Ray*

Professor Debiprasad Chattopadhyaya asked Professor Niharranjan Ray in an interview in Calcutta in May 1974:

> Professor Ray, to your readers and to the large number of those who had occasions to hold discussions with you, you give the decided impression of taking an absorbing interest in a very wide range of intellectual disciplines, both academic and professional. Indeed, one knows that your interests are almost encyclopaedic in character. Nevertheless one feels that there is a unifying principle behind this apparent diversity of interest. (Debiprasad, Chattopadhyaya, ed.; *History and Society*, 'Essays in Honour of Professor Niharranjan Ray', K.P. Bagchi & Co., Calcutta, 1976)

In reply, Professor Ray said with his characteristic humility:

> I must try, even at the outset, to disabuse your mind of any idea of my scholastic and intellectual mastery of any of the fields you have just mentioned; indeed I have no such mastery. But you are perhaps right that I take a great deal of interest in a fairly good number of intellectual and professional disciplines.

Simply and lucidly expressed, the question and answer sum up the personality and work of Professor Ray, the liberal humanist, the man and writer, at home both in Western and Eastern thought, sensitively responsive to the literary, performing and plastic arts, a keen observer of life in all its facets and an active participant in political life. A breadth of vision, catholicity of outlook, a sophisticated sensitivity, combined with an uncanny capacity to draw people of different outlooks, social strata and disciplines together, with an infectious zest for life characterized the man—author, politician, academician, administrator, guide and mentor.

Son of a dedicated teacher, the late Mahendrachandra Ray, Professor Ray was brought up in an ardent nationalist home and an animated

* *The Indian Historical Review* paid homage to the memory of Professor Niharranjan Ray, Chairman of the ICHR (from 10 April 1981 to 30 August 1981), and Mr. Amalananda Ghosh, Director of the ICHR project "Encyclopaedia of Indian Archaeology", and published tributes to these two eminent scholars. Reprinted from *The Indian Historical Review*.

Brahmo Samaj environment. Mymensingh (now in Bangladesh) along with Chittagong were active centres of the Swadeshi Movement. The first seeds of a social and political awareness must have been ingrained in the young Niharranjan in this milieu of the large joint family. Understandably, Professor Ray participated in the first Non-Cooperation Movement as a student and, like other contemporaries, was externed from college. He completed his chequered educational career as a student of history and began working as an editor of a Bengali weekly.

The late twenties was a period of great ferment and creative activity in Calcutta. The place hummed with the poetry of Rabindranath Tagore and was dominated by the towering personalities of Jadunath Sarkar, Subhas Bose, Sarat Chandra and a host of others. Professor Ray was drawn to them all and was affectionately encouraged by Professor D.R. Bhandarkar, Professor Benimadhab Barua, Professor Suniti Kumar Chatterjee, Professor Hemchandra Raychaudhuri, Dr. Stella Kramrisch, Dr. Kalidas Nag and Professor Sarvepalli Radhakrishnan. Professor Ray has repeatedly acknowledged his indebtedness to these teachers, particularly Professor Raychaudhuri, Professor Barua and Dr. Kramrisch. About the last he said:

> I feel proud to record that it was she who opened my eyes to the magic and mystery of Indian Art and inculcated in me the love and regard for the subject which I retain to this day. My perceptions were sharpened by her and whatever insights I have been able to develop in regard to this field of knowledge have been because of the initial training she imparted to me.

This statement epitomizes Professor Ray's approach with regard to his teachers because, although he graciously acknowledged his debt, he felt absolutely free to depart from their approaches and methods of analysis. This was true also in respect of Coomaraswamy and Zimmer whom Professor Ray admired, but whose approaches he differed fairly radically.

Indeed what is true of Professor Ray's attitude towards these art historians is also true of his feelings towards all others from the disciplines of history, sociology, philosophy, language, aesthetics and literature. He does not follow Professor Hemchandra Raychaudhuri in his treatment of history, Professor Sarvepallli Radhakrishnan in philosophy, Professor Suniti Kumar Chatterjee in respect of language and linguistics, and yet each of them stimulated his intellectual enquiries and sharpened his sensibilities. This ability to understand and imbibe the ideas of others and yet to be dispassionately critical and questioning characterized his writings from the first dissertation on 'The Political History of Ancient India from c. AD 600–900' to the last. It was while working on this dissertation, which won him the Mrinalini Gold Medal in 1926 at Calcutta University, that he came to feel that "there was nothing in this kind of dynastic and political history in which I could find creative intellectual delight or satisfaction." Such an insight would be taken for granted today, but seen against the background of the historical writing in 1926, its value is clear and unambiguous. A similar self-awareness was evident after the first studies on Burma, entitled Architecture in Burma, which earned him the Premchand Roychand Studentship of the University of Calcutta in 1927. This time, Professor Ray realized that "no study of art and architecture could be adequate without a study of the socio-religious background of the art."

Thus, whether it was art or architecture, history or politics, Professor Ray's concern was a multi-dimensional enquiry into the concepts, the socio-religious and socio-economic background and the concrete manifestation, be it creative literature, political movements or artistic works of sculpture or painting. For some critics, the *prima facie* range and diversity of his concerns is an enigma, a puzzling multiplicity of themes and disciplines, but seen against the background of his chief concern—to place the phenomenon, the text and the artistic creation against its socio-religious and socio-economic background—all these concerns ranging from political and religious movements to colonial rule, regional history, literature and the arts fall into place and provide the central axis around which enquiries were conducted.

With characteristic candour Professor Ray introduces the subject of Maurya and Sunga art and asserts:

> I am not bringing to light any fresh find, nor am I trying to say anything strikingly original as to the character or form of the two periods under review. My aim is to read this art in the larger context of life and hence as a related phenomenon, i.e., as one of the aspects of our cultural life in that distant past. Whilst recognising the identity and integrity of this art existing independently from other sociological phenomena, my aim is to correlate it with the latter ..... Frankly my method is sociological *(Maurya and Sunga Art*, University of Calcutta, 1945).

He continues:

> I have, therefore, taken into consideration the current tastes and preferences, individual and collective, the social background, the political circumstances, the trend of thought, ethnic components, root forms, traditions of influences, history

of technique, etc., to elucidate the coming into being of what we call the Maurya and Sunga art.

This statement was made in the forties and not in the eighties when any serious student of art begins with the premise that for a proper and total understanding of artistic manifestations, all these factors must be taken into account. Indeed, Professor Ray was one of the first among art historians to draw attention to this method called today by any of its various appellations of the socio-economic approach, the holistic approach or the centre and the periphery paradigm or the text or context model. What was clearly stated and elaborated upon in this short work in relation to Maurya and Sunga art was developed in other studies, particularly in *Sanskrit Buddhism in Burma* (H.J. Paria, Amsterdam, 1936) and *An Introduction to the Study of Theravada Buddhism in Burma* (University of Calcutta, 1946). In both he attempted to unfold the processes of interaction between Indo-Burmese historical and cultural relations in the aspects of autonomy and diffusion. The approach of identifying the factors which determined the creation of artistic forms and styles, particularly socio-cultural, was further refined in a much later work entitled *Mughal Court Painting: A Social and Formal Analysis* (Indian Museum, Calcutta, 1975). In *Maurya and Sunga Art* Professor Ray attempted to show the influence of Achaemenian art and Maurya Monarchy on the character of Maurya art. In *Mughal Court Painting*, he describes at length the nostalgia for the homeland in the beginning which developed into a broad cosmopolitan attitude which the Mughals shared, even if indirectly, with their counterparts in the West when the Renaissance was as its height. Boldly, Professor Ray suggests that in Mughal art, the emphasis shifts from the collective to the individual, from Man in Nature to Man and Nature, and succinctly concludes:

> A look at any Moghul court painting would at once convince anybody that in theme of the painting, even if it be the portrait of a bird or of an animal, it is not the bird or animal so much as a man's particular interest in it that has brought it into being. In portraiture the pivotal quality of man is evident, and in the narrative-descriptive paintings, man is indeed practically the only theme, man one upon and by the side of another, centering round and flanking another, teeming dozens of them; everything else subserves him.

These observations, much debated today, could have been made only by one who was deeply immersed in the development of Western thought and history and who could correlate cognate developments in different cultural milieus. Imperceptibly, Professor Ray moves from a purely narrative descriptive study to an identification of world views and fundamentals of speculative thought.

It puzzled some readers that Professor Ray should move from sociological concerns to speculative thought, especially as seen in the two works, *Idea and Image in Indian Art* (Munshiram Manoharlal, New Delhi, 1973) and *An Approach to Indian Art* (Panjab University, Chandigarh, 1974). When asked whether there was a deviation from his own stated approach, Professor Ray's answer was convincingly clear and simple:

> No, l do not think l departed or deviated from my general sociological approach to the understanding of the problem I had before me. Rather I tried to find out if I could apply, meaningfully and effectively, the same approach and method of analysis but at a higher and subtler plane of study and investigation..... The problem before me was to study the dialectical interrelationship between an abstract idea or concept and its concretized manifestation in a meaningful aesthetic form. As case studies I chose three such abstract concepts from our traditional repertoire and tried to find out how and to what extent these concepts were sought to be given concrete form in terms of sculpture, and conversely, how and to what extent the aesthetic forms themselves conditioned the growth and connotation of the abstract concepts. The method I adopted was that of social analysis, namely, I tried to study the story of the origin and evolution of the concepts along the arrow line of time, taking care to find how social changes had affected them. Simultaneously and side by side I studied the story of the evolution of the concrete aesthetic manifestations in terms of images, in other words, of the formal changes that were taking place, again because of changes in the socio-religious or socio-economic situations as much as in the tools and techniques of stone-cutting and carving. I also took into consideration the question of material, that is, of the quality and character of the stone (or bronze) that was used, in regard to the concept on the one hand and the concrete image on the other.

Finally, this enquiry into speculative thought, historical socio-religious and socio-cultural situations, themes, content, form and technique came together in the series of essays in *An Approach Io Indian Art*. Here, Professor Ray moves freely in time and space, examines in depth Upanisādic thought, brahmanical literature, the indigenous Lokayata traditions and the socio-cultural background to present a thesis. The approach differs from Coomaraswamy, Zimmer and Stella Kramrisch in a highly refined manner. He does not negate the role of metaphysics and mysticism, but does not make it the central pivot of his enquiry. The book opens up several avenues of exploration and it remains for contemporary art historians to question or follow the many interesting and fresh approaches suggested. Quite clearly, Professor Ray's approach moves from pure chronological studies, identification of dates and iconography to an analysis of form and content within a context.

The art historian was only one facet of Professor Ray's personality and work. Simultaneously, he was deeply concerned with larger cultural history, especially that of Bengal, and wrote *Bangalir Itihasa: Adiparva* (Book Emporium, Calcutta, 1949). Although the second volume could not be completed, this work has to be seen along with Professor Ray's biography of Tagore entitled *An Artist in Life: A Commentary on the Life and Works of Rabindranath Tagore* (University of Kerala, Trivandrum, 1967), which won him the Sahitya Akademi award. The two together, one in Bengali and the other in English, are perhaps the most comprehensive critical studies of the creativity of Bengal in the medieval and modern periods. Professor Ray's command of Bengali prose in *Bangalir Itihasa: Adiparva* will remain a landmark and it is unfortunate that he could not complete the second volume on which, as far as one knows, he had done considerable work. The two studies are clear evidence of Professor Ray, the historian literary critic and biographer.

The politico-social historian in Professor Ray manifested itself in the two thought-provoking studies, one entitled *Nationalism in India: An Historical Analysis of its Stresses and Strains (*Aligarh Muslim University, 1973) and the other *The Sikh Gurus and Sikh Society: A Study in Social Analysis* (Punjabi University, Patiala, 1970). Professor Ray's enquiry into the nature of the colonial rule and the rise of nationalism shows a singularly dispassionate and catholic view. He brings to this study a cool discriminating viewpoint which stays clear off narrow affiliations and ideological biases. Here, as elsewhere, the early liberal humanist in him is dominant and it is evident that Professor Ray was at no point and in no sphere willing to fall into a groove of thoughts, concepts and ideologies. He explored his subject from many angles and many viewpoints.

To these major writings, one could add the hundreds of others which appeared in journals of archaeology, history, politics, literary criticism and sociology but the few cited above are a testimony to his breadth of interest and vision.

Early in life, Professor Ray had received a degree in Library Science and this interest was sustained throughout his life—many people in the field of Library Science remember him as a stimulating colleague and an exacting taskmaster. One of the first tasks he undertook as the founder-

Director of the Indian Institute of Advanced Study, Simla, was to establish an important library of source material.

As editor, teacher, professor and politician, Professor Ray participated in many activities on diverse forums including the Rajya Sabha. However, as the founder-Director of the Indian Institute of Advanced Study, he translated these multi-faceted insights into a concrete institution. The multi and inter-disciplinary approach was fundamental. His personality, warm and outgoing, was the human tool and he could gather together here intellectuals, artists, politicians and scientists, men and women of different generations who could deliberate on issues. The seminars, discussions, the initial and concluding remarks of the Director, the tenacity of ensuring the publication of reports were all result of Professor Ray's vision and his administrative and organizational capacities. All those who participated in the programmes of this Institute will testify to its stimulating environment and if the institution later came under a cloud, the reasons lie elsewhere and not in the lack of dynamism of its founder-Director.

Professor Ray, despite his years, was never dated: an unusual capacity to communicate with the young and modern always kept him abreast of the latest developments. He could participate with vigour and enthusiasm on any aspect of modern art, theatre or the performing arts, respond to new creations and be alive to all that was and would be. He never wore the mantle of a "guru"—had sufficient distaste for it—and could plunge into contemporary problems and controversies—social, political, artistic, literary—with unusual felicity. During the last ten years of his life, he was again active in Bengal, was busy writing, discussing, lecturing and, above all, had plans and dreams for the future. He lived fully, tasted life, was the participant and observer who carried in his personality India's cultural discovery of itself. His passing away is the end of an era, but further explorations of insights embodied in his works will be a more meaningful continuity of his life and work intellectually and creatively. Professor Ray had often spoken of the two streams of '*sastracara*' and '*lokacara*' in Indian culture and the need to correlate them. Perhaps the new generation will realize this goal more fully.

28.

Tribute to Dr. Daya Krishna

Where do I begin to talk about Daya, Dayabhai, Dr. Daya Krishna? I still cannot believe that he is not physically present with us, because beyond his physical presence, there is still the presence of his aura, of the presence of his scintillating mind, the presence of his modest human personality, as informal in his pyjamas, as free flowing in thought. He represented a certain attitude to life, particularly towards learning, today called the intellectual cognitive enterprise.

After my matriculation early—a little too early for people to believe—I was already in college, not quite 14. The college had seven or eight girls and a thousand boys. The girls were escorted to class by teachers from the chicked ladies room. We learnt much in class, from botany to history and literature. But we learnt as much from the naughty boys whistling in the gate and from other good boys who were protecting you. Justice was instant. Despite the adolescent dramas, this was all exciting and challenging. Also, amongst the teachers were some who were not only protecting you but those who became your life-long friends.

This is not to recount personal history in Hindu College; instead it is an attempt to situate and contextualise the presence of Daya in that Hindu College of Kashmere Gate 1942 and thereafter for six years. While we took part in the processions of the 9th August, and escaped imprisonment because we were still under-age, the atmosphere was charged with heady mix of British education and patriotism. While courses taught British history as also ancient and medieval history, there was an equal calling for exploration beyond courses. Amongst the faculty there were some who welcomed debate and encouraged what would be called 'out of course' reading. One amongst them was Dr. S.K. Saksena, who was a teacher of Daya—today I would say maker of Daya in many ways. It was he who said to some of us, particularly me: 'you are very interested in talking and doing *gup-sup*. Go and talk to them, that group of boys more senior to you. You will enjoy the *gup-sup*'. And so it was that hours after classes we sat on those wooden benches listening with rapt attention to Daya and Vivek Dutt and Ram Swarup. So, despite the fact that the Principal

Mr. N.V. Thadani was not very encouraging about all this freedom of sitting and talking to boys, here was this group of seniors, who were the 'good boys', seniors who were the talking boys. There were also those active in the Parliament of the Hindu College, such as Giri Lal Jain, who later became the editor of the *Times of India*. There were others who were active in debating and in social causes, such as Lakshmi Jain and Som Benegal.

This group of seniors was different, who talked about philosophy, who talked just about everything that was happening, who referred to the latest writing in any field. They taught us through this *gup-sup*—and what would be called in Bengali 'adda'—to interrogate. To interrogate what we were learning, be it western philosophy or history—interrogate every proposition. This was training in sharpening the intellect. There were heated debates, differences of points of view, and all this in a most affectionate atmosphere. We laughed with each other and called it the *gulli-danda*—the game that we played—*gulli-danda* of thought!

For me this is the abiding Daya, him sitting there, almost lording over these discussions and heated debates between him and Vivek Dutt and Ram Swarup and Sita Ram Goel. We heard these with rapt attention, a trifle intimidated at the extent of their reading and familiarity with authors and names—Socrates to Shankaracharya—but we were engaged. They in turn had been encouraged and nurtured by two philosophy teachers totally different from each other, viz., Dr. S.K. Saksena and Dr. Indrasain who later left for Pondicherry to be with Sri Aurobindo.

I believe that the inherent genius of Daya was nurtured by these two, not so much for the content but more the attitude to the entire intellectual enterprise of philosophy. The encouragement received from Dr. S.K. Saksena played a very big part. But for his incisive and persuasive techniques, Daya may have continued his informal dialogues.

This is the Daya that I remember, the Daya with whom you could argue just about anything, argue with passion, argue with heat and as much love and affection. He just needed any proposition which he could break up and then argue about it. This was the Daya of the 40's and this is also the Daya of maturity and ripening that I saw from near and far five decades later. He could question just about anything, whether it is of western philosophy or thought or Indian philosophy or thought or pandits or different texts, be it the *Nātyaśāstra* or *Rg Veda*.

In this argumentation there was no question of first accepting a hypothesis, then marshalling evidence selectively. Instead, it was an exercise of examining and analyzing a phenomenon, thought or a text without bias. He was a free mind, who was exploring, interrogating, and appropriately he has been called a Socrates. I also recall the many wonderful and meaningful meetings with him in Hawaii and when he came to Berkeley—we happened to be in Berkeley at the same time. Daya, matured, ripened, was both the teacher, philosopher and the original thinker without subscribing to any 'isms' or any ideological positions rigid or inflexible.

Thus Daya holds a very unique position in the tradition of thinking not confined to a single discipline. One of the explicit results of this manner of deliberation is a book which he edited entitled *India's Intellectual Traditions*, with his remarkable Introduction. Only two sentences need to be quoted here:

> 'Concepts, however, are not just tools for the understanding of what exists, as is usually thought by many people. Rather, they are modes of organizing what we experience in a particular manner and give it a certain meaning and significance, thereby making it intelligible in a distinctively human sense. Beyond this, they also constitute reality in a certain sense, particularly at the level where the reality they ostensibly seek to articulate or understand is itself the creation of human beings. And, even beyond the *constitutive* function of concepts in certain domains, there is the other function of determining our attitudes towards what we perceive and guide our actions with respect to it.'

This extraordinary ability of interrogation, of what today in modern discourse could be called deconstruction or post-modernism, was uniquely his, not to be framed within the confines of these 'isms'.

In this brief remembrance as tribute to Daya, who has played a very important part in my life in learning to explore, in learning to debate, in learning to look at textual material with a free and open mind, I want to draw attention to what he has said in the Introduction to the volume *Developments in Indian Philosophy from Eighteenth Century Onwards: Classical and Western.* Here, with the sharpness of a knife, he begins to interrogate the entire cognitive enterprise of history. I think that in this introduction he makes some very fundamental statements which we need to recall because they have a bearing on the nature of the debate, specially in the domain of history or more specifically the larger corpus of what we call the intellectual traditions of India. Let me quote just a few paragraphs which are of relevance to us because it is with this talisman, so to say, that Daya looks into what had happened in what we call the thinking in philosophy during the eighteenth century.

'History, as a cognitive enterprise, seems to be amongst the strangest of endeavours undertaken by man for it claims to know the past, that is, something which does not presently exist. But, how can that which is 'not', be understood? For to understand that, it would be to endow it with some sort of 'being'. The anomaly and paradox inherent in this attempt to know and understand the past has generally been ignored, as it raises questions about the very foundations of the enterprise in which historians are engaged. For the 'past' that one tries to know was at one time existent and hence cannot be regarded as 'a pure nothing'. If it were so, it would not have left any evidence of itself. 'Non-being' does not produce effects or leave any evidence from which it can be constructed as the 'cause' of that which is in the present and on the basis of which we try to understand what was. Thus, the cognitive justification for the enterprise named history is said to lie in the relation between the present and the past and the linkages that can be established between the two.

'But even it if this is accepted, the question remains of how one who claims to be a historian 'validates' this linkage between the present and the past, as the past, that is no more and can never be there, in principle shall never be 'present' to verify the linkage that is postulated. Normally, the hypotheses that one forms to explain or understand what is in the present are supposed to lead to further consequences which can be observed or met with the future, which would be the 'present' at that time, and thus establish, to some extent at least, the plausible truths of the hypotheses that were formed. This is, to a large extent, the established method in most of the cognitive enterprises of man. But as far as history is concerned, the situation seems to be just the reverse. Here the evidence which is supposed to be in the present, validates or corroborates or establishes the truth of the hypothesis which is postulated about the past without any further attempt at finding whether the hypothesis so postulated is itself valid or not. In fact, the terms 'hypothesis', 'postulation', 'validation', 'corroboration' are seldom used in the cognitive enterprise known as 'history'. Rather, the whole thing about the past is presented as if it were 'really' so, and that the historian has somehow got access to it and 'knows' it as if he himself had been a star witness to the events he is writing about and that his veracity is itself the guarantee of the truth of what he is writing about.

'.....A 'real' encounter with the texts, is thus, not just a reconstruction of past thought but rather stepping into a living stream where the thought currents of the past, both visible and invisible, carry one into the future as they gently 'force' one to move in directions one had not dreamt of before. The encounter with 'history' is, thus, not a movement into the past as has generally been thought but rather a movement into the future because one has stepped into the living currents that flow from the past and have sufficient vitality and force in the present to carry one onwards into the future. At least, this is what we have 'experienced' and the sensitive reader will find on every page the marks of this living encounter, leaving an exciting challenge to carry on the dimly-seen possibility and develop it into directions which are only faintly indicated there.

'...How professional historians will respond to this effort is difficult to say. But new departures are generally not welcome and intellectuals, as a class, happen to be as 'conservative' as anyone else. Perhaps I was 'saved' from the usual traditions of history writing as I was never trained as a historian and, even in the field of philosophy, I have been an 'outsider' as I have not belonged to any 'school', whether modern or traditional. I have been, if anything, a 'thinker' at large for whom the activity of 'thinking' has always been more important than the products of that activity, and hence have always questioned the obvious, so easily accepted by most. My encounter with 'history', or rather, the practice of historical writing, fortunately or unfortunately, is of the same character evident in the other subjects/ topics on which I have written'.

Why does Daya, who was primarily a philosopher, commence his introduction with a piercing insight into History? He convinces his readers that any enterprise, any cognitive enterprise, or any investigation into the past, becomes an essential ingredient of the discipline of history. And it is here that his remarks have special value. As we know, the discipline of history has not been considered the Humanities and by volition has been called a part Social Science. There are more recent debates on the discipline. Daya's remarks acquire a contemporary significance. What is cognitive enterprise of reviewing the past?—is the simple and complex question he asks.

In this context, it is then well to remember that while Daya looked at or interrogated the cognitive enterprise of history, his dear friend and contemporary, and with whom he had such an enduring relationship—they were in dialogue over the last few decades—D.P. Chattopadhyaya—also examines the discipline of history and takes us through the historiography of looking at history as art or history as science. In his very short but meaningful monograph entitled 'The Ways of Understanding the Human Past', D.P. Chattopadhyaya gently raises the question of whether history should be looked at as art or as science and probes into whether myth, epic and the chronological texts provide the basis for reconsideration of the past. He takes the reader through the historiography of looking at history as either art or science. Thus, he says that he will endeavour to show that 'the recognized sources of history being what they are history is bound to be primarily in the nature of art, marked by imagination and construction, disappointment and hope, irony and contingency'. Alongside he traces the historiography of viewing history as science by examining the evolution of the classificatory systems of disciplines in the West, e.g., *trivium* (Grammar, Logic and Rhetoric) and *quadrivium* (Arithmetic, Music, Geometry and Astronomy), on the one hand, and *Vidva*, on the other. According to him, critical or scientific research is causal history. 'Causal account of historical events is said to be scientific account'.

To return to Dr. Daya Krishna: in the volume which speaks of the developments or contributions of philosophers in the 18th century, Dr. Daya Krishna draws attention to the nature of the scholarship, the contributions of the 18th century—19th century scholars. During the course of his investigation he hits upon the fact that the nature of discourse and the methodology of discourse in this tradition was very different from what we would call the western tradition. And thus in juxtaposing those who were known as the traditionalists and those philosophers who have come from the western stream or route in the English language, Daya played a very important role in drawing attention to very distinct epistemology or, more accurately speaking, the nature of commentaries and argumentation. As we know, Daya himself travelled through the entire journey of western philosophy to return to Indian sources and Indian philosophy. He came to acknowledge the nature of argumentation within this tradition and that is why his book 'Indian Philosophy—A Counter Perspective' has been dedicated to the memory of the late Pt. Badrinath Shukla—'the outstanding representative of the Ancient Philosophical Tradition who made us all realize how rich and alive it still is in this country'. It was from Badrinath Shukla that he realized that the nature of originality in this tradition was a very different understanding nature of originality. Here it was not a matter of constructing something absolutely new in a unilinear fashion. Daya appropriately observes that we have to re-look at what is known as cognitive enterprise in the Indian tradition. I quote from his Preface to the book:

> 'The context of contemporary intellectual life in India, even in the field of philosophy, has no relationship with India's intellectual traditions of the past, but rather with the way these disciplines have developed in the west and the way they are developing there at present.'

I think that for us today Daya's role of a bridge-maker between two traditions, between two domains, between different ways of looking at thought itself—and he is the master player in the exercise of thought—is unique and unparalleled.

As in the days of old Hindu College, so in the days of India International Centre in the last few years, on every visit to Delhi there would be this call: 'Kapila, I am here, coming over. Shall we talk?' So we talked of countless things, of all kinds, we talked about the Nātyaśāstra. He and I held very differing views on the subject. He wrote a provocative article, which was published in the journal of the Indian Council of Philosophic Research—*The Rasa, the bane of Indian Aesthetics*. He sent it to me with a long letter saying that, look, now if this does not provoke you to send a rejoinder, I know that you have not been reading your Nātyaśāstra! I wrote back and I rang him up and I told him that I was not rising to the bait. Nevertheless, we spoke, we wrote, we argued and I told him that Bharata is not the last word but then the question to be asked is why for 2000 years did the people keep talking about him and people still keep taking about Plato and Aristotle, and not to speak about Socrates himself. There was the perennial and ephemeral in everything, the *rasas* and *bhāvas* included. Our dialogue would have continued.

It was 'fun', fun most invigorating. Talking to Daya it was obviously more than fun because it was recharging of the intellectual batteries, every moment of it. Every moment of it was exciting because Daya was literally the dancer of thought. The last conversation that I had with him was just on this. 'Kapila, we are today going to talk about dance as thought.' And so sitting in my little office in India International Centre we talked for nearly two hours, on whether one could really categorize the nature of movement, the nature of kinetics as the cause and effect of the workings of the mind. And from mind we went into the brain, from brain we went into the sensory and motor senses, and then to deconstruct the concept of *indriyas* on which I had written, and much else. The dialogue could continue.

This was Dayabhai. It was also Dayabhai who had the largess and the capacity to change, to re-question himself on something that he had said. It is to this Daya, the dancer of thought, that I pay my tribute. Daya floated lightly on the sea of thought with discernment and freedom, watching the constant changes of the tides and waves. Himself an iconoclast of sorts, his spirit would not allow itself to be made into an icon.

29.

Philosophy as Samvad and Svaraj

Shail Mayaram succeeded in persuading me to write a Preface to this impressive volume, *Philosophy as Samvad and Svaraj: Dialogical Meditations on Daya Krishna and Ramchandra Gandhi*. I told her that I was no philosopher nor was I a frequent participant in the seminars held in Jaipur and understandably not present in any one-to-one dialogues between them. It reminded me of my long association with both of them, particularly Dayabhai. Yes, I did know both of them at a purely personal level and was aware that they dialogued with each other openly and freely with depth and incisive argumentation. It is difficult, very difficult indeed, to write, comment or evaluate the contribution of those you have known at a personal level, more so, when they have risen to the status of gurus and teachers of another generation.

Shail Mayaram's own proximity to Dayabhai and her communication with Ramu in the *Satsangas* he held must have been an advantage though not without some intrinsic or certainly tacit challenges. Reading through her introduction, so beautifully and sensitively textured, it occurred to me that I would restrict myself to making some observations in regard to a few issues of great importance and value raised in their dialogue.

As I perused the introduction and some articles and the imagined dialogue between Daya Krishna and Ramchandra Gandhi that Shail Mayaram has constructed with such finesse and sophistication, my thoughts went back to many, many decades. These are the memories of Hindu College around 1942. It was Prof. S.K. Saxena who first identified the genius of Daya, and he was sure that irrespective of his making any grade in the examination, he would certainly travel a long way and ascend many peaks in the realm of philosophy/cognition. And the other teacher, Dr. Indrasen, who later relinquished teaching to join Sri Aurobindo Ashram in Pondicherry, instilled in Daya the desire for exploring uncharted paths. The presence of these two intellectuals in the very absence of explicit statement about them, for me, was not just a matter of nostalgia but instead a renewed awareness on the method of the transmission of knowledge and inculcating attitudes of exploring the realm through innovative methods.

Prof. Saxena was not only an unconventional teacher but was also very caring of those he nurtured. Daya was very special for him. As far as I know he succeeded in taking Daya as a Fellow at the East-West Centre in Hawaii. The seeds of 'interrogating' any proposition, to my mind, were laid by Prof Saxena. Daya travelled a long way with Prof Saxena but also beyond his mentor in this intellectual journey of investigating and interrogating with ease. Daya was not alone because he had three other lifetime friends. I refer to Vivek Dutt, Sita Ram Goel and Ram Swarup. Gosh! How heatedly they could debate over any issue sitting on those wooden benches in Hindu College in Kashmere Gate. Prof Saxena always encouraged the very few girl students, just about a score to a thousand boys, to participate in these discussions. Of course, I heard Daya and Vivek converse, argue and differ in college and yet stay close. This volume brought back very many memories of these dialogues.

As far as I am concerned, my communication with Dayabhai continued intermittently—at times frequently and at times after long gaps. Invariably, I was a silent listener to the dialogue between Daya and other philosophers, particularly Prof. D.P. Chattopadhyay, Balasubramanian and D. Prahlada Char, never having the courage to intervene.

During the last decades of his life, on his visits to Delhi he would stay at the India International Centre. Whenever he found time or had the inclination, he would walk up to my office, enter with a smile and then pop up the question as to what subject we both would have a conversation on. I teased him, "Dayabhai, you should be with the Buddhist monks where debating is done with wooden plank and physical movements." He would respond with a laugh and say, "You mean that I do 'fencing'." I said, "Well, Dayabhai, you do 'fencing', for you know the art of 'fencing'. Attack and defence is the sophisticated art of training the physical movements in philosophic arguments. You are a master in this art of 'fencing' in the realm of thought and intellect (*buddhi*)."

I had heard Daya speak at the seminar on the *Natyasastra* and also read his article, *The Search for a Conceptual Structure of the Natyasastra*, in the volume, *India's Intellectual Tradition*. I told him that while I appreciated the views of the participants, especially that of K.J. Shah and V.Y. Kantak, and particularly his introduction, I had some questions as a humble reader for decades of *Natyasastra*. We had a very engaging discussion on whether a *Rasa* theory propounded by Bharata in the *Natyasastra* should be held responsible for all the ills of the trajectory of Indian aesthetics, whether at the level of theory or practice? I said to Dayabhai, "Don't you think that you should then also question what is it within the Indian tradition which allows for dialogue, divergences and even counter questions without invading the very earth of fundamentals of the worldview?"

We argued for long. On my part, I thought it was imperative to place before Daya my own journey of investigation on the many, many texts not only on aesthetics, but also the Indian arts, where this premise is both followed and interrogated within the textual tradition. I also said to him, "You have not addressed the question of its transmission and how it travelled across. Why didn't you ask the question where was the *Natyasastra* composed, why did one find the earliest manuscripts in a place like Nepal and how did centuries later the commentaries of Abhinavagupta reached Kerala? All these questions also need to be addressed." He laughed and replied, "OK Kapila, why don't you publish a rejoinder? I think you have a point." Our affectionate bond didn't allow me to publish a rejoinder, although Dayabhai egged me on.

Reading Neelima Vashishtha's *The Applicability of Indian Aesthetic Theory of Rasa to Visual Arts—A Rejoinder to Daya Krishna's article, 'Rasa The Bane of Indian Aesthetics*', revived memories of those conversations.

The most exhilarating moment was when Dayabhai wrote me a long letter after reading my book on Mewari *Gita-Govinda* and said, "Kapila, *anand aa gaya, anand aa gaya."*

And in the very last meeting with him, at the outset he said, "Today, we are going to talk about dance as 'thought'." I said, "Dayabhai, am I going to talk about dance or dance of thought'?" He laughed and said, "You know, I have been thinking whether there can be thought without word, and therefore, whether dance or movement is pure thought?" Shail Mayaram's volume reminded me of these and many other dialogues with him at a personal level.

The articles in the volume are based on a stimulating seminar, *Philosophy as Samvad and Svaraj*, that took place in Shimla at the Indian Institute of Advanced Study. My mind instantly went back to the first decade of the institute. I remembered Dr. Niharranjan Ray, the first Director of the IIAS, as also the many engaging and path-breaking interdisciplinary seminars. It was in one of those seminars that I heard Ramchandra Gandhi at his dramatic best.

As for Ramu, this association goes back to the bonding between our mothers, as we were almost neighbours in Connaught Circus. Only a few Indian families were residing in this part of the city. So, my mother would often say that she was going to meet Lakshmi, that is, Ramu's mother. I would also visit their house and also get to meet Ramu and his siblings, Gopu and Tara. Later, Tara was my student in Miranda House and she has continued to be a close friend. Ramu was a constant in the premises of India International Centre and I watched him in his role as a guru. He leaves behind many an admirer.

Let me now share some responses on Shail Mayaram's Introduction, and the Imaginary Dialogue between Daya Krishna and Ramchandra Gandhi. With great care and industry, she has structured her volume in a manner that there are some explicit threads which run through both the Introduction and the Imaginary Dialogue. This is an awesome task that she has accomplished with great sensitivity as also analytical skills.

Shail Mayaram says that Dayabhai was an iconoclast. I would modify that by saying, no, not an iconoclast, he was an interrogator, whether it was eastern or western philosophy, whether Socrates or others in the Indian tradition.

She refers to reading of the *Purush Sukta* of the *Rg Veda* and how Daya points at the solidification of a verse to validate societal hierarchy, normally understood as the *Varna*. Here I am taking the liberty of quoting Raimundo Panikkar: "*Purusha* is the cosmic Man; it is also the primordial aspect of the whole of reality." As for me, I would humbly like to ask, tell me of another civilization where feet are venerated. So, here is an ontological and epistemological problem, for if a culture venerates feet, then by the same analogy the 'Shudras' must be part of an inclusive vision. The distortions and the disjunctions that have taken place reflect a very complex dynamic of thought and social structure.

Daya pertinently refers to the exclusion of the 'Shudras' and the reluctant inclusion of the women in the Vedic *yajnas*. As someone who has been involved in the organization of these *yajnas*, especially when the *agni chayna* was held in Panjal in the '70s and the subsequent *yajnas* held in Kerala under the direction of the late Dr. T.I. Radhakrishnan, it was clear that the *yajna* was the concretization of the vision of the primordial man, step by step, brick by brick, person by person, certainly in defined roles in specific time. It would be a partial statement to speak of either hierarchy or total exclusion and inclusion at the level of societal structure. I can go on and on to give instances of reversal of roles, reversal of hierarchy in specific space and time. This is evident to anyone who has witnessed performances of ritual dance-drama in all parts of India.

To turn now to Daya's views on Indian philosophers writing in English. I happened to introduce Professor Jay L. Garfield to Daya, when Garfield and Nalini Bhushan (a cousin) were engaged in editing a volume *Indian Philosophy in English*. As quoted by the editors in their Introduction to this book, Daya Krishna said,

> 'We have been fed on the Western presentation of Indian philosophy, which hardly captures the spirit and history of Indian philosophy .... If I were not to know Indian philosophy myself; I would say that (their presentation) is wonderful, that it presents it clearly, with great insight and understanding. Now that I know a little Indian philosophy, I say that they did not .... They are not concerned with the problems that Indian philosophers were concerned with'.

As one knows, Daya travelled a long way himself. He acknowledges his debt to Badrinath Shukla in this journey. It will be remembered that it was Daya who initiated a meaningful, active and on-going dialogue between traditional pandits and contemporary Indian philosophers. In his remarkable introduction to the volume entitled 'Developments in Indian Philosophy from the Eighteenth Century Onwards: Classical and Western' (brilliantly edited by him), Daya interrogates the very cognitive enterprise of history and then develops his argument in regard to the nature of both continuity and discontinuity in the intellectual journey of Indians.

> 'History, as a cognitive enterprise, seems to be amongst the strangest of endeavours undertaken by man for it claims to know the past, that is, something which does not presently exist. But, how can that which is 'not', be understood? For to understand that, it would be to endow it with some sort of 'being'. The anomaly and paradox inherent in this attempt to know and understand the past has generally been ignored, as it raises questions about the very foundations of the enterprise in which historians are engaged .... '

The contributions in this volume assume significance as indicators of the continuity of the philosophic discourse in the 18th century. Daya played a seminal role in making these bridges of communication.

Shail Mayaram draws pointed attention to the 'intellectual decolonization' and asserts the need for adopting 'non-western categories' to comprehend the trajectory of not only Indian philosophy, but extended to the social structure and contemporary disjunctions. The relevance of *sva*, i.e. selfhood, *svaraj* in the deepest sense of intellectual freedom, and *samvad* not to be equated with dialogue, is her concern. Quite deftly, she recreates the *samvad* between two unusual minds of our times.

She highlights the difference between Daya and Ramu's perspective on Indian civilization. For Daya, it's the plurality of the intellectual traditions and a relentless questioning spirit, while for Ramu it is '*Advait*', the non-duality, which defines the truth of India. For Daya, it's not only the spiritual quest but he lays due stress on the knowledge quest, the philosophic quest, the scientific and aesthetic quest in equal measure. As for Ramu, *samvad* is all about self-understanding and arriving at the truth.

The dialogue between Daya and Ramu continues whether it is in the understanding of the philosophic principle of *Advait* or its ramifications in the life of thought, intellection, not to speak of experience.

Understandably, there is an interesting reference to Martin Buber and his much discussed book, *I and Thou*. Now it reminded me of a major seminar, *Intercultural Dialogue and the Human Image*, held at IGNCA in 1994, which revolved around Buber's formulation *I and Thou*. Ramu's perspective is not *I and Thou*, it is instead *I am Thou*, the title of his own book. Although an ardent admirer of Ramana Maharshi, Ramu's own musings, alas, cannot quite reflect the experiential depth of the Master. Also, there was some difference between Daya and Ramu in respect of *Advait*. Daya had critiqued *Advait* and Sankara and asserted the universality of the Upanishad. Oh, there is more one could say, but no more.

Let me now refer briefly to the imaginary dialogue so poignantly and meaningfully created by Shail Mayaram. Reading through these pages, some images come to my mind. It was like two boatmen on the same boat, sometimes oaring in consonance and sometimes in great dissonance. The boat, however, remained afloat on the tides and waves of a vast ocean with fathomless depths and unbound horizons. The two boatmen not only sought to measure those depths but also navigate on those waters and yet look up to the skies, to identify, if not reach, the *saptarishis*. Had they? Finally, the boat, the boatmen, the dancers of thought was in the realm of razor sharp intellect. The *saptarishis* of the sky and the *saptarishis* of experience may have led to silence.

30.

Sumatheendra Nadig and the Panchamahabhuta

One day as I sat in my office, walked in the renowned Kannada poet Sumatheendra Nadig. Of course I knew him as Chairman of the National Book Trust. I had heard him speak; I was familiar with his writing. I wondered what was it that brought him to me with a sense of urgency?

After a very brief conversation, it was clear that when an idea captivates the mind of a poet then it is all-engaging and almost consuming. Nascent but potent, the seed begins to flower slowly but surely. In a sudden flash, it flows in manifested form as poetry or drama, sound or music, line, brush or colour, or for that matter even the organization of a seminar or conference. The basic stimulus is the same. The idea captivates. The moment of igniting the mind is also the moment of creation. In the case of Shri Sumatheendra Nadig it was the idea and concept of the Panchabhuta. Nothing new, and yet ever fresh. Perhaps one of man's primordial consciousness, articulated in words, was that of the primal elements. The human must have realized early that he or she cannot live without water, or fire, the earth that sustains him, the air he breathes and the vast measureless expanse—*Antariksha*, sky and *akasha,* that envelop him. Spontaneously he invoked them with poetic fervour.

All civilizations or cultures have been conscious of the primacy of the primal elements. Some identified four as the Chinese, others like the Vedic five. Articulation of each of the elements, singly or together, was a natural corollary. Philosophic systems and sophisticated arguments in speculative thought developed. In India there is very early evidence of a self-conscious comprehension of the nature of the primal elements. This consciousness is sustained, nurtured, for many millennia in different hues and colours.

If the Rg Veda begins with evoking *agni*, Atharva invokes *bhoomi* (the Prithvisukta), *Vayu, Varuna* and *akasha* permeate the Vedic corpus. The vedic ritual (*yajna*) is a manifestation in concrete form of the consciousness of the five elements, their confluence and inter-dependence. A mighty system of correspondences is developed. The

Upanishads built upon the primal consciousness which is so elegantly articulated in the Vedas into yet another system of speculative thought. Throughout the Upanishads there are some of the most astonishingly impressive dialogues on the subject. The Chandogya and the Brihadaranayaka upanishads bring home the message that each of the primal elements are inter-dependent. Also that there are no absolute hierarchies.

The preoccupation with the elements, their materiality and non-materiality at a micro and macro levels, is central to all branches of the Indic knowledge system, creative and critical. Ayurveda understands the body system in terms of the primal elements, *agni (pitta)*, water (*kaph*) and *vayu (vitta)*. Charak describes the embryo as the aggregate of the five *mahabhutas*. He says,

> 'Embryo is the product of *akasa, vayu, tejas, ap* and *prithvi,* being the seat of consciousness. Thus, the embryo is the aggregate of the five *mahabhutas* being the seat of the consciousness which is regarded as the sixth constituent of embryo.' (Charak Samhita)

Chemistry dwells upon them as *dravya* and philosophic systems. Specially Sankhya dwelt upon them.

In course of time the Puranas adopt yet another strategy to incorporate this consciousness in the mythic image and iconic form. Another monumental and complex system or symbolism emerges. Shiva is the embodiment of the primal elements. As Nataraja he embodies the five elements. As ashtamurti he is also the elements. The prologue to Abhijnana Shakuntala by Kalidasa visualizes him thus:

> 'May the Lord protect you, He who is endowed with eight visible bodies: Brahman's first creation, the carrier of oblations offered according to the Rule, the Sacrificer, the creators of time, the world-pervader whose quality the ear grasps, the celebrated source of all seeds, that which gives the breath of life to living beings'.

They are respectively water, fire, soul (agent of sacrifice), sun and moon (base of the calendar), space, earth, wind.

There are other great examples in Sanskrit literature where poets have visualized Shiva as the embodiment of the five elements. Indian sculpture is replete with these images throughout India from the North to the South, West to the East. Bhartrhari was also concerned with the five elements but in the Vairagya Satak he is almost taking his final plunge into the Supreme Brahman when he says,

> 'O earth, my mother, O wind, my father, O fire, my friend, O water, my good relative, O space, my brother, for the last time I salute you and I fold my palms to you. By virtue of my association with you I accumulated merits from the abundance of which arose in me the pure knowledge, dispeller of all delusions. Now I merge in the Supreme Brahman'.

Vishnu is no exception. His embellishments, whether it is the Sankha or Chakra or Gada, are symbols of the primal elements. The Vishnudharmottara Purana addresses Yadava thus:

> 'O Yadava, in reality these are not weapons; they are the great elements borne by the Lord Hari. The conch-shell in the hand of the Lord should be known as being space, the disk as wind, the club as fire, the lotus as water (and earth?) as placed between his feet. Thus these great elements are (manifested) by Hari'.

So also the Devi. Devi is also the embodiment of the primal elements. There is a monumental body of literature in the texts of Tantra on the subject. The Devi consists of the five elements. She is also the embodiment of the primary sounds, i.e., phoneme. The Yoganisutra states,

> 'The universe consists of five elements and the divine goddess herself is inherently present in it. The root *mantra* of her is made of her essence, I am telling this to you. From the phoneme *h* space emerged and from *k* wind was born, from *r* fire, from *s* the principle of water, from *l* earth. Therefore she is immanent in everything'.

The Isanasivagurudeva Paddhati articulates it differently:

> 'Space, wind, fire, water and earth are denoted by the phonemes *h, y, r, v* and *l*. These five (phonemes) are the material causes of the universe in its form of *matrika.*'

It is natural that S. Nadig, the poet, should be sensitive to the legacy of this consciousness in the Indic tradition. It is also natural that a contemporary poet's sensibility should be equally concerned with the manifestation of the primal elements in our time and space. Also it is equally pertinent that our time and space may not allow only an abstract, positive evocation. For the poet S. Nadig is as consciousness of the ugliness of the manifestations of *agni* not only as life giver as the pure sun and the eternally pure dawn, *usha,* but *agni* as the diesel fumes, the devouring flames of destruction. Mother Earth, *Bhumi*, is the desecrated woman, and *vayu, prana*, contaminated with greed, and water polluted by our own human psyche.

Shri Nadig's poems impel us to ask these questions even if the interrogation is couched in the language of metaphor. No longer then are the poems about the idyllic, beautiful and abstract. They are of the here and now of the existential state of our living and the fractured psyche of the micro-man which is causing havoc to the macro-universe.

I am no literary critic, or have ceased to be one, and therefore will not comment on the poetic images or the prosody or the meter of the poem, nor on his positive attitude in the poems on Dampatya. I write because Shri Nadig and I share the fascination with the idea and the concept of the Panchamahabhuta. The primal elements are ever young and ever new. The ancient is transmuted to the most contemporary and modern. Shri S. Nadig with poised ease can converse with Rilke on whether there are four or five elements. Equally he can invoke Vagdevi, the goddess of speech, but in tone and tenor totally different from the *Vak Sukta,* and he can turn around the image of the tree of life to reflect upon the late flowering of one of the twin coconut trees and he can castigate the caste system by reminding his readers that creativity is no one's especial privilege. Nadig reminds us that Vyasa was the son of a fisherwoman, Doorvasa, the son of a cobbler, Kashyapa, the son of an ironsmith cobbler, to conclude,

'Come let us have a discourse.
Before you come forget your caste
leave aside your politics
throw away your prejudices
come, let us talk soul to soul'.

The pain of our existential state of turmoil is evident when he calls out:

'What a milky ocean is this mind!
The intellect is like the MERU mountain
We make it the churning rod
and we make our ego the churning rope
and we have gone on churning
getting more poison than Ambrosia'.

I have no doubt that the poems will find a resonance in many hearts and minds.

31.

The Legacy of Dr. Grace Morley and After

Thank you for inviting me to deliver the Grace Morley Memorial Lecture. This is indeed a great honour. I readily accepted the invitation, not because I consider myself or am considered either a professional Museologist or Art Historian, but because this would give me an opportunity to deeply reflect upon some issues of both disciplines which have been the subject of discussion in the past and the present in contemporary discourse. These issues, amongst others, it is my understanding, have to be discussed against the larger and wider backdrop of the varying points of view in regard to cultural heritage as also the institutional structures which were in part, if not wholly, a consequence of these perceptions. Also, as important for me was the opportunity to acknowledge not only my personal debt to Dr. Grace Morley at many levels but also the gratitude that she deserves from a whole generation of museologists, conservationists and art historians. Soon after her passing away I had paid her a personal tribute. I am not repeating that.

Thank you again for inviting me.

I thought it may be pertinent to situate Dr. Grace Morley's legacy against the background of historical developments of a century or half-a-century preceding her arrival in India, in short the legacy or inheritance which Dr. Morley carried with her from Europe, the USA and UNESCO and the legacy that was handed over to her in India of the state of discipline of art history, but, more, the institutional structure of museums in the country. Her contribution to India and the legacy that she left behind can only be evaluated by placing her in the spatio-temporal context of that era and that historical moment. It was logically the result of what she carried and what she was recipient of. It was not given to her to reshape and redefine the disciplines and the institutions. She was neither personally so constituted nor was the time ripe for initiating radical departures.

Her strength lay in consolidating—and enlarging—and building upon what she received and shared with her contemporaries. In so doing she nurtured the institution National Museum at a seminal time and provided leadership and energy to the discipline of Museology and the institutions called Museums. For two decades, her impact was effective in more ways than one. Subsequent developments, beginning with the late seventies, but specially in the eighties and the nineties, were understandably affected less by the dynamics of changes and transformations of perspectives and sensibilities in regard to cultural heritage, or heritage—bio and cultural—in the countries of the West or North, as also India and the countries of the South. These changes were a direct consequence of the awareness of developments in science and concern for the environment, and naturally the experience of the new political states of the post-colonial era. Cumulatively this brought about shifts both at the level of theory and, to an extent, practice in respect of the disciplines of archaeology and anthropology, extendable to art history and museology and the institution called Museum, i.e., as structures. Now there was ethno-archaeology, new anthropology and new museology, and the latest being new art history.

So to return to the legacy which Grace Morley carried from Europe and what she received in India. Although all of you here are more familiar than I am with the history of the founding of museums in Europe, the USA, not in the distant past of Greece and Rome, or even the sixteenth century, but the eighteenth and nineteenth centuries, let me make an effort to recount not the chronology but the philosophico-political underpinnings of these perspectives, more specifically in the eighteenth and nineteenth centuries. It is well to recall this again, despite the sizeable, although not sufficiently analyzed, critical literature on the subject in regard to the founding of the great museums in Europe and even the USA. Perhaps it is to be reiterated that the institution of museums received a fillip in no small measure as an inescapable concomitant of the twin psychological needs and political motivation of (a) establishing the antiquity of European civilization through detour routes of investigating other civilizations—this was specially so in the sphere of languages and archaeology; (b) to claiming patrimony of the evidence of natural and cultural heritage of these other civilizations and cultures. Both had much to do with maritime trade and colonial expansion. Economic power, acquisition of objects and appropriation of knowledge went together. Enough has been said and written on Enlightenment, positivism and liberalism, but few political historians have chosen to identify the links of these with the establishment of museums. Of course, in the field of art history Partha Mitter critiques these processes in his book *The Much Maligned Monsters*. In our context it may be pointed out that there was also a lurking sense of psychical insecurity. There was a consciousness that the politically poor were culturally rich. Thus it became necessary to evolve theories of common or allied ancestry. This is not the occasion to dwell on this more fully. I have done this elsewhere.

The emergence of the disciplines of archaeology, anthropology and natural history was to an extent the result and explicit expressions of these perspectives. Not un-linked were the theoretical discourses in the domains of science, philosophy and psychology, the last, then, a new discipline. Thus all dimensions of the socio-political, scientific and philosophic discourses have to be considered together for a fuller comprehension of the forces which accelerated the growth of the disciplines of archaeology, anthropology and the tertiary and then nascent discipline of art history and the establishment of the major museums in the metropolitan cities of Europe and the USA. This history, or, may l say the chronology, is well documented, and you are all acquainted with it. However, often it is overlooked that the history of the establishment of the four Surveys in India—namely the Archaeological, Botanical, Zoological and Geological—was an integral part of the European discourse, and perceptions at a theoretical level and integral to politico-philosophic-psychical imperatives. Resultantly, 'archaeology' became the study of the past, dissociated from the present, to put it in simplistic terms, and anthropology the investigation of the 'other' also belonging to the past, or certainly assessed as a lower level of human development in a hierarchy of scales, and natural history, the collection of flora and fauna of geographical areas, largely also of the 'other'. The past was to be discovered and excavated and the natural and cultural world which was destined to extinction, collected and documented. The unilinear progressive path parallel to Darwinian evolution, Newtonian science and Cartesian dualism of mind and matter, constituted the implicit, if not explicit, theoretical underpinnings.

Naturally and understandably, archaeology focused on excavating the past with a view to establish linear chronologies through the assembly of material remains, anthropology of collecting human specimens of skeletons and skulls with a classificatory model of racial types, and flora and fauna as objects dissociated from human interaction. In short, a vast, complex, interlocked, interconnected holistic system was perceived and preserved through fragments and units, de-contextualized. It was believed that through the collection of specimens or fragments, some postulates could be made on the attributes of specific civilizations, in this case Indian. Integration, or re-construction, of a whole by juxtaposing the natural with the human was neither the motivation nor the purpose. A clear distinction was made between the material and non-material, Nature and Culture. Besides, in the domain of archaeology stratification was established in a linear order, not on the acceptance of multi-layering and concurrency. Also, the yardstick of comparison was Greek or, more precisely, its Roman incarnation. This was the normative.

Anthropology was clearly impacted by the notions of higher and lower civilizations. It was accepted that there was a linear progressive development from savagery, barbarism, agrarian societies to urban societies. Gordon Childe offered a classificatory system of attributes even if he modified it later. No more need be said here as elucidation.

The remembrance of this discourse is of vital importance before reflecting upon the term 'Museums', not necessarily from the primary association with Muses or creativity. Whatever the etymology, by the nineteenth century, it was accepted that museums collected the objects qua objects of the dead past, to be looked at objectively, dispassionately, distantly; and the natural history, flora and fauna, which was rare or that would disappear, become extinct, and anthropology would investigate the physical traits and material culture of the less civilized and underdeveloped. It must be reiterated that the evaluative categories of the uncivilized and lower civilization and higher civilization were not only 'cultural' categories, these were also political categories. This notion of high and low civilizations was widely debated and finally accepted in the sphere of political and legal discourse. While this is not the occasion to offer a more detailed account, today there is a body of literature which comments upon the implications of this at the socio-political and economic level. As cultural historians we must also be aware of the implications of these categories to museums and to the interpretation of archaeological remains. Just as a reminder in our context, perhaps two quotations will be illustrative. Samuel Johnson had written to Hastings: 'You who are familiar with the riches of Persia will no doubt bring the riches of Ind to enrich the isle of Eng,' and in turn the statement by Hastings: 'The sword which gave us the domination of Bengal must be the instrument of its preservation, and preservation of its past." For our purposes, it is interesting to note that the theory of sovereignty which emerged during Europe's imperial expansion, the development of certain ideas about 'civilization' as a juridical notion was crucial. The entry of the concept of 'civilized' and 'uncivilized' at a theoretical level in the political and juridical discourse enabled the European powers on the one hand to deny certain rights to the subjects and concurrently have the right to appropriate the wealth of the 'uncivilized' without any compunctions of respecting territoriality. The development of the concept of 'civilization' and the positivist's interpretation and extra-territoriality not only provided the basis of legitimization, but also of appropriation. Although this empowerment did uncover many riches, and there is ample reason for acknowledging debt, we must also not overlook the philosophico-political ideology. As cultural historians we often forget that the principles which distinguished civilized and uncivilized states, which became integral to the domain of rules of international law and international legal rights, had far-reaching effects in the evolution and establishment of several strategies of state policy in India in the fields of archaeology, anthropology and natural history.

It is important to bear this in mind, also because while historians, political and cultural, have or often redrawn the contours of the Anglican and Orientalists' discourses and commented upon the polarities of views, it is not sufficiently recognized that although they appeared at opposing poles, i.e., Mills, Grant and Macaulay at one pole, William Jones, Princep, H.H. Wilson and of course Max Mueller on the other, there was an unvoiced acceptance of the notions of civilization, as also the right of 'appropriation'. It was thus not a question of acceding to the aspiration for the benefits of science and mathematics, as Raja Ram Mohan Roy wanted and which Macaulay used to the fullest for his famous or ignominious Minute, but also a strategy of legitimization of appropriation in international law. Consequently the educated Indian was doubly distanced. No doubt we imbibed science and liberalism through the cloaks and gowns and forks of the intellectual discourse, we also became unknowingly, as Macaulay said, their representatives. Macaulay had prophesied that 'there will be class of Indians who will be our representatives when we are no longer there to rule.' In short, the internalization of the language of 'thought' penetrated deep. The Orientalists gradually essentialized the East, spoke of the spiritual East, but they too were suffused with a missionary zeal to 'civilize'. One may respectfully and with great admiration mention that despite the monumental contribution of Max Mueller, one must not forget that he too wanted to 'civilize' the Indians and hoped that one time or the other they would reach a higher degree of civilization (in his case, the Christian). This may seem like flogging a dead horse and yet it is relevant for a clearer understanding of the era and consequently the manner in which there appears to be some lingering of these perceptions. It may be added that what was true of India, with a difference was true of Africa and other countries in Meso America and Asia.

Logically European museums collected the fragments of archaeology and specimens of natural history to demonstrate not only the distinction between Nature and Culture but also the distinction between the less and more civilized, the East and the West. Understandably this could not be made explicit in India, nor was it perhaps a sharply self-conscious awareness when the Surveys and or/the Indian Museum were established in 1814.

The subsequent history is all too familiar and needs no recounting. Archaeology, anthropology and the museums were built on the premise of the clear division of Nature and Culture, antiquity, past and present, the more civilized and the less civilized. The last was implicit in archaeology, explicit in anthropology. It is not necessary to elucidate the developments in the last half of the nineteenth century and first part of the twentieth. The gains were not minimal. Sites were located, mapping done, fragments and specimens collected, scripts deciphered, flora, fauna, monuments listed, and equally or unequally distributed. Interpretation of the culture on its own terms through its own categories of thought and knowledge, and revitalization of a living civilization and a pulsating vibrancy of local communities, was not in the intellectual or political consciousness. While education, or modern education, distanced the Indian from both his past and the living cultures, it empowered the Orientalists and the archaeologists to uncover the past. Only a handful of Indians participated. Also, state policy did not always encourage the enterprise of archaeologists. This is amply borne out by the repeated pleas of Prinsep, H.H. Wilson and others for funds. The Surveys continued to document archaeological remains, flora and fauna.

Concurrently there was the political movement of the struggle for independence. At the political level it was an awakening of a national consciousness. At the cultural level, it was a rediscovery of the past by the 'educated' Indian. Understandably, the rediscovery or re-acquaintance meant 'reconstruction' or reinterpretation. The contribution of the pioneers—Tagore, Rukmini Devi, Vallathol—is recognized.

However, both at the political level and to an extent 'cultural', there was an emphasis on the pan-India, the unified India, with a single perennial tradition. Diversities were contained, but regional autonomy was eschewed. Today it is called the 'Nationalist discourse' and has been under considerable attack. The protagonists of the critique of 'Nationalist discourse' have naturally been critical of the Bengal School and the art historians, A.K. Coomaraswamy, Stella Kramrisch and others. This background of pre-independent India has to be taken into account.

In 1947, a politically independent India was the inheritor of this dual legacy of asserting national identity as also being obliged to continue pre-independent India's policies in respect to these domains. Thus, while in other spheres of policy the State intervened to make major changes and bring about reforms, in the matter of educational policy, the division between the modern and the Oriental learning continued. Even Gandhiji's concept of Basic Education was abandoned. There were no major changes made at the policy level in respect to archaeology, anthropology and museums. Elsewhere l have elaborated upon this at greater length. Although there was great sensitivity at the level of political leadership, e.g., Azad, Nehru, their idealism was not translated into a radical transformation of the policy orientations of pre-independent India. In 1948 the Burlington exhibition was a high water mark of representing excellence of achievement; it was a magnificent show of representation, but not of asserting or reaffirming another theoretical position. Like many great scholars, my guru Vasudeva Saran Agrawala, who was an active participant in the assembly of objects, was at that time not an articulator of an alternate model of comprehending India, although later he was one of the most outspoken expositors of both value as also differences of attitudes and modes of expression. The National Museum, as we all know, was founded on the nucleus of this exhibition.

Dr. Grace Morley came from Europe and the USA about a decade later. Undoubtedly she carried no baggage of the political and legal discourse or subscription to the Orientalists or Anglican debate, but she too has to be situated in the history of the establishment of the great museums of Europe—Louvre, Indische Kunst, British Museum and the Metropolitan, to name only a few, besides the Museums of Natural History in the UK and the USA. This was her inheritance. Good or bad, she was neither an Ananda Coomaraswamy nor a Havell. She was neither a Ruskin nor an Eric Gill, nor a Birdwood or a V.A. Smith. She was a sensitive scholar of cultures, with no prejudices or biases—open, free and empathetic to all cultures. Her advantage lay in her catholicity on account of her being the chief architect of the Museum of Modern Art in San Francisco and closely associated with the Museum of Modern Art, New York, with a deep and abiding interest and scholarly research in pre-

Columbian and Mexican Art. Coupled with this was her experience of the early idealistic phase of the UNESCO in the first decade. All these combined to give Dr. Grace Morley, the gentle, graceful, generous human being, the ability to look at all cultures and civilizations through the perspective of equal 'dignity' and not placing any one in a scale of hierarchy, major or minor. Undoubtedly she inherited and received the legacy of the institution of 'Museums', born and founded as a consequence in part of all that I have mentioned above. However, at no point did she subscribe to the theory of the higher and lower civilizations, nor was she a missionary. She respected the boundaries created between archaeology and anthropology, science and natural history. This was the state of the art in these disciplines. However, she worked assiduously and with incomparable commitment to preserve the integrity of each 'domain'. Hers was a mission to deepen and enrich, to refine, not to break walls or to create new models. This was also her inheritance from a highly altruistic generation of Americans. Upgrading of skills and techniques was her mission. Her leadership in the UNESCO is legend even today.

When she arrived in India, there was enough, more than enough, to transform Indian museums from 'Ajyabghars'—collections of unequal quality, poorly housed, badly maintained, with minimal conservation techniques. No doubt Indian Museum was a century-and-a-half old. The Madras Museum had rich collections and the Prince of Wales had enlightened leadership and the National Museum had a core collection, but there were hardly any systems of housekeeping, accession, inventories, catalogue cards, documentation, ideas on exhibitions, permanent and temporary, display methods, and above all, conservation, with exacting standards. The commitment she brought to these tasks both at the National Museum and others has been exemplary. At the National Museum she classified the galleries Pre-History Archaeology, and then by genre—sculpture, paintings, manuscripts and decorative arts. Further by region—Central Asian Antiquities. In short, she made a miscellaneous collection into a systematic museum.

She was not exhibiting objects from any ideological position—Western colonial or nationalist. Her task was to reorganize and sift and re-arrange. For this she was convinced that training of museologists and specially conservationists was a dire necessity. With uncommon and unconventional modes of philanthropy she succeeded in training and shaping a whole generation of museologists who are today leaders of the Museum movement. Appropriately even pioneers, like Dr. Devakar and

Bedekar, have paid her rich tributes, not to speak of others. She was modest, humble but resolute. She communicated with a C. Sivaramamurti, a Rai Krishnadasa, and a Moti Chandra on equal terms and with respect. Above all, she nurtured a younger generation of conservationists, such as O.P. Agrawala. Generosity and grace she carried with unassuming dignity. But art museums were not her only passion. Dr. Grace Morley was concerned about museums of all kinds and all descriptions. As Head of the Asian Agency of ICOMs she was indefatigable in setting up and reforming museums of ethnography, crafts, personalia museums. She was the fairy godmother of the Natural History Museum and S.M. Nair was encouraged. She explored all avenues to give the younger generation the widest exposure. Truly dedicated to science and technology museums, she was a guiding spirit for the Birla Museum, the Visveswaraiah Technology Museum in Bangalore and the Pilani Museum. The Indian Council of Science Museums was established as a result of her active and successful advocacy. Saroj Ghosh was the receiver of great encouragement and guidance. She made it possible for the curators and directors to have the widest exposure to the Museums of Science, such as the Hall of Science, Berkeley and the Science Museum, Chicago, etc.

In her writing and in her work, Dr. Grace Morley was deeply conscious of the relationship of museums with education. For her, outreach educational programmes were essential, both in art and science museums. She was conscious of the fact that museums had to serve the community. She referred to this repeatedly. Dr. Grace Morley gave the National Museum a method of acquiring and housing antiquities and objects of art and designing galleries, finding innovative ways of display for permanent and temporary exhibitions. In addition she was anxious that the Museum reached out to the community. It was her decision to have mobile vans of the National Museum as educational outreach and her insistence for a community base for the science museums. I distinctly recall her anxiety to create a network of science and technology museums which would be operative at both urban and rural levels. She was sensitive to the vibrant craft traditions of India and Asia. She advocated the establishment of ethnography museums. She said, 'Ethnography museums are greatly needed in Asia. Most countries have not only traditional handicrafts, often with a very long history from villages and rural centres, each with a very long history, each preserving its distinctive character, but also a living tradition of creativity. The performing arts of mime, dance and drama are often an integral part of this heritage. These museums must become the centres of presenting the richness of the living traditions.

She strongly supported the work of the Gurusaday Museum in Calcutta, the Crafts Museum in Delhi and the Calico Museum in Ahmedabad. She bemoaned the fact that the museums of the Anthropological Survey had rich collections but not enough was done to involve the creators of the crafts. She suggested several times that approaches in anthropology needed changes. No longer could one group of people look at some others. In fact, she advocated a change in the USA, specially in the Museums of the West Coast. In India she was convinced that steps should be taken to ensure the continuation of these creative skills. She was a great supporter of Kamaladevi's initiatives. She could do no more than voice her concern, placed as she was as an Adviser, and not a policy maker. She welcomed the proposal to establish a Museum of Man. She articulated her concern simply: 'Now fortunately all the countries which have distinctive folk and tribal cultures are giving serious attention to find means to preserve them, for it is very evident that the processes of westernization, industrialization and urbanization encroaching on the styles of living everywhere are tending to eliminate this aspect of the heritage.'

It was at her initiative that UNESCO and ICOM decided to hold a special regional symposium 'The Role of Museums in changing Asian societies, with special reference to the role in strengthening traditional rural and tribal culture." She also advocated the establishment of a museum devoted to the struggle for independence. Her concern for training of museum personnel is well known. She supported and helped the few universities which had departments of Museology, e.g., Baroda and Calcutta. What I learnt from her as a pupil when the Teen Murti was converted into a Personalia Museum is yet another chapter.

I can go on to elaborate upon her concerns and her ceaseless efforts at many levels. In Europe and the USA she initiated a movement of not acquiring antiquities which were not legally imported. Resultantly a consortium was established amongst some leading museums to ensure ethical practices of acquisition. The ICOM document of Ethics of Acquisition was drafted by her and later accepted by the UNESCO. This was certainly a change from the colonial position of the right of acquisition and appropriation. While she could not ensure the repatriation of the original objects, she did persuade V&A to return the regalia to Burma. She participated actively in the Government of India's programme of conserving the murals of Pagan. I have watched Dr. Morley at work not only in different parts of India but also Burma, Indonesia, Vietnam and Thailand.

Her dedication was deep, her sense of detail impeccable and her generosity boundless. She nurtured young and not so young talent, and embraced all with open arms: she was called Mother appropriately and like a mother she showered her care and affection on all children—human and institutions—without distinction and with no sense of superiority or advocacy of any ideology she may have inherited.

Thus, although she was the last of the Children of Enlightenment, she shed the ideology of enlightenment to become the follower and practitioner of the middle path. In private conversation she sometimes said, 'May be I really belong to this part of the world. I do not know Buddhist or Hindu but middle path is my way,' surely the middle path of restraint, altruism and compassion.

The legacy that Dr. Morley left was precious and extensive. Radical departures were not her way, nor was she so situated. Nor was there an alternate voice. Nor was it given to her to theorize on the discipline of museology or museums. Nor for her to dismantle existing institutions. She was a bridge-maker between the East and the West, the national and the international, the rural and the urban, and specially India and Asia and India and the West. Her strength lay in refinement, consolidation, expansion and deepening. This she demonstrated in her work in full measure across the globe.

Concurrently, beginning in the seventies, there were deep rumblings about the institution of Museums and their mission. Understandably but ironically, this too began in the West. This time it was not the consequence of colonial expansion, or acquisition of the patrimony of an alien civilization, or a commitment to conserving the ancient and contemporary heritage; instead, a psychical insecurity of another type. A section of the 'thinking' and sensitive West or the developed world was concerned about the consequences of 'development'. They were of the view that the very 'development' processes and mindless exploitation of resources had impoverished high civilization both in the matter of Nature and Culture. Besides, minority cultures or marginalized people began to assert their identity, e.g., American Indians, Samis or Laps in Sweden, indigenous people in Canada, Hispanic and Chikanos in the USA and others. There was a concern for the depletion of the natural species and the imminent prospect of extinction of many human groups and societies. Also some countries of Europe and the USA no longer had a single mono culture; there were immigrants, and nation-states were becoming multicultural. This was also true of Australia with a difference. In Stockholm, away from the city, was established the cluster of museums and parks, today recognized as Swenska model. Here it was sought to bring Nature and Culture together. Canada, with its multi and varied environmental zones and indigenous people, rose to the occasion. The Quebec Declaration was the result. Others followed.

The Stockholm and Rio de Janeiro conferences on environment voiced anxiety. The Johannesburg conference admitted defeat. The international community, at least at the level of theory, admitted that bio-diversity could not be fostered without cultural diversity. The two were twins. The Nature and Culture dichotomy had to be broken or rejected, or certainly redefined. Thus, just as a century or more ago the philosophico-politico-scientific discourse impacted the institution of museums and the disciplines of archaeology, anthropology and ethnography, now too it was these discourses which impacted the need for a redefinition of the institution of Museums. However, it should not be forgotten that the dominant discourse continued to be on the exclusive prioritization of economic development, growth and GDP, and unilinear progress. The new museum discourse had affinities with minority discourses in ecology and politico-economic theories, not with the dominant discourse of the progressive development model. Of course the older museums continued with their policies of acquisition, enlarging permanent collections and showcasing expensive temporary exhibitions. These travelling temporary exhibitions to the West were also good business for some in the industrialized world. Motivations were not always totally altruistic. Young nation states participated in the hope that their cultures would be internationally recognized.

Hugh de Varina coined the term 'Eco Museums' in 1971. It alluded to the need for conserving and creating an awareness of the heritage, natural and cultural. However vaguely defined, the concept of eco museums spread in France, Canada, Latin America and Africa. The Quebec Declaration called the movement New Museology, to be followed by the Santiago Declaration of 1980 'Integrated Museum', to be followed by the Guwahati Declaration in 1988.

Other terms were used—Integral Museum, Identity Museum, Community Museum, Neighbourhood Museum, Tomorrow's Museum, and finally both new English terms of Heritology, Museumalization and de-museumization. The last three terms have perhaps not yet entered the Oxford or Webster's dictionary. I do not have to elucidate the history of these developments, because for those of you who are students and scholars of museology, you know it all too well, and many of you are active participants in the Association of Museums and its deliberations. However, it still remains to be said that all the theoretical and academic debates and, more, the conceptual framework of the Museum of Man—IGMRS—the last as visualized by the present Director General, K.K. Chakravarty, points to the fact that a genuine concern is about sustainable development of the community, and alternate and plural models of fostering, promoting, regulating, even ensuring self-governance. In short, it is a plea to recognize self-organizing systems of nature and culture, bio- and cultural diversity.

Whether this can be done through dismantling the institution of museums or by adopting more appropriate methodologies of human development and growth, through redefinition of development, and much that is contained in the term 'sustainable development' and empowerment of all those communities who continue to live with or in Nature, remains to be seen. The issue is complex, and there are no easy answers. Museums as institutions are always or have always been within a socio-political context. Policies and perceptions have to be modified at the politico-economic level, even the academic, before museums can be redefined or dismantled to become focal centres or instrumentalities of an alternate 'development' model.

I have carefully perused the conceptual plan of Chattisgarh. The concept and the programme is truly impressive and, if it fructifies, obviously this is a blueprint of an alternate development model of plural societies, where rupture between Nature and Culture has not taken place. The blueprint obviously cannot be conventionally replicated because its foundations lie in respecting the eco-system, bio and cultural diversity, and thus the integrity of distinctive eco-cultural zones, in short, the natural and human landscapes and the specificity of the ecology, natural and cultural. Fluidity and liquidity and flux appear as the attributes of these de-museumization. This is all welcome. But the plan can be realized only with the full support of the politico-social, economic system and, more, as they say to-day, a 'U' turn in the mindset at both the level of State policy and society. Naturally, the processes and programmes of education, specially primary as also the mindset of 'educated' and empowered civil society, will only then undergo radical changes. No longer would schools be the agents of 'uprooting' or merely preparing human automatons for a consumerist, fiercely competitive, market economy. If the school system seeks to stress 'uniformity'—mono-culture educated Indians—obviously no amount of transformation of the museums is going to bring about a change. So also is the issue of interface of policies and programmes of conserving the natural environment with those which advocate a single model of development at all costs. This is a vast field which calls for urgent serious attention. Science or New Science, and what is today called Swadeshi Science, has to be an indispensable partner.

Can only a new type of museologist or art historian achieve this without full participation or support at the political and administrative level? The answer to these questions is, 'perhaps it will happen, perhaps not.' The fast pace of the industrial sector and new communication tools indiscriminately used could well swallow up the fragile cultures. Also, realistically speaking, would it be wise to dismantle the existing museums of specific disciplines in urban centres? After all, the fragment and dismembered objects are there, and they are housed. Whether these museums should be promoted only as tourist attraction, devote themselves only to showcase, or should they become active partners in education at the tertiary level is the moot question. Despite the fact that museums exist, there is no structural interlinking between museums and universities' Departments of Art History and Archaeology. These are issues which should continue to engage the community of museologists and art historians, at least in India.

Thus it would appear that there is scope for building upon the legacy of Dr. Morley and concurrently breaking fresh ground and adopting new innovative methods for future museums, specially in the hinterland, providing space for adopting plural strategies specific to the eco-cultural zone. As important is plurality of models of development and thus plurality of approaches. Indian civilization rests on the foundation of the acceptance of the adage of plurality of paths and interconnectedness of dimensions. Obviously one dogma must not be replaced by another fixed conceptual frame. There is room and appropriateness of several types of diversities and, as they say, alternate modernities and a middle path.

To conclude, it would appear that the professions of museologists and art historians have been by and large impervious to identifying the larger and deeper context of the socio-economic, political and philosophic underpinnings of the disciplines and the institutional structures. Grace Morley carried a legacy, received a legacy, and gave or left behind a legacy. This comprised systemization, consolidation and opening many new avenues in the matter of types of museums, interaction of India with the West as also the East. The generation following could have built on the legacy by finding ways of greater interaction with Asian and African civilizations, and not always focusing on showcasing, exhibiting to the West. Many positive developments have taken place in the institution of museums.

However, there is need for redefining the role of museums or spacio-temporal areas wherein a continuum could be established between past, present and future. For this, distinctive zones, specially eco-zones, have to be identified, eschewing the earlier classification of forest, cultivation and urbanization of the tribal-rural and urban, and non-literate and literate.

In such a programme it is most fundamental to see education, culture and rural sustainable development together as a whole, and not in isolation. At the tertiary level, redefining of disciplines and boundaries of disciplines, and a structural interchanging between institutions of higher learning in both science, philosophy, history and those of archaeology, anthropology and the arts, is absolutely necessary.

32.

Tribute to Alice Boner

Allow me, first and foremost, to express my sincerest and deepest sense of honour and privilege to deliver the Alice Boner Memorial Lecture here in Switzerland.

As one who had known the person in whose name this lecture is instituted as both artist-scholar and thinker and meditator, I feel that it is a singular compliment to be asked to deliver this lecture in her memory.

Before I commence speaking on the subject, I would like to take the liberty of speaking for a few minutes on Alice Boner I knew and what she stood for, both in India and in Switzerland.

For this audience, Alice Boner—young, enthusiastic, creative and vigorous sculptor—is not unknown. The collections of the Reitberg Museum donated by Alice Boner bear testimony to her unfailing eye, her immaculate taste and her generosity. This too is known and recognized. The Alice Boner that I wish to speak about is the Alice Boner who travelled from Western Europe physically and psychically to another culture, both physically and psychically. Her encounter with Uday Shankar the dancer was, perhaps, accidental but it proved to be God's gift, instrumental in changing the course of Alice Boner's artistic, intellectual and finally mystical and spiritual journey. The shaping of mass and volume into sculpture, the moulding of clay into shape, the chiselling of stone, the arresting of movement in line was her passion. This is evident from her early works. The dance of Uday Shankar enchanted the sculptor because dance was movement before and after the moment. It is significant that another contemporary scholar came to the field of Indian art through dance. I refer here to Alice Boner's friend and near-contemporary Stella Kramrisch. Herein lies a key to understanding why some or, one may add, many have begun the journey from sculpture to dance or from dance to sculpture.

To return, however, to Alice Boner's journey, it is the dance which brought her to India and it was the dance which took her to the mysteries and magic of the forests of Kerala. Her early writing in the Journal of the

Indian Society of Oriental Art of the late 30s is replete with revelations of the dance as she knew it. It was this writing of Alice Boner which awakened my curiosity to see the author behind the work. It was the search for finding an appropriate costume for the dances of Uday Shankar, which took Alice Boner to the caves of Elura. It was one such moment of experiencing Elura that compelled Alice Boner to take yet another journey. It was no longer the outer trappings of the formal technical elements or of the technique of sculpture which aroused her curiosity; instead, it was a revelation almost like an explosion, which opened her third eye. As she herself recalls in the introduction to her book *Principles of Composition in Hindu Sculpture*:

> "It was before the magnificent panels carved inside the cave temples of Elura that in 1941 I had the first intuitive perception of a deliberate compositional planning."

Day after day, she sat in front of these images, lost in contemplation, passively allowing their mysterious presence to work on her mind and to penetrate her inner perception. The more she meditated the more the sculpture revealed to her: not only the essentials of form but more the essentials of the spirit of the dance which permeated her being. These were truly intuitive insights conditioned no doubt by her training as a sculptor and her response to dance but qualitative of another dimension.

The result was a book almost 20 years later: *Principles of Composition in Hindu Sculpture*. Alice Boner's experience of Elura in 1941 could hardly be called an intellectual analysis. From all that she did then and later it is clear that if Uday Shankar's dance was instrumental in bringing her to India, it was the caves of Elura and Śiva the Lord of Dance which opened other vistas and levels of comprehending Indian art. From the form of sculpture, she moved to delve deeper into the sources of this creativity, both at the level of theoretical formulations as also artistic expression. Had the impact been of lesser intensity or of a different quality, Alice Boner could not have taken the decision to settle down on the banks of the Ganges, watching its eternal rhythm.

It was the Alice Boner as a resident of Assi Ghat whom I came to know in Banaras as a student. I was familiar with her writings on dance, her association with and her great contribution in introducing Uday Shankar to the West. I had avidly read every bit of her writing in the journals and now I was face to face with the sculptor, the painter, the searcher for the Indian *Śilpa Śastras*, the meditator and the contemplator. She was all this.

But she was also, or, may I add, continued to be also, the bridge-maker between the East and the West, between Assi Ghat and Konarak on the one hand and Switzerland, on the other.

Between 1941 and 1964, she moved in and out of two worlds. She also moved within from the world of dance of the body to the world of spirit and essence of Indian sculpture. More, she searched for the textual basis of the artistic activity. I recall vividly, or rather too vividly, her presentation in January 1964 at the 26th International Congress of the Orientalists on the manuscript on Konarak. The archaeologists and the Sanskritists both were skeptical, if not critical, of the authenticity of the manuscript and the contents. Doubts were raised on Alice's command over her material and yet the curiosity and the animated discussion of her work aroused was difficult to quell. Alice persevered, despite the ambiguous response. Her search was to identify the textual base for the complex structure of Indian art, both temple architecture and sculpture. She had proved through her work on the manuscript of Konarak even if the authenticity of its actual date has not yet still been established that there was a textual base. She continued until she could prove beyond doubt the existence and efficacy of other texts. She not only located but also collated and edited and translated the *Śilpa Prakāśa* and the *Śilpa Śarini*. The publication of these books firmly established the Śastric textual basis of the Indian arts, particularly architecture and sculpture in the Orissan traditions.

While Alice Boner herself delved even deeper to find the philosophic and metaphysical basis of the artistic tradition, she had succeeded through her books on Konarak, *Śilpa Prakāśa* and the *Śilpa Śarini*, to create a renewed interest in textual studies and the *Śilpa Prakāśa* and the *Śilpa Śastras.* She identified the *Vāstu Śilpasutra Upaniṣad* which constituted the firm bridge between the philosophic and metaphysical thought of the Upaniṣad and the language or grammar of artistic form.

While the intellectual journey was unceasing and unending as her search for materials, Alice Boner, the meditator and contemplator, moved inward into yet deeper psychical levels of consciousness. She became both a worshipper as also the painter who created icons: concurrently she was also the watcher, almost like Siddartha of Herman Hesse, of the eternal flow of the Gaṅgā.

33.

Stella Kramrisch

She came to India after years of dreaming about India. Her teacher in Vienna, Professor Joseph Strzygowski, had exposed her to Buddhist art. Her thesis under his guidance was on Buddhist art entitled 'Dissertation on Early Buddhist Sculpture'. But her quest was for more. Trained as a dancer, she was sensitive to movement; she was perhaps torn between pursuing dance as vocation and preserving with her studies on India. She took the daring journey to England in the hope that it is from there she would ultimately reach India. It was a propitious moment, the poet Rabindranath Tagore was visiting. After her stirring lecture and his altogether too magnetic an appearance in his flowing robes, the petit, short Viennese girl walked up to him and said: 'I want to go to India'. It is said that the poet opened his arm, enveloped her in his embrace, and responded spontaneously, 'Yes, you will come to Shantiniketan'. Hope filled her bosom, her round eyes lighted up, but the journey to India was still far away. She had to put together the wherewithal for a boat journey, seek confirmation from the poet after his return to Shantiniketan. The poet wrote to Rothenstein, the guardian angel of all those who were interested in India. Rothenstein wrote back to Rabindranath Tagore: 'Never respond altogether too readily to all those with round eyes who wish to search for India.' The poet was generous. He said, 'She was welcome if she could find the means to get to India; the rest would be taken care of.' Stella Kramrisch, the Viennese daughter of a distinguished family, was adamant. She worked in all kinds of ways, including being a char-woman, cleaning steps, and undertaking all kinds of menial chores, to put together the fare for the 'boat' to India. She made it after saying fond farewells to her family in Vienna, never knowing if she would return.

And so she arrived in India after an eventful journey. She landed in Bombay, and on the very first day went to Elephanta, the Elephanta she had known through her reading. The visit was no less than a spiritual experience. She stood before the many forms of Śiva, and something within her revealed to her the essence of the Indian spirit. Here was the manifestation of the manifest in all its power. The figures of Śiva surrounded her in their multiplicity, but they were all the diverse images of the Unform, the No form, of the *lingam*. She was charged with this energy, although as a scholar she was yet to explore the many, many layers of what she beheld. As she walked out of the Elephanta complex, she saw a pool of fresh water and in the pool of fresh water was a rosary almost floating. She clasped at it as good luck or good omen. A Christian rosary in a Saivite shrine, a pool of fresh water in a rock surrounded by the azure waters of the sea. What could all this mean?

Her journey continued until she reached Shantiniketan. The poet welcomed her, and she like some others from far off lands, e.g., Sass and Elizabeth Brunner, made this abode of peace, Shantiniketan, her home. Here in the late twenties of the twentieth century, she began to unravel the different aspects of Indian art. No longer was it only Buddhist art; it was Indian art in all its diversities. One of her first perceptions was the relationship of Nature and Art. She wrote: Indian art is a part of nature itself and is nothing else but man's ratification of his own thankful reality, as a part of nature.

Through this one insightful perception, Stella Kramrisch had, as if in one stroke, given a new direction to the study of Indian art. No longer was this art Pagan or Pantheistic, in the words of Fergusson, nor was it an art devoid of portrayal; instead, it was an organicity of nature and the human. Ceaselessly, she explored different periods from the earliest to the medieval. She discovered that the art pulsated from within, it was breath in the mass and volume. Her writings along with those of her teacher, Professor Strzygowski, appeared regularly in *Rupam* and in the Journal of the Indian Society of Oriental Art. Ashutosh Mukerji, the enlightened Vice-Chancellor of the Calcutta University, immediately spotted extraordinary talent in the Viennese young scholar and appointed her as the first professor of Indian Art at Calcutta. An unconventional appointment brought rich dividends to India. She began a new school of thought in Indian art studies, complementing but going beyond the heated controversies between an Auroville, A.K. Coomaraswamy, G.B. Havell, Birdwood and others. The pioneers in Indian art history—S.K. Saraswati, Niharranjan Ray, K.R. Ganguly and K.K. Dasgupta—were her students, later to occupy the prestigious Bageshwari Professorship at the Calcutta University.

Herself she continued to write. Her little book, 'Indian sculpture', first published in 1936, was a landmark. Here she condensed, with incomparable precision and lucidity, a fresh approach to the study of

Indian sculpture. Undoubtedly there was chronology here, but more importantly there was an unequivocal rejection of the theory of 'decay and decline', propounded by her predecessors, specially Vincent Smith. With uncanny insight, she traced the history of Indian sculpture from the Mohenjodaro to the medieval times. However, this was no narration of dynasties or cults. It was a history of the evolution of 'form' qua 'form', of course, not uninformed by content.

Her observations on the treatment of mass and volume, weight and configuration of planes, gave Indian art a new vocabulary. Also, she established firmly the view that 'medieval factor' in Indian art was not to be equated with the art of middle, dark ages, in the European context. Also, she referred to the specific Indian vision, without subscribing to the theory of the Greek origins or certainly Greek and Roman influences. At that time these were fresh perceptions, the last shared with A.K. Coomaraswamy's writing. The little great book 'Indian Sculpture' was a watershed.

However, her journey of search continued ceaselessly to delve deeper and deeper. On the medieval regional developments she had written, but this time it was a search for the metaphysical and textual basis of Indian architecture. Khajuraho, a monument long discarded as the epitome of decadence and abhorrent eroticism, was her focus. She identified the literary sources, specially the Brahmanas, the *Satapatta* and others and unfolded the dynamics of the paradigmal model of *Purusa* as the basis of the Hindu temple. With impressive photographs by Raymond Burnier, charts, figures, she argued convincingly on the emergence of a concrete structure on the basis of an abstract principle of the *Purusa* (the Image of Man) as cosmos on earth. Her magnum opus, 'The Hindu Temple', in two volumes, appeared in 1946. I recall as vividly as if it was yesterday the desire to acquire the two volumes (expensive as they seemed for a student) as also her book 'Indian Sculpture'. This was the beginning of my journey into Indian art, as also of others of my generation—educated and trained in English literature and Western Art. While there was an emotional affinity with the art of our country, there was little or no understanding. The writings of Stella Kramrisch and the popularity of A.K. Coomaraswamy's 'Dance of Śiva' were eye-openers at another level. They obliged us to look at the tradition with the same critical faculty as we had been trained to do in respect of English literature, extendable to Western Art. A whole new world opened up. I longed to meet the author, but that was only to be much, much later.

Stella left India after the Second World War around Indian independence after the invitation of the Indologist scholar, Norman Brown, to serve on the faculty of the University of Pennsylvania (Philadelphia). Here she produced more students, and as Curator of the Indian and Asian Department of the Philadelphia Museum, gave yet another vision both to Indian studies as also representation of Indian Art in American museums.

Although I was in the US in the late forties and early fifties, I could not meet Stella. However, when we met in the early sixties, it took not a minute to be friends, and friends we so remained till her very last.

It was 'dance' that brought us together. I had given a lecture on 'Sculpture and Dance', had also demonstrated. Stella's positive response with her unfailing critical eye was a source of great encouragement and affirmation. It was then she told me how she had been torn between her desire to be a professional dancer and her search for India. We talked of Khajuraho, which I visited several times, thanks to her book, long before it was declared a protected monument. Each conversation was enriching, exhilarating, as were her public lectures, without any piece of paper, delivered as if she was reading a text.

She continued to visit India, if not often, regularly, made countless friends with the famous and the ordinary. Everyone recognized the brisk walk of a person committed, deeply committed, to what she set out to search. She visited temples, shrines, dressed in Indian saris. She wanted now to breathe the living India of the pulsating frozen stone.

The visit to Elephanta she had never forgotten, even if Śiva lived academically in the subaltern of her consciousness. For decades she read, reflected and interpreted on the Unmanifest and Manifest. All this introspection and the probing into literary sources culminated in the desire to hold an exhibition, on the Manifestation of Śiva and the book 'Presence of Śiva'. In Khajuraho she had encountered and made manifest the paradigmical model of *Purusa* in the *Kandriya Mahadeva temple*. In her masterly article on Elephanta she had made explicit the schema of the architectural plan and the sculptural imagery. Now she pierced an arrow with swiftness of her protagonist Rudra, to comprehend the multi-dimensionality of the primordial myth. In the 'Presence of Śiva', in chapter after chapter she follows Rudra, Śiva—in the different aeons of time, in His numerous aspects. She moves freely in space, time and sources, epic, Puranic and others to recount with great alacrity, the forms and significance of the numerous interlocked myths of Śiva.

It was during her planning of the exhibition 'Manifestation of Śiva' that I came to know Stella even more closely. She shared her original vision and conception. She identified the sculptures she wanted India to ban. We travelled to some sites together, at other times spent hours pouring over her lists to make sure that the thematic, unifying vision would not be compromised in the logistics of loans and borrowings from several sources. Each session was a learning experience, even if at times an arguing experience. She listened carefully, not because I happened to be officially entrusted with the project, but because she had unhesitatingly admired my visualizing in the best part (along with others of course, T.S. Maxwell, etc.) the 'Image of Man' exhibition in London. On that occasion, she had spontaneously exclaimed: 'Brilliant, beginning with water cosmology and ascending to the dance of the cosmos in Śiva as Nataraja'. Each time we discussed it was to that Kapila that she spoke.

Fortuitous circumstances so had it that I was on the faculty as visiting professor when the exhibition was mounted in the Philadelphia Museum. It was the experience of assisting in planning and mounting the exhibition, that made me the friend into a pupil of sorts. I watched her day after day in designing the exhibition. Śiva lived inside her, and it was once again the original revelation of the Unmanifest (Unform No form) and the multiple forms which engaged her attention. Logically, within the halls she began with compact cluster of the *Lingams*, the *Ekamukha* and *Chaturmukha* all together under dark lush green foliage. This was the centre, the focus half lit, and half hidden and half revealed. The narrative of the other forms began thereafter with meticulous care but no over-statement. Rough chronology was observed. However, what was important was not chronology and regional representation; instead, it was literally the unfolding of the diverse manifestations of Śiva. Her joy was unbound. For me, the experience of sharing was a precious gift ever to be treasured.

Stella however did not rest on her oars. While the Śiva of Elephanta continued to be closest, she embarked on a fresh journey of the 'dateless art of India'. She made the important distinction between the dateable and dateless art of India. Terracottas, bronzes of what she termed as the 'art of unknown India', engaged her attention. She called upon Haku Shah to be her Indian collaborator. The result was the magnificent and significant exhibition entitled 'The Art of Unknown India', which travelled to the different museums in the US.

Her impish delight in miniature painting was joyfully playful. The exhibition 'Painted Delight' and the book 'Painted Delight, was the expression of childlike delight of ripe maturity. She had delved deep, travelled far, and now the whole of miniature painting, with the same myths and legends, transformed into the pictorial frame of Indian miniature paintings, gave her an easy delight, which she shared in full measure with her audience.

Stella, the human being beneath the scholar, art historian and thinker, collector and museum curator, was reserved, but not uncommunicative. We could sit for hours, in almost silence, exchanging few words, but being in communication. Our dear friend Irene was by her side through her illness. I sat by her bedside holding her hand in the twilight of one evening. She said: 'It has been a long eventful, fulfilling journey. And, Kapila, will you just do a few movements of the dance for me, the dance which lives deep inside me still? I sometimes wish I was a dancer'.

And then with care, affection, she handed over a 'mellakite' egg amongst the many others by her bedside. She held my hands, I hers, that was 'farewell'.

A few weeks later she passed away, only to live with me, as with many others, for ever. For me she was the revealer of the 'essence' of the artistic tradition to which I was born, but one which she lived and breathed to her last.

34.

Kathleen Raine and India

Kathleen Raine says in *India Seen Afar*, 'as I think back I realize that perhaps it was not I who chose India but rather that India chose me'. Although this simple, direct statement is in the context of Tambimuttu, the Ceylonese (Sri Lankan) poet who was the publisher of her first work, there is a deeper significance to the statement. Tambimuttu, as she goes on to say, 'discerned in my work some quality India looks for and recognises. Tambi heard in my verse some music of the soul, the music of the goddess Saraswati, the goddess as Muse.'

The explicit recognition of a quality which in Kathleen's view India recognises, was the quality that she chose to explore through many meandering paths and, in her words, 'crooked roads'.

Her childhood had prepared her to take these journeys at many levels. She had learned to communicate with nature unself-consciously: the forest and the flowers, the insects and the animals were her friends. As one knows from her *Autobiographies* and other writings, the forest, the sea and the creatures that inhabit this world were never strangers or entities to be feared or destroyed. Little wonder that, more than the stories of Kipling, it was the narrative of Puran Das, who left home to retreat to the forest, which caught her imagination. 'Why did he renounce the world to be in the forest? And if he went to the forest 'why did he not communicate joyfully with the trees and the birds in the forest?' were questions that arose, long before she comprehended intellectually the concept of 'renunciation' in the Indian tradition. She could not, understandably, come to terms with the concept, although it kept teasing her off and on over many decades. Her mother had also instilled in her a curiosity about the life of the Buddhist monks in Sri Lanka. Aunt Meg had lived there and had seen the forest monasteries of Sri Lanka. Her mother, through many implicit and explicit ways, had shaped Kathleen's inner life. 'Was my pilgrimage already forecast in my mother's most secret life?' Kathleen asks. Her mother, she tells us, had the gift of communicating imaginatively. 'Had my mother, that secret theosophist, already made her passage to India? Or dreamed of it? I do not know, she was the native of a country which has no name.' Perhaps it was her mother who embedded the seeds in young Kathleen's mind and consciousness, long before any intellectual or physical journey to India took place. For her India was not a geographical region or country, not even an 'idea'; it was 'the place of every arrival, the term of every spiritual quest.'

But before she could embark upon this journey and identify India as the place of arrival, Kathleen traversed many circuitous paths at the intellectual and psychical level. She recounts with characteristic candidness her involvement with many movements of the twenties and thirties. The more she encountered the Marxists and the ideologies of the left in their Cambridge versions, the materialist discourse of Locke, Bacon and Newton, the more she recoiled to the sources of inspiration and imagination of her childhood. Yet there was no reprieve. She entered many taverns of thought and ideological groupings. She read Eckhart, but could not respond to him beyond a point. She visited the Churches of Rome, Assisi, Subiaco, was appreciative of their beauty, but 'they could not become companions of her soul'. She could also not be a 'Catholic poet' despite having embraced Catholicism at one stage. She could not live by the rules, however much she told herself that she should do so. Although sceptical of all groups and formal organisations, she nearly joined an organisation, 'Shanti Sadan', participated in a Magical Society akin to Yeats's Order of the Golden Dawn, and there were others. She 'dabbled', as she says, in all of them, but none satisfied her. This 'eclecticism' Kathleen does not regret nor the fact that the 'strait path was not hers' and yet it was these wanderings which prepared the ground for her to penetrate into the world of Platonism through the translations of Thomas Taylor, and to sit intellectually and spiritually at the feet of her 'Master' William Blake. Through him she explored Boehme, Swedenborg and others. Henry Corbin's writings opened other doors of perception onto Islamic mysticism. All this prepared Kathleen to encounter India at its purest and subtlest, not necessarily 'real', 'temporal' and actual. Only then could she declare India to be 'another name for that knowledge absolute to which we all strive.' It was for her a 'predestination'.

The physical journey was important, late as it was, but not of paramount importance. It would be hard to make a distinction between the India of the imagination, which Kathleen lived with before the actual journey, and the India she saw and experienced after the several visits to India. For her India was not an idea, as in the case of Raja Rao. It was more, because it stood for and symbolised for her all that the Occident had rejected, turned its back on. Thus India was the Orient, the East from where the Sun begins its journey each day, every day. Time and again, she juxtaposes the material West (Occident) with the Orient, only to underline not two geographical areas and civilizational trajectories, but two distinct world views, two attitudes, which can be discerned both in the geographical West as also the geographical East.

She was also fully conscious of and sensitive to the fact that Europe too did and continues to affirm a spiritual mystical tradition, despite the dominance of its subscription to the philosophy of 'materialism'. She was also not blind to the fact that despite the continuously rigorous and revitalizing traditions of India, embodying the messages of the Gita and Upanishads, India was herself poised on the perilous and precarious path of making choices, and even rejecting its own inheritance of looking inward and upholding values grounded in the spirit rather than 'matter'. Nevertheless it is the 'India of the imagination' which she explored with utmost finesse in the innermost processes of the working of the mind. It was this which engaged Kathleen with 'India'—and with all that she identified as the 'Orient' and the Oriental tradition.

As is well known, Kathleen's acquaintance with the sources of the tradition came to her gently, again through oblique paths, and not as a scholar of Indology, or through command over languages or primary sources. Her journey to the East, apart from the early influences of her mother, appears to have begun, as in the case with some others, through the reading of the Yeats's translation (and description) of Rabindranath Tagore's *Gitanjali*. These poems 'display in their thought a world I have dreamed of all my life long. The work of a supreme culture, they yet appear as much the growth of the common soil as the grass and the rushes. A tradition where poetry and religion are the same thing, has passed through centuries, gathering from learned and unlearned metaphor and emotion, and carried back again to the multitude the thought of the scholar and of the noble.'

While Kathleen's imagination may have been fired to explore the many regions and layers of the culture which constituted the soul of Tagore's poetry, it was not until she turned her attention to Blake that she began seriously to pursue the sources, the *Bhagavad Gita* to begin with, and later the Upanishads. She was acquainted with the principal characters of the Ramayana and the Mahabharata. It was through Blake that she made her journey to Boehme and Swedenberg and of course the long chain of the Neoplatonists. Philip Sherrard opened the doors to the writings of René Guénon, Henry Corbin to the world of Islam, and Coomaraswamy's writings sharpened Kathleen's sensibility and ability to make extraordinary and often unexpectedly convincing connections between cultures and civilisations, religions and artistic traditions. She affirmed with total conviction her commitment to a Perennial Philosophy, universal and pervasive, immutable and of ultimate value.

In the Editorials written by Kathleen for the last two issues of the *Temenos Academy Review*, she lucidly traces her journey through these many meandering paths. In the first (1998) she looks back at herself as the child of her age, the early twenties and thirties of the last century, and the multitude of influences, only to conclude: 'As to India there is too much to tell here: for I believe that if the West is to re-learn spiritual knowledge, it can only be from the Orient, where Buddhism, Islam and above all the great Vedic heritage, threatened as they are by western materialism, remain intact. India, a deeply wounded country, is still the mainstream of spiritual civilization. Can India teach the West before the West has destroyed India?' These words come from a mind approaching India with all its contrasts of riches and poverty, of affluence and destitution, of austere simplicity and vulgar consumerism. She was acutely aware of an empowered but rather derivative intellectual India, yet was also conscious of the continuation of indigenous, authentic but marginalized stream of speculative thought. She imbibed all this graciously with no—or only gentle—questioning. Her faith in a perennial or eternal India remained unshaken. It almost became a credo, because this India of Kathleen was not spatially or temporally bound.

In the second Editorial (1999), she takes the theme further, to assert the quintessential universality of all religions. She begins her Editorial quoting Blake's 'all religions are one' only to remind us of 'Jesus, the imagination,' the 'Divine Humanity' innate in every individual—a term taken from Swedenborg, by which term Blake did not mean the Christian religion but what is now called the 'Perennial Philosophy'. She goes on to compare the concept of Perennial Philosophy, first expounded by Agostino Steuco during the Italian Renaissance and the school of Ficino, with the concept of Sanatana Dharma, the original name for Hinduism. Ultimate authority has a human nature 'As all men are alike in outward form, so (and with the same infinite variety) all are alike in the Poetic Genius'! It is this universal imagination she hopes Temenos will explore and illustrate.

She enlarges her scope to comment on the divergence between the civilizations of Orient and Occident, only to point at the contrast between the thought of Blake and that of modern West. Also she returns to the East and to Hinduism to emphasize that Hinduism takes 'as axiomatic and self-evident that the ground of reality is consciousness.' It is evident from her earliest to her latest writing that she sees an affinity between the concept of *sat-chit-ananda* (being-consciousness-bliss) and 'our own past (of) the Platonic trilogy of the Good, the True and the Beautiful.' As almost a final statement, in her second editorial she articulates her perception of Hinduism:

> Hinduism is like the great range of the Himalayas from which many streams take their rise. It is a great creative matrix, it pays sole allegiance to the Guide within, seated in the cave of the heart; it has put forward from time to time many teachers and sages of incomparable power and vision. Buddhism, Jainism, Shaktism, Sikhism, Advaita, are children of the same mother. Nehru, in his book *The Discovery of India*, describes the Buddha as India's greatest gift to the world. The austere philosophy of Shankara, the passionate devotion to a personal God of the Bhakti tradition of the mystical poets Mirabai and Kabir; are different modes of the experience of the one living reality. Hinduism is not a religion but a civilization. The difference between western materialism and the oriental philosophy is the difference between a lifeless and a living world.

Kathleen's encounter with India had many dimensions and layers. This was one; the profoundest and the deepest. There were others, more human and feminine, of which she gives us an account, not only in *India Seen Afar*, but in her poetry and her editorials.

Kathleen Raine, the poet and scholar, had communicated with the India of thought and idea, of poetry and perennial teaching, before her physical journey to the 'place' and 'space' of India. The physical journey facilitated an encounter with India at other levels. She vividly describes her first impressions as she landed in India in the early hours of the morning. She breathed the spiced air, was enchanted with faces of children and, of course, beggars and poverty did not escape her. All this she received graciously. Unlike Arthur Koestler, she was not repelled by the reality. Her attention was drawn to these bewildering facets, but nowhere was she disenchanted. She did not allow these to shatter the vision of the India of her imagination, 'the human beauty and richness of life itself everywhere'. For her, 'it is not the *rishis* and the 'Masters' alone who are the custodians of that spiritual civilization of beauty and crafts and skilled handiwork, it is the people'. That India is 'everywhere like a fragrance—the beauty of the cotton saris of the women who carry earth to the men repairing the road'. Perceptibly she observes, 'It is not certainly the westernized intellectuals who are custodians of India of the imagination..... it is the people'.

Throughout her narrative in *India Seen Afar* Kathleen juxtaposes her interaction with the intellectual world of urban India with the simple enchanting world of the people in the streets, the children selling artefacts in the vicinity of temples, and the multitudes of humanity. It is said that C.G. Jung had come prepared to meet the 'collective unconscious' in India. He visited Varanasi, saw the crowds, heard the loud tympanic breaking music of the temple bells, breathed the heavy incense smells and was bewildered beyond words. He admitted that he could not take it. The 'collective unconscious' as manifest in the multitude of humanity was altogether too much. An associate of his decades later told me, Jung exclaimed loudly, 'Enough of the collective unconscious. I am sick and want to return to Ascona'. Whether the story is absolutely true or not, it is significant.

The enchantment with the idea of a distant culture intellectually is one matter, the experience of it in raw flesh and blood another.

Other perceptive minds from Europe have been engaged in the thought and spirit of India. For example, Heinrich Zimmer wrote on India with great sensitivity and uncanny insights. Despite the understandable lacunae of information at the level of chronology and dates, Zimmer opened a new world of understanding. His interpretation of myths in that masterly, lucid book *Myths and Symbols in Indian Art and Civilization*, became a guiding light for many, both abroad and in India. It inspired, or certainly encouraged them to turn inwards and return homewards. Zimmer, however, never visited India. It is difficult to speculate as to what may have happened if he had actually visited and seen the monuments and sculptures he wrote about so effectively.

Early in the twentieth century came another seeking eternal truths. Stella Kramrisch hoped to engage with India in reality after her intellectual pursuits. She arrived in India and one of her first encounters was with the art of Elephanta. Although it was a rosary she found in a pool of water in the rocks, it was Shiva who enraptured her. Although she explored many highways and byways of Indian art, it was Shiva, unmanifest and manifest, which became for her a life-long journey. Her writings were, from first to last, a journey investigating the relationship of latent and potent, unmanifest and manifest. The architecture spoke to her. Sculpture pulsated in her veins and the dateless terracottas were her perennial companions of many births. Gradually she made India her home and became the mentor for many Indian art historians. Through the staggering multiplicity of forms, she could pierce into the 'metaphysical' and the ideational heart of this art. Her erudition and command of sources was matched with a rare, almost psychical, insight into this art. Through the delight of the manifested form she grasped the silent unmanifest core of this art.

Another, a contemporary of Stella and predecessor of Kathleen, Alice Boner came to India as a sculptor, initially to assist Uday Shankar, but stayed on to watch the flow of the Ganga. It was a visit to Ellora which revealed to her the principles of form of Indian architecture. She continued to investigate deeper layers of the spiritual in the art. Kathleen visited these sites. But her response was of a different order. Although she resonated with this art Kathleen remained strongly grounded in her psyche, was ever the disciple of Blake. India, or its art, did not transform her nor convert her artistically or spiritually. She responded to the beautiful in all spheres and at many levels without being persuaded to abandon the paths she had already taken.

Thus her journeys to the great monuments, Konarak and Ellora, evoked responses clearly different in tone and tenor than those of a Stella Kramrisch or an Alice Boner. The latter wrote a significant book on Konarak, which remains the centre of discourse on many accounts to this day. Kathleen also visited Konarak, to see the monument of the East where the sun rises. She was all too sensitive to the night and the dawn, the sea, and the wait for the moment of the red globe sun to rise. Indeed, it is through many irrelevances and detours of associative memory that Kathleen 'approached the precincts of the Gods'. She was never oblivious of the contemporary culture which surrounds the ancient monuments. Her penetrating eye saw the Sun Temple, but she was not unaware of the bead and tinker sellers. And yet it was the eternal which called. She exclaimed, 'the great Surya with sublime indifference, sheds his light on backward sellers of coconuts and crates of bottled Campa Cola-Limca'.

Then she sat in 'contemplation of that amazing temple the imagination of India had raised to him'. For her the temple can't be called architecture in the western sense or in the sense of those superb tombs and mosques and palaces of the Moghul rulers of India. One could argue with Kathleen whether Konarak is architecture or not in the western sense, yet one cannot but appreciate her sensitive response as an artist and poet, not as an art historian and scholar. It matters little to her if the temple was constructed on the basis of a highly sophisticated architectural style or whether the architecture was a concrete illustration of a chiseled language of form of the Indian arts. Neither chronology nor text nor techniques interest her. It is in the intrinsic value of symbolic and the universal which interests her. This is as evident from her description of Konarak as it is from other accounts of temples. The following passage from *India Seen Afar* is characteristic of Kathleen's observation and perception:

> Here the sun-god's temple takes the form of a huge chariot of stone rising as a pyramidon carrying all sentient beings, the sun's retinue, all praising and delighting in that god, source of life of the sensible world and all its creatures, from animals to the gods themselves. Round the base, in that deep relief carving that in India so subtly plays with sun and shadow, are elephants, creatures of earth; next, the beautiful naga-women, human above, serpentine below; next, friezes of dancers, and musicians, each with her instrument of music, tabla or flute or vina or mirror, all adorned as for the god with earrings and ankle-bells, girdles, bracelets, dancers beneath the overarching branches of some tree; all is joy—religion be it of Durga and Shiva themselves, not only of the life-giving sun, is celebratory, and expresses a delight, be it terrible, like that of Kali with her black mask and protruding tongue, or Shiva whose indifferent foot tramples all that is mortal and deformed; or as here at Konarak ecstasy and bliss in all its modes. For above those dancers and musicians again, and mingled with them, are those famous 'erotic' sculptures of blissful embracing lovers. All is expressive of life and delight and fecundity. Nor are the lovers life's sublimest expression, for higher yet are the *apsaras* and the gods themselves and high on each face of his chariot laden with all life, Surya himself is depicted, his round solar face shining on the four directions of his world, also those magnificent stone horses draw his chariot for ever from the East. His lions overwhelm earth-born elephants, animals of fire triumphant over creatures of clay. In what country has the solar kingship of the fiery lion ever been challenged? Yet here in India the hooded cobra also, the deadly one, is not without honour in that teeming fourfold chariot life.

Kathleen observes Konarak, but in observing and responding to it she also observes her 'self'. Thus, significantly, she adds,

> But, brought up as I was to believe reality to be Beauty, Truth and Goodness and the virtues of Faith, Hope and Charity all-sufficing, those hooded cobras, those necklaces of skulls, those demon-trampling feet of the Nataraja, those fangs, the blood-lust of Kali, all these *m'effrayent,* like Pascal's infinite spaces, sent me running back for shelter and security of the all-good all-merciful all-protecting Christian pantheon. No, I had not yet made my peace with the wholeness of what

> is, whose joy and ecstasy is celebrated in Surya's temple at Konarak more fully, surely, than in any other temenos on this earth he enlightens.

As always, Kathleen is true to herself, always observing the 'self' which observes. This is evident in another instance. She visits another temple where Krishna is worshipped as baby Krishna or child Krishna. She cannot relate to him. For her 'Krishna' is the Krishna of the Mahabharata, the expounder of the Gita, and not the baby and child of Brindaban. Candidly she states, 'For me Krishna of the Mahabharata stands with the Lord Jesus, truth universal, but the little swings for the child Krishna at his play are cultural and I felt it was not for me to play with the child'. It is the soul of India which Kathleen discerns, be it in the streets of Jaipur or the palace where Gandhiji was jailed. She is not interested in placing her experience in any socio-historical context. She constantly sees in her inner eye 'that refinement of the soul that touches everything in India from the poorest village (those beautiful faces) to the richest sculpture'.

Kathleen could not have been trained or prepared to hear classical Indian music. However, again in this sphere, it is this refinement of the soul she hears in the music of the Dhrupad singers, the Dagar brothers:

> The music comes from afar, with slow approach, arrives like a retinue of the gods, without our knowing how or at what moment they came, yet we know they are there, we are taken up into the cosmic music, for the sound current of the universe flows through us also, through our unawakened occidental senses and crude flesh like unfired clay, yet of what else are we made, being within the one creation, unless of that music, that octave that is colour, sound, light, the flow of tides and rivers? On that ever advancing sound current the gods arrive in their splendour. The Dagar brothers so refined by that music, seem almost luminous, and carry with them, even in a room full of people, a listening stillness. Seeing them, always, as it seems, together—or when in the same room listening, as it were, to one another—it was as if the music flows through them always, when silent no less, or only a little less, than when they sang; like two wonderful instruments—violins—their human frames sounding-boards of the unheard music. Like the sound *OM* their music is a bridge between men and God, transforming and purifying the dull senses, so that even we for a moment seem to discern those unheard sounds of which Pythagoras taught that heard sounds are but a crude approximation, and who
>
> Fingered upon a fiddle-stick or strings
> What a star sang and idle muses heard.

No, even Yeats's words are too Western, too secular for that absolute.

The same sound current flows through all India, one hears it under an awning in a village festival, in temples, in homes everywhere. 'It is the sound of India, the India of sound.... On that sound—*OM*—India is upheld.'

Unexpectedly, she juxtaposes this sound and music with the raucous mechanical sound of 'muzak' which disseminates disintegration from every supermarket. 'Are we not doomed by our music?' she asks. 'In India one can understand that a civilisation is sustained or destroyed by its music.' She discerns refinement here and believes that every villager and beggar is participating, to be formed by the sound *OM*. And suddenly, even the all too generous Kathleen halts; 'for how long can disintegration defeat the sound of creation? Does not our popular music proclaim our irreversible dissolution?' Truly Kathleen heard the sound of eternal India, but was equally anxious about the possibility of disintegration of a civilization through its music. As a footnote, which should bring us down to earth, one may add 'Heaven knows how loud and threatening' are the polluting sounds of popular Indian music in contrast to the music of the refinement of the soul which Kathleen heard?

She had eyes and ears only for the True, the Good and Beautiful and could be blind or deaf to the ugly and the disturbing. She looked for 'essence' and grasped it; distortions and disfigurements she ignored. From somewhere deep within her she was confident that India's soul would not be lost and that India of 'essence' would be the redeemer of the 'materialist' West she denounced.

Countless other examples could be cited to illustrate Kathleen's unshakeable faith in eternal India, the India of the imagination. Some shared her vision, others, both in India and abroad, were sceptical. Was not the India of the Imagination being systematically devoured by the lure of the material West? Be that as it may, Kathleen remained resolute to the last. She said that her life 'could be divided into two parts: the first before I went to India, the second after'. How could it be otherwise?

Perhaps a slight amendment should be made, 'No, it was not in two parts; the India of Kathleen's imagination remained the India of her inner experience.' The ephemerals and the irrelevances she could brush aside. No reality of India which exhibited the fracturing or distortion of this vision could change Kathleen Raine's faith in the 'India of the Imagination'.

35.

Kathleen Raine and the Temenos

KATHLEEN RAINE, poet, critic, scholar, inveterate devotee of the learning of the Imagination, walked the earth softly with her head, as she says, in the clouds. The earth and the world she knew brought with it the knowledge that the quantitative had to be replaced with the qualitative, the measurable with the immeasurable.

Turning away from the natural sciences to poetry, from the positivist discourse to the world of the learning of the Imagination, she grasped at 'Beauty' in all its immaterial hues and colours, only to reaffirm the Platonic vision of Goodness, Beauty, Truth, and the European legacy of the Neoplatonists. For her this approximated the vision of *sat-chit-ananda* in the Indian tradition. Dreams were as real as actuality. Freud's interpretations she rejected. Jung was closer, but her experience was uniquely her own. This she made visible through her poetry and her critical writing. Her *Autobiographies* turned her gaze upon her contemporaries and herself with unparalleled candour and ruthless severity.

She came to India to speak about Yeats and his and her master Blake: her lectures and interventions were undoubtedly a profound learning experience. More, the many meaningful encounters of deep significance succeeded in making me re-examine and re-read the English poets I had read and even taught for decades. Understandably the comprehension had been coloured, if not conditioned, by the critical discourse of the 1930s and 1940s of our century. With the lightness of a feather's touch she demolished the critical apparatus of my academic training in reading and comprehending the Romantics, especially Shelley and Coleridge.

I was left with no option but to read the Romantics afresh, with new perception. All assessments of the poetry as an escape into a romantic idyllic world of fancy had to be revised. Soon it became clear that the so called West, the material West which Kathleen vehemently denounced, also had a long and sustained tradition of the 'mystical' and 'spiritual.'

I had read and recited 'Kubla Khan', and taught Shelley's 'Ode to the West Wind' and of course Keats's 'Ode to the Nightingale', 'Ode to a Grecian Urn' and 'Autumn'. How had I failed to see the deepest layers of this poetry couched as it was in sensuous imagery? I returned to these familiar poems, favourites no doubt of my early years, with now fresh and deep perception. This was Kathleen's gist through her writing specially the book *Defending Ancient Springs*.

This was homecoming of another kind. Decades ago, my attention had been turned away from this poetry and the English and European legacy of my upbringing to the Upanishads and Kalidasa, to return to my roots. Now, decades later, I learned from one who had been drawn to the perennial sources of the Indian tradition to look at and re-read perennial messages of those whom I had decided to disown or forget. Kathleen's critical writing enabled me to re-establish bridges and tread the two worlds without tension and conflict. Her free-flowing, smooth but sharp and incisive analysis of the imagery and symbolism of 'Kubla Khan' was the beginning of a new journey to the 'Ancient Springs.' I returned to this poetry with a new pair of eyes. I was enchanted by the essays 'On the Symbol' and 'On the Mythological,' having myself attempted to decode the world of symbols and myths in the Indian tradition.

Kathleen's insights were fresh and challenging. Never before had I realized why Coleridge used the image of the dulcimer and not of another musical instrument. Her insights penetrated into the tradition with the sharpness of a needle. The 'tree' and the 'river', more universal and familiar images, acquired new significance as metaphors across cultures. It became clear that although the poetic image provided cultural context, it transcended the specificities of any single culture. Altogether, Kathleen's criticism gave me a new impetus to rediscover the multiple layers of meaning of perennial knowledge and wisdom which knew no boundaries of East, West, English or Sanskrit. Her exposition in the essay 'On the Symbol' reaffirmed my own, however superficial, comprehension of the law of correspondence in the cosmos, a subject on which I had written in the context of Indian literature and the arts. Quoting René Guénon, she reminds the reader that a natural consequence of the law of correspondence is the plurality of meanings contained in the symbol. For me this was a talisman, a theoretical premise, enabling me to probe more deeply the many layers of meaning of the symbols and mythology that had preoccupied me. Kathleen thus proved through an oblique path, to be a guru, a teacher, in the Upanishadic sense.

What other tribute can I pay to her for this precious gift? I am indebted to her for making my journey come full circle.

Kathleen, the person who came to India late in her life, physically was at home with the India of the learning of the Imagination for many decades. The physical journey was only a return to familiar ground. From the very first moment of touching the ground of India she was with family and friends of yore, although in flesh and blood she met them only now.

I watched her with Kamaladevi, two women totally separate in experience and attitude: Kamaladevi, the freedom fighter, social activist, pioneer of the revival and restoration of theatre and the crafts; Kathleen Raine, the poet, committed to the vision of the visionaries. How could they meet, on what plane?

Kamaladevi was like a mother—my mother and she had been friends since the twenties of the last century; Kathleen was the potential new mother, teacher and guru. I waited holding my breath; how would they meet? Kamaladevi had little use for the spiritual, although aesthetics and beauty of all kinds were her calling. Kathleen floated in the clouds to grasp the ungraspable, the infinite. Was there a possibility of sharing space? Yes, they met and I watched and listened with childlike wonder at the ease of the communication.

Kathleen shared Kamaladevi's unshakeable commitment to the beauty of the ordinary, the humble. Kamaladevi enabled Kathleen to be acquainted first hand with the beautiful which is the work of the hand rather than the mind. Kamaladevi's presence permeates the pages of Kathleen's book *India Seen Afar*.

But Kathleen communicated with others who lived at the level of the idea and spirit. Kathleen and Raja Rao, the author of *The Serpent and the Rope*, spoke in soft whispered tones about India—not the country, but the idea of India. There was an air of mystery in these conversations, with many significant silences. Kathleen recounts with utmost sensitivity their last meeting, when he called on her in London. This was a meeting of kindred spirits.

Kathleen could also wield, with razor-sharp wit and humour, the sword of the intellect. She gave me vivid accounts of her arguments with many in India. She could argue with a younger generation with vigour. Her encounter with Ramu Gandhi's mind is a case in point; her response to Nirmal Verma's fiction, another. To Keshav Malik's poetry she responded at another level, commenting with sensitivity, understanding and comradeship.

Kathleen had known the visual image—Barbara Hepworth, Ben Nicholson and Winifred Nicholson. It was natural for her to be interested in the work of Indian painters, especially K. Khosa and Kishori Kaul. She compared Kishori's preoccupation with nature and flowers with Winifred Nicholson's flowers. Of Biren De's works she was particularly fond. She discerned in his visual imagery the power of the geometrical form.

Kathleen, as we know, could also be effective as a diplomat, in her own style, not through socialization but through human communication. Gopal Gandhi was like a son and the Nehru Centre became almost an extension of Temenos. She charmed many Indian High Commissioners, such as Mr. Rasgotra and Dr. L.M. Singhvi. For my part I could tease her about her great diplomatic skills and whether she had not lost a vocation!

Our friendship gave me the liberty to say, 'Dear Kathleen, what about Blake, the Master, and Yeats and Coomaraswamy, and the spiritual life? Where are they with your altogether too successful, social, diplomatic life?' With a gentle, benign smile, the question was brushed aside, to be answered with the draft of a new poem. 'Perhaps, Kapila, you would like to read this!'

There was constant correspondence. As everyone knows, the small typewriter was overworked. No one could match her promptness. I responded only unsatisfactorily and intermittently. Instead I took recourse to the easier option—I picked up the phone to speak to her long distance. She was delighted, attentive and shared the moments of both elation as also depression. Often her concerns and anxieties, especially about the future of *Temenos*, would surface. *Temenos* was her child. She worried about its survival, both at the level of finances and of vision. She wanted to withdraw, as all parents do, and could not, as few parents can. She rejoiced at its recognition and took the recognitions that came to her late with detachment, almost aloofness. The state of the world disturbed her, and she wrote the atypical poem 'Millennial Hymn to the Lord Shiva' and sent it to me, as also to other friends. I was taken aback for a moment. The singular calm and composure of a radiant visage had concealed the red flames of anxiety and concern far too long. Now they leaped out in the poem. There was a rapier sharpness, which cut through the darkness which seemed to loom across the modern world.

The last meeting was memorable. I had delivered the L.M. Singhvi lecture at the Nehru Centre on her birthday. I spoke, not without trepidation: she was my special audience. She listened with attention, but said nothing. I thought I had not been able to get across, much as I tried to speak of the multiple levels of meaning of myth of the mountain in literature and art. I should have known better. After all the celebrations of the birthday were over and as Kathleen walked down the stairs, she gently held my hand and said, "Thank you, Kapila, for this special birthday gift. I am glad you spoke of the perennial myths. You know, I have lived with some of these all my life!' No more words were necessary. There was a renewed bonding beyond the specificity of time and space, cultures and languages. I had no words to thank her explicitly. Silently I said, 'But you taught me to look at the myths again'. She had denounced the dictionary meanings of the mythological in her essay and had identified the significance of the mythical image beyond social, cultural boundaries. I had attempted, although inadequately, to elucidate the myth of the Eternal Mountain, Meru, as *axis mundi* in Indian literature, monuments, and poetry. Both the mountains and the clouds were my theme, as humble tribute to Kathleen who had always soared in the clouds of the mystical. The gentle grasp of the hand, the 'Thank you', was the quintessential. Transcendence was in the moment here and now. The good, the beautiful, and truth had enveloped Kathleen gently and genially, radiated with translucence. She responded, wherever she saw them.

Although Kathleen has been gone now for some time, she is strongly present in her absence. There is the sense of a void, not without the consciousness that the 'void' is all 'fullness'.

I read and re-read her poetry and her writing, the autobiography and the scintillating editorials of *Temenos*. I am seized by the anxieties which she shared for the future of *Temenos*, crave for the response of the voice from Paultons Square, and yet I know that she is present in the ever-giving of 'gifts' of perception. She said often, 'I have lived too long.' In her passing away she continues to live in the many lives of many people in many lands. My *pranams*, obeisance, to this Guru of the learning of the Imagination.

36.

Homage to Guru Amobi Singh

The name of Guru Amobi Singh, the grand old man of Manipur, brings a number of images to one's mind. These images are connected with the cultural history of India during the last 70 years: his life and work provide the milestones covered by Indian art, particularly dance, in this century.

Ojha Amobi, as he was endearingly called in Manipur and outside, undoubtedly belonged to that virtuous land which has been the envy of not only human beings but also of the Gods. Legend has it that it was in this beautiful valley that Shiva and Parvati lived until Krishna felt that this was the place for him to hold his moonlit night rasa dances.

Nature has silently and unobtrusively shaped the character of the inhabitants of this valley; and so has it given a unique character to the dance style of its people. The sinuous, waving trees have left their mark on the undulating movements of the dance. On the hills, there is a stronger and fiercer nature, with storms, wild animals and sudden violence. Nagas inhabiting the hills match the virility of nature with their dance.

The two traditions, that of the Nagas and the inhabitants of the Manipur valley, of the Maibas and Maibees and the Vaishnavites, have flourished in harmony, coexisting and supplementing each other. For, the younger traditions have not been uprooted or replaced the earlier ones.

It is often believed in the context of Manipur that Chaitanya transformed the valley into Vaishnavite "temple" leaving little or no traces of the earlier traditions. This is not quite correct because these traditions continued, and still continue, even if they had Vaishnavite veneer on them.

Ojha Amobi was a true representative of this process of Indian Culture where, while one form grew out of another, the original has not been lost or obliterated. It was perhaps this solid foundation of Meitei culture that enabled the guru to be modern and, at the same time, a ruthless and uncompromising traditionalist, believing in the sanctity of the ritual, an unquestioned Vaishnavite *bhakta* (devotee), and modern experimentalist who did not fear to break fresh ground in life or artistic activity. He was a pioneer in spreading the message of the Indian tradition in all its vitality, sanctity, capacity for assimilation and continued reformulation.

The guru began his life young and, so far as one knows, as a member of a family which had long served the Manipuri army. Dance was undoubtedly ingrained in him but his vocation was not that of a traditional dancer in the temple. His mother had, however, danced in the temples and had taken part in the varied repertoire of Manipuri dance form. She was inheritor of the Raas traditions of Maharaj Bhagyachandra, being none other than his great grand-daughter.

With the spread of the British rule to Manipur, the father of the young Amobi was exiled. This exile proved to be a blessing in disguise as he was obliged to spend many years in Brindavan, more particularly in the Vaishnavite temple of Radhakund. It was here that the seeds of the Vaishnavite faith sprouted and flowered beautifully in the form of song and dance in the young Amobi.

From braj bhoomi the *leelas* and *rasa* dances of Krishna had travelled to the secluded valley of Manipur. Now, once again, Amobi, amongst a few others, was instrumental in carrying the vibrant atmosphere of braj bhoomi with a new flavour back to Manipur. He returned to the valley a transformed man; while the life of action he did not forsake, in spirit he was a *bhakta* dedicated totally and completely. Back in Manipur, his performance and extraordinary talent both in *sankirtan* (devotional songs) and the *rasa* tradition caught the eye of the Maharaja, and he was appointed court dancer and guru for many years.

Perhaps in recognition of the restlessness of the earlier years, or perhaps destiny had ordained it so, the guru had to leave Manipur again. For he was apparently born to be a transmitter of the traditions from one part of India to the other. This time he was sent out of Manipur with the command that he should propagate the art of Meitei dancing to other parts of India.

This was a propitious time, for this was also the time for the revival and rediscovery of the Indian tradition. The Bengal School was at its height: Tagore was looking for fragments of Indian classical traditions in music and dance so that he could recreate a genre distinct from the prevalent nautch. The poet had been inspired by his visit to Japan and to Indonesia; he knew that his country too had the same traditions but it was not until he found genuine gurus of the Kathakali and Manipuri dance forms that he was personally confronted with them.

The impression produced by the Kathakali and Manipuri dance forms on the poet gave rise to the dance style which came to be known as the Shantiniketan School of Dance. Guru Naba Kumar's and Guru Amobi's contributions were not minimal in this movement. They had sparked off an interest in the tradition with which the educated Indian was not acquainted. Soon there followed another movement on the return to India of Uday Shankar from Europe.

The message from Uday Shankar to the guru inviting him to Almora again reminded him of his ordained duty. Without a moment of hesitation he decided to accept the invitation. With him, he took a young dancer named Mahabir Singh who had received training from Guru Amobi and had been trained in the art of Pung playing by other traditional maestros.

At the Almora centre there were doyens of dance from various parts of India. These included Guru Kandappa Pillai and Guru Namboodripad; among the pupils were Shanti Bardhan, Simkie, Amala Nandi, Narendra Sharma and others. The guru had known how to use the elements of Manipuri for dance dramas. Here he learnt to use the rich and intricate repertoire of Manipuri dance for short, presentable numbers in a modern concert programme.

For a traditional master this could have proved fatal. He could have been uprooted from his tradition, swept away by the glamour of the stage. He could have diluted the tradition and polluted it by a series of compromises. But the guru was much too deeply rooted both in Brindavan and Manipur to allow this. He taught, he composed, he insisted on the purity of the movement: the chastity of its execution was a must, no matter what external form in composition it took. This then was the secret of his power.

The guru could be ruthless if the characteristic movements of Manipuri dancing of the fingers and the wrist were not rendered properly. He could shout and weep if the foot contact was stronger or weaker than it needed to be and yet when it came to compressing a four-hour Vasantraas to a 10 or 15 minute piece he could do so with ease. The guru also trained the eye to see the dance and the ear to hear correctly. This was the second phase of the guru's life.

After the Almora centre was closed and Guru Namboodripad and Guru Kandappa Pillai passed away it was once again left to Guru Amobi to take the message of the tradition to different parts of India.

Amongst those who remember him in Gujarat are Mrinalini Sarabhai, the Jhaveri sisters and others. The wheel had come full circle: from braj bhoomi the *rasa* went to Manipur and from Manipur it was brought back to the Saurashtra region of Gujarat.

To Delhi the guru sent Mahabir, a true disciple, uncompromising, imaginative and adaptable. But Mahabir Singh's career was cut short as he died in Delhi under tragic circumstances. Such a loss of a pupil so dearly would have broken another guru's back, but not Guru Amobi's. He offered to come to Delhi to continue the uncompleted task of his pupil.

For the first time in Delhi there was a realization of the genuine, authentic Manipuri style, as distinct from oriental dance. To Delhi he also brought another disciple, Babu Singh. Babu did not have the fire of a Mahabir but he had an unparalleled ability to imbibe subtleties of dance techniques from the guru.

The guru's pupils in Delhi will long remember him for the variety of ways in which he could teach movements exactly. He would make patterns on walls, draw lines on the floors, narrate anecdotes from the Puranas, could mimic and if need be catch hold of the ankles to ensure accurate footwork; often he would support elbows so that they would not limply fall down. He would gently move the head with his hands so that the feel of the movements could be recognized by the learner.

And if the pupil continued to be clumsy, heavy-footed, he or she would hear the roar of a lion. "Do not hurt mother earth," he would say. And gently the threats would turn into Saraswati's wrath who punished the dancer if he or she used an *ashuddha svara* (corrupt note) or rendered an *ashuddha* (wrong) movement. Dance was part of his life, an instrument for cultivating the self, not a skill to be imparted: lack of vigilance was punishable in this life—and, in the life hereafter.

It was about this time that the Sangeet Natak Akademi decided to set up a training centre of Manipuri dance, known as the Jawaharlal Nehru Dance Academy, in Imphal. The guru was invited to undertake this assignment. He was initially of two minds: he felt that his task in Delhi had not been completed. He had not been able to impart the right recipients with sufficient knowledge. The words that he used were;

> "If I found a *satpatra* (a good recipient), I have been able to give him enough. But often I have not found the perfect *satpatra*. Whatever I have is for the giving; it was given to me by Saraswati and Radha to be given away so that I can repay my debt".

This was another aspect of faith which continually inspired him to carry the message of dance. He was only the carrier of an art which was bigger, greater than he himself; it was his mission to transmit it. In this way alone could his life's mission be complete.

However, it was under his guidance that a strong institutional framework was established in Manipur ensuring the continuation of a classical tradition into modern times. While the guru was teaching in Manipur he sent Babu Singh to Bombay to enrich groups like the Little Ballet Troupe.

Such foresight and imagination combined with dedication are practically unknown in the modern artistic world. Like a master planner of strategy, he spread the style to all parts of India. The guru as well as his pupils were traditionalists on one plane and bold experimentalists on the other.

An austere teacher, a strict disciplinarian and a meticulous keeper of institutions' accounts, the guru was first and foremost a *bhakta*, a devotee for whom dance was only an instrument of transcending a narrow self to a godhood. This inner life of the guru determined his actions and also gave his dance just that quality which transforms the skill of the execution of movements to the creative art of ecstasy.

Out of his 90-odd years perhaps 70 years were thus spent in dedicated work. When government assistance was offered to him during his last illness, he refused it unequivocally. He wanted nothing for himself. If money had to be given it must be for the propagation of Manipuri dancing, for the recitation of the Srimad Bhagawat—or for the needy and the poor. For the guru death was no enemy nor a stranger; it was a milestone in a journey. If money could save man from dying why had kings and saints passed away? "Like all men born I too must die. My time has come and although my work is incomplete I hope that my disciples will carry on the work of Manipuri dance," he said.

Here then was an amalgam of a yogi of the *karma marga* and the *bhakti marga*. He had played his part in life with vitality, with a sense of duty, of joy; but the guiding spirit of the activity was somewhere else. The still centre, which made him sing and dance the pada of Gita Govinda before the images of the yugala in Radhakund, was the essence of this ease and abundance.

The words *sadhana* and *yajna* have been used in the context of the Indian arts from time immemorial; they stand for this inescapable demand for impersonality. The guru 'lived' and 'danced' the concept through every act of life, through every movement, through the sound of dance and music. How many of us know this in our being outside the intellect?

37.

Rukmini Devi as a Teacher, Guide and Mother

My emotions, feelings and experiences clash deeply with my intellectual and analytical inclinations today. How do I and with what authority, claim and experience, talk about my mother? Rukmini Devi was a teacher, guide and surrogate mother to me. At that level, the kind of communication that takes place is silent, participatory, and does not rest on explicit articulation but is communicated through the act of silence alone. I would like to emphasize that difference. That is one aspect.

I have had the great privilege of having several mothers in my life. I shall not be autobiographical beyond this, except one last statement, which I shall make later. But amongst those I want to remember are my second mother Kamaladevi Chattopadhyaya and the third, my biological mother. It is these three women in their own unique ways and working in manifold domains, intersecting, disagreeing and agreeing, who broke paths which were not contained, and not thought of in terms of 'box categories'. I want to say that it is this unselfconscious breaking of paths that this generation stood for. They were, unlike modernists or traditionalists, not motivated by thoughts, they just acted.

As we go along, perhaps we should keep in mind the general milieu and, in particular, the intellectual dimensions of that period. I would also like to draw attention to the recent writings on that period, from 1928 to about 1947. In the intellectual discourses there has been a great deal of bashing of the nationalist ranging from Kamaladevi to Rukmini Devi, Stella Kramrisch to A.K. Coomaraswamy, all of them being branded as people who were constructing a nationalist discourse. That is the other end of a pendulum.

Since that was my childhood, I can tell you about it, whatever may be the opinion of the people who are engaged in the post-modern discourse on the subject (and I have read that literature with care). I want to say very humbly, but most sincerely, that for all these people, this was its search for identity and at no point at all was it merely an intellectual stance or for that matter ideology. I am someone who has known all these people personally and I want this on record today, because there has been so much written of late on the unnecessary nationalist discourse from which a reconstruction unrelated to reality is being made and, in particular, in the political arena. But these women, whether they were in social fields or in the arts, were exploring different levels. Some like Rukmini Devi returned as pilgrims; thanks to Anna Paylova (whom I hope we shall honour one day for giving us back our dance and three Indians). Also, the search was one which was not individual or in isolation, nor was it an external movement, and that distinction has to be made.

It is not as if what Tagore did during the same period had not influenced Rukmini Devi in what she did. Again, it was not as if what Vallathol did, meant that Rukmini Devi would follow by saying 'let me also try something'. That happened in the post-independent period, not in the pre-independent era. Nor was the search motivated by personal ambition. For the preceding generation it was in the process of exploration that they got their insight. Illumination came to them through the scattered fragments of a mirror. And, they had to piece together that mirror. They knew that what they had were the pieces. Through an enthusiastic but tortuous journey they put it together—whether they merely put it together or they put it in a kaleidoscope to make new images, I cannot say with certainty.

This exploration was not restricted to the fields of music and dance; it was also happening in the fields of literature, painting and the crafts. It was as if those who had been the inheritors of a tradition had found pieces of the tradition. Tradition, we all know, is conservative in some respects, but it also flows. These people possessed a sensibility which enabled them to piece together and rejuvenate a tradition, so that it could breathe in open spaces. No doubt they were important constituents of the social, cultural, political and historically contextualized space. It is from the ground of their times that they emerged. Just as students of a particular art get understandably focused on form and technique and a little bit on content, the larger manure which sustains the ground, the tree and its organic growth is not visible; it is the flower that is seen and not the process. Critical appraisal of the period has overlooked or certainly slurred over these aspects.

The third dimension that I would like to speak about which emerges from this is dance, undoubtedly dance; the body, undoubtedly the body and the body alone and all the discourse involving the removing of the dance from the context of the temple and everything that has been written, re-written including the critique of the history of the *devadasis* or the *maharis* and so on. What is involved in all this is another kind of discourse that relates at a much deeper philosophic level, to attitudes towards the body and deals with where the dance is located—whether in the context of the temple or outside it. Therefore, the double bind and the paradox of dissociating an art from its immediate context with its sociological background, but retaining the content of dance outside the sociological religious milieu in which it was nurtured, that was the challenge; a challenge of the deepest kind. That which was performed at the level of feeling and emotion was then given an intellectual dimension and then a platform. *Sahitya* became important in order to sustain the dance; the musical score became important and thus we enter the question of technique.

I cannot elucidate here the changes which ensured from this re-location of space. Instead, I would like to share two reminiscences. I saw Rukmini Devi in 1947 in performance of the *Kumarasambhavam*. I will never forget that curtain and those two feet. As that curtain went up, it was as if Parvathi had come to the earth. Rukmini Devi in that static but fully empowered pose of Parvathi was electrifying. She stood as icon; and soon the icon became the body and flesh. Kalidasa's poem became alive, and Rukmini Devi a legend. This was the beginning of a new journey for my generation. From that day to the many years which followed, there was learning, participation, much sharing, and some disagreements, altogether most enriching. All I can say is that I am grateful and deeply indebted. A book could be written on the many levels of the communication. This is not the occasion even for a summary.

Let me confine myself to significant disagreements. Many decades after *Bharata Natyam* and its dancers had travelled away from both the temple and even *Kalakshetra*, it occurred to me that it was time to relocate the dance in the precincts of the temple. Of course, the *devadasis* were banned, and the Act was not repealed, Kamaladevi, Rukmini Devi and my mother were there as guarding spirits. It was decided to request dancers to dance in the *Tillai Hall*. Yamini and Chitra agreed. When I spoke about my intention there was a strong negative response from Kamaladevi and my mother who said, 'you are mad', 'you are not my daughter'. Rukmini Devi said to me, "is that what I taught you all these years, Kapila? I thought you might even be my successor here and yet you want to go to Chidambaram and make them dance as *seva*, *nritya seva*. I said, 'but their dance is all about *Tillai*, and what is *Natanam Adinar*; why should they not have an experience of dancing in *Chidambaram*? This I believe will reconnect them to the source'. There was so much love that there was no question of doubt in anyone's motivations. But l think this was one of the great learning experiences.

All my three mothers were against taking the dance back to the temple. My mother said, 'is that why I started a school in Delhi when no one danced? And you want to go back to where we rescued it from?' Kamaladevi said, 'well, you happen to be Vice-President of the Sangeet Natak Akademi and you can do this, but I am not going, I shall not be seen dead anywhere near it. I am ringing up Rukmini Devi and you should first go and talk to her'—which I did. I tried to convince her. I said, "Athai, I am not suggesting that we attach ourselves to the temples and become part of the whole *Agraharam* and *Devasthanam* system and revive the *devadasi* system. Nor do I intend it as a show. I only ask for them to have that experience so that wherever they dance it would be Siva as *Nataraja* which would inspire them."

The initiative was a success, altogether too much of a success. The *Arudra* festival became an annual festival. Now it was my turn to disagree with other colleagues and associates. Dancers from all parts of India came. Once a group from Manipur was invited. I love *Manipuri* dance and am a disciple of the great Guru Amobi Singh. I thought it was inappropriate to have a Manipuri rasa revolving around Nataraja. Again there were protests. 'Now what has come of her? She is inflexible and conservative.' I argued that I want Manipuri in the courtyard of the Govindaji temple and even other Vaishnava sites, but not in Chidambaram. No one understood, they still don't. I wanted to ensure the integrity of each religio-cultural site. Authenticity of experience could only be thus possible.

As for the path finders in the context of *Chidambaram*, I had said, 'You were right when you did it. I am right when I am doing it. That dance which was taken out of the temple has also faced the dangers of dissociating the dancers from the cultural context and thus essence. I want them to reconnect. This is a challenging task. Perhaps an experience of context will enable them to reconnect, even when they dance on urban stages.'

Rukmini Devi, aside from her many other contributions, was chiefly an institution-builder. She treated it as not merely a finite structure with a linear progressive movement. Her insistence was on organic growth. She revived textiles; she collected great musicians; was also instrumental in bringing in the U.S. Swaminatha Aiyar Library, among other efforts. The institution thus became a confluence of many streams of the tradition, which had the possibility of revitalisation.

And that brings me to my conclusion. What is the relationship of life and dance for a woman with a holistic vision that was Rukmini Devi? The difference is not whether she came from Theosophy, or some other larger background of values. What matters is the values that this body holds and manifests in time, and the values which the body communicates. Not through the *Sahitya*, not through the great music and not through the *Adavus*, the *Thirmanams* and the *Jathis* and so on. It is communicated through what one is; through what you are. And in this communication is the moment of revelation. Rukmini Devi was life that was whole, whether as *Pranimitra* or a social reformer, as an institution-builder or an educationist; or above all, a 'dancer' who facilitated the flow of a tradition into 'contemporaneity' of another kind.

38.

Balasaraswati

T. Balasaraswati was unique—the dancer, musician and the person. Truly she was the Bharatanatyam dancer of the century, never to be excelled.

Ever since one began to be interested in 'dance', and Bharatanatyam, specially in the forties when Bharatanatyam was not known to the North and had just re-established itself in Madras, two names kept coming up—Rukmini Devi and Balasaraswati.

Ramgopal came to Delhi to participate in the first All India Dance Festival, held at the Ferozeshah Kotla stadium. He was accompanied by Nina Thimmaya and that exquisite dancer who was bronze come to life, Janaki. Of course, Ramgopal's dance was impressive, his presence spectacular, but it was Janaki's performance which ignited a curiosity, a burning desire to go to the South and see, if not learn. This style was altogether different from all that one had learnt and practiced under my great guru of Kathak, the late Achchan Maharaj. Of course, one was totally committed to the style and devoted to the Master; nevertheless this other style held an attention of another order. Here the gods of yore, the sculptures in stone, and the bronze icons came alive. It was stone and bronze made kinetic. The musical score was different from the *nagma* of Kathak, the *bols* (*solukattu*) had another metallic quality. What was it? How could one enter into the structure, technique and the psyche?

A few years later. Yes, the journey was taken. The Grand Trunk Express was a fast train, but the journey was long and tiring. Forty-eight hours was a test of patience. But it was worth it. The moment I reached Madras began the ceaseless hunt to meet scholars, musicians, *nattuvanars*. Thanks to my dear friend Sita Chari, to whom I shall ever remain indebted, access was possible, although not always easy. Dr. V. Raghavan was sceptical of my intentions first, but later not only relented, but became a teacher-friend figure in many other enterprises—dance, Oriental Studies, Sanskrit theatre, and much else. It was he who introduced me to Bala and her family—mother, brothers, daughter, et al.

I came back to Madras after having sat at the feet of the great tutor—Meenakshi Sundaram Pillai—and with many animated discussions with the other guru Bhagavatar Bharatam Narayanaswami. Each of these visits and later repeated visits to the first were rewarding and enriching. Elsewhere I have described this in detail, but it was in Bala's home and her morning teaching lessons at the Music Academy that the secret of the inner structure of Bharatanatyam began to unfold itself. Day after day I sat silently and patiently watching, listening and observing her teaching. She had few students. Dr. V. Raghavan's other daughter Pape (Priyamvada) was certainly the one with great promise. At the Egmore home, the atmosphere was different, less formal but suffused with music. Jayamma sang as she cooked, Viswa played the flute, Ranga struck the mrindangam as he joked, and Bala as if spontaneously tucked her *pallu* and began to dance or to do *abhinaya*. There was no demarcation here between art and life. *Sahitya* music (singing) or dance, more worship and dance—it was all of a piece.

In deep contrast, and equally impressive, was the experience in Kalakshetra. Rukmini Devi too I admired. The austere regulated discipline was of another order. I learnt much from it, and my own training in Bharatanatyam was in the Kalakshetra style with S.V. Lalitha, whom I brought from Kalakshetra to Delhi.

There were two distinct schools within a single style in Bharatanatyam. Of course, I was familiar with the *gharanas* in North Indian music and dance, specially Kathak. I belonged to the Lucknow *gharana* under Achchan Maharaj, but there were the Jaipur and Banaras *gharanas*. Rivalry was endemic in the *gharanas*, the differences lay in content, modes of delivery and varying degrees of emphasis on the sung word, Thumri, Dadra, etc.

The differences between Bala's approach and Rukmini Devi's were of a different order and scale—it was not a case of the Pandanallur versus the Vazhuvoor Ramiah Pillai, etc. etc. It was a question of a different sensibility to both content and form. Both were Bharatanatyam, each school with its own integrity but totally different in spirit and import. If one came from the intellect and cognition, and critical understanding, the other flowed like a river, naturally related to the source, with awareness but not self-consciousness. I relished both, one was intellectually stimulating, the other was vibrating with deep-felt experience.

Be as it may, I made friends with the two, separately, cautiously avoiding confrontation or taking positions. For me it was a delight to relish both separately and never ask for their admixture. For decades the enriching friendship and communication continued uninterrupted. Rukmini Devi symbolized, like Kamaladevi, a mother figure, teacher, preceptor and woman activist in many fields. But for a Rukmini Devi and Kamaladevi we would all still be wearing georgettes and chiffons. They changed the educated woman's taste and provided another basis of Indian identity. Bala was the unalloyed tradition with all turbulence and its social ups and downs of respectability or otherwise. Music and dance was in the marrow of her bones, the blood in her arteries and the pulsation of her heartbeat. The more frequently I visited Egmore, the more enchanted I was, although at an intellectual, pedagogical level, I understood somewhat more (not enough) of Rukmini Devi and Kalakshetra.

The movement-analyser in me saw clearly the differences in technique and the kinetic vocabulary. I could distinguish between the modes of delivery and of movement and the structure of the compositions. At a technical level, some of this has been said in other forums.

However, the greatness of Bala's art urged me to find ways and means of presenting her outside Madras. Rukmini Devi was of course an acknowledged international figure and needed no support from tiny persons like me. I did make the effort, first to present Bala in Delhi. Not easy, tickets had to be sold from door to door, explanations given and eulogies from her performance in Varanasi quoted. She performed and as usual splendidly. Few were magnetized, most others did not resonate with the greatness of her art and only commented on the frequent entrances and exits to wipe off totally unself-consciously her face. I was disappointed and desolate but did not give up.

It was at the first Dance Seminar held under the aegis of the Sangeet Natak Akademi (1957) that Bala made her presence felt both as dancer and personality. She demonstrated her style, spoke flawlessly. Rukmini Devi and she had a heated exchange on the social aspects of the dance—Rukmini Devi with great sophistication spoke of how the style had needed cleansing; Bala asserted that that brought in its wake lack of depth, etc. etc. Admirers of both were left speechless, if not bewildered. These were the towering figures, sincere and dedicated and with matchless integrity, but at different poles. The later critiques, and something that continues today, have taken rigid positions, attributing all this to the Brahmanical and non-Brahmanical. All this is far from the truth; the societal structures, the sociological background and breeding certainly had a role to play but the 'art' and the distinguishing characteristics of 'style' within Bharatanatyam was an act of art and creativity, and not sociology.

This is not the occasion to dwell at length on the nature of discourse in the performing arts, specially dance. Alas, it has been impelled with considerations outside the 'art' and not from within. Some of it was existent there too, as the following will reveal.

To return to Bala, now I made another effort. I wanted her to go to the erstwhile USSR. I rehearsed with her. Moscow would be cold. Coats and shoes were made. All was ready. The Soviets had accepted her. And then came the bombshell from the Ambassador: 'What we want is a pretty young dancer and not a heavy weight football champion. Her visit should be forthwith cancelled'. The Ambassador had obviously received communication from another eminent dancer who was anxious to go and had access to him. The Ambassador was senior and powerful. The Minister also had been advised against sending her and asked to revise his order. More, he was told to be very cautious about accepting my 'biased' advice. There was nothing else to do but to be the helpless, unfortunate instrumentality of communication to Bala.

I took a trip to Madras. I thought it may be better and more polite to let her know personally. Hell let loose. She cursed, fumed, threw the coats and shoes at me, wanted me to take them and myself back. I took it all, because she was right. I was as humiliated in her humiliation. There was not a word I could say to console her, because I the person was on her side, even if I the representative of government was the instrumentality of breaking the news. It took some time for the dust to settle before we could be friends again, so that she could do her *abhinaya* of Tamrajakshi in the twilight of her courtyard.

Inside me, I was hurt and lacerated and disillusioned with the lack of understanding and taste and, more, the role of personal rivalry and petty intrigues, not uncommon in bureaucracies, but destructive in artistic spheres.

However, I did not give up. An opportunity came, and this time was somewhat easier to 'fight it out', as they say. The occasion was the East-West Music Encounter to be held in Japan in 1961. An international committee comprising Nicholas Nabakov, Alain Danielou, Earl Harewood, Narayana Menon had been formed. Margot Fonteyn, Maya Plisetskaya, Yehudi Menuhin, amongst others, were to be there. Nicholals and Alain Danielou identified the Dagar Brothers and Ali Akbar Khan as musicians, and Balasaraswati and Kathakali Ramankutty Nair (group of Kerala Kalamandalam) as dancers. Whatever the informal discussions with friends Nicholas and Alain, the formal suggestions came from world renowned musicologist, and could not be turned down. Naturally, there were murmurs of disagreement. I was delighted and ecstatic. At last an opportunity had come to make up for the earlier disaster. I rushed to Madras, meticulously rehearsed each number. Worked with Viswa and Ranga to notate the musical score, the *sahitya* the music and *tala* in staff notation but with a difference, with a view to making explicit the multi-layered structure of the word melody, notes, *tala* and the dance performance. Day after day Bala danced with ease and joy, explaining each metaphor of her interpretation. With childlike simplicity she said, 'Don't you think if I could write I would be like Rabindranath?' Both laughed and hugged each other. It was beautiful. I had tears in my eyes.

But the storm was still brewing in the corridors of power. This time it was also on the Kathakali and my dear friend Ramankutty Nair. The Indians who mattered did not think that the tympanic breaking sounds of the *chenda* and the 'grotesque' make up of Kathakali was fit for the delicate sensibility of the Japanese, and as for Bala this was a repeat colossal mistake. How would she ever hope to compare with a Margot Fonteyn and Maya Plisetskaya and their large group? The Minister summoned me, wanted to find ways and means to alter decision. I gave all the arguments of an international commitment, etc. etc., but when all else failed, in desperation I burst out: 'If Bala fails I shall resign, and please put this resignation in your pocket'. He roared back 'What arrogance'. I replied: 'Not my arrogance, it is pride in Bala's art'. Of course, reinforcement was needed from the international committee, which enthusiastically obliged, including Narayana Menon who had been under immense pressure. We were both relieved though still nervous. I more than him.

And thus the trip to Japan at the East-West Music Conference in the great and grand theatre of Ueno Park. It was an impressive gathering of anyone who mattered in the field of music and dance. Apart from the performers, there was the respected musicologist, Thakur Jaidev Singh.

For Bala I ensured that there would be morning workshops where each number would be broken up into its constituents—the Liberto, (the *sahitya*) the music, both the words and notes the *tala*, and the *sollukattus* of the *nritta* as also the variations and improvisations in the *abhinaya*. In short, I tried my best to prepare the audience for the performance. I did the same with Ramankuty with whom I had travelled to the Soviet Union a few years earlier. Nevertheless, my nervousness was persistent. I remembered my exchange with the Minister, and was also anxious to uphold in every possible way Bala's art.

All very well, what will she do in a stage with a 60 feet opening and 40 feet depth, and automised lighting with a pre-arranged timing. I was at my wit's end, but I found a solution. I had the orchestra pit lighted up and darkened the rest of the stage and gave Bala a 14×12 space to dance. I told her: 'Now forget everything, and just dance as you do in Egmore and remember Jayamma's singing'. That was it. Vishwan, Rangan and all others were at their best. Her Varnam in Todi was a tour de force, the *Tamarasaksha* held the audience spell-bound and *Krishna nee Begane* had them in tears. I stood in the wings trembling. At last the deafening applause. Bala had made it, or was made an international figure. I was fulfilled. Margaret Fonteyn came up to the stage, held my hands and stroked Bala's shoulders in the most gentle of gentle gestures, looked at me and said: 'Kapila, I thought I was a dancer! This is dance incarnate'.

No more is necessary to add. Of Ramankutty's great performance was *roundra* Bhima, I shall not say any more here; that is another story.

Yes, Bala was made in the external world of recognition. Rave reviews and accolades followed. I pleaded with Bala in Japan, as I had in Madras, that she must teach Lakshmi. She would hear none of that. She reminded me of her personal suffering, the social injustice and rejection, and not for anything in the world would she make Lakshmi, her one and only child, a dancer. Lakshmi too, at that time, was not particularly drawn, however it was clear that dance was also in the marrow of her bones and the blood in her veins, latent if not potent.

But such are the ironies of destiny or circumstance, the moment of Bala's glory and her recognition was also the moment of her departure from India, both physically and psychically, for long periods. Directly or indirectly, and ironically, I was instrumental.

A year earlier I had spent a year in Berkeley, California, as the wife of the Regent Professor, the late S.H. Vatsyayan. To keep myself in dancing shape and to keep myself occupied, I gave dance lessons largely only of the basics, the *adavus* in Bharatanatyam, and somewhat more to others in Kathak. Two Americans took lessons in Bharatanatyam. One was Louise Scripps, wife of the business doyen, Sam Scripps. When I was going to Japan, I told Louise of the event, and suggested that she may like to visit Japan. Louise did come. Louise was enchanted as all others were, and she took Bala to the US. Louise of course visited Bala in Madras and took lessons from Bala. But Bala, the person, had been appropriated, although no power on earth could appropriate her art.

The rest of the story of Bala's art, her performances, and her many admirers in the US and her recognition and renewed acclaim in the Music Academy is all too well known and narrated several times in several versions. All I need to recall is the memorable occasion of doing a lecture demonstration with Bala at the Cord Conference held in Hawaii. and her memorable speech.

As I moved her body, she was pliable like a reed or a leaf. She knew when to let go and when to take control. Also, when the audience insisted that she only do *abhinaya*, she said to me, 'Kapila, they do not realise that unless I have danced the *varnam* and the *nritta* has made butter out of my body, I can do no *abhinaya*'.

The more Louise possessed her, the less I could keep in touch, but in communication we always were. I reminded her about teaching Lakshmi. 'Yes, you were right, and now Lakshmi desperately wants to learn'.

Later, in the twilight of her days, and when she knew the end was close, one evening we had a long conversation in her home in Madras, with many silences and deep communication, holding hands. She said, 'How right you were, this art can only be passed through the blood. I want Lakshmi to sleep next to me, so that I can without her knowing give everything I have. Time is running out. I am rather ahead in the queue. I want to give, give, give. Will there be time?'

And so, while she gave and Lakshmi received, Lakshmi herself was ahead in the queue. Strangely and ironically, but understandably, it will be the son who will carry the legacy.

Japan, East-West Encounter, for Bala was an India-US encounter for herself and her family, both Vishwa and Ranga. The story of achievements and suffering is out of a novel, heroic and tragic in proportions. Art and Life are enmeshed. If artistic creativity would also lead to making the greatest art, the art of living, if only, if only.....

39.

Shantha Rao*

In what words do I recall the life and work of this incomparable dancer, painter, musician, writer and above all, an extraordinarily generous human being, as strong from the outside and as sensitive and delicate from the inside? To me it is difficult to put in words the character of this human being and her journey for more than half a century through many vicissitudes of life, the courage and the tenacity that she had and the commitment, uncompromising commitment, to the art which she learnt and performed and communicated to the world.

Her life story is known: from a family of affluence to a decision to respond to this call of dance; the difficulties that she faced as the first woman to have rigorous training in Kathakali under no less a master than Ramunni Menon; her having the courage to learn and perform Mohini Attam at a time when the dance was neither recognised nor acknowledged, to be with Meenakshisundaram Pillai—*thatha*—from whom she imbibed not only the rigorous training of the Pandanallur style but also broke path by having the courage to perform compositions like the *Thanavarnam*; and then to sit in that, or to dance in that spacious, beautiful floor of 6–B, Brigade Road and to sing whenever she wanted to with that gentle supporting voice of Vasanti.

What memories do I have and how many, and on how many different planes? I see her in that 6–B Brigade Road where I was always welcome and where one partook of a delicious meal besides hours and hours of communication on dance, her own performances and her understanding of the movement of the vocabulary of dances that she performed.

Throughout her life she was as dedicated as uncompromising with her art. For this she suffered. She was a path-breaker of another type, quite different from the contributions and the path-breaking steps which were undertaken by Rukmini Devi in giving a new institutional framework to

---

* This is a message on the occasion of the memorial meeting for the great dancer and my dear, dear friend Shantha Rao. Recorded on tape by Dr. Kapila Vatsyayan.

Bharata Natyam, or Balasaraswati bringing out a tradition of what we loosely called the *Devadasis* into another social context. Shantha Rao was in her own way a path-breaker because here she established that it was possible to have an individual style within the larger framework of what we call classical Indian dances, specially Bharata Natyam and Mohini Attam. Whenever she danced it was fire and lightning. The strength of her movements was matched by the nimbleness of her feet, the lightness of the touch with the earth.

This is not the occasion to reminisce, but it is the occasion to mark her journey from the early 40's to the early 50's and her first performances in Bombay, then in Delhi and later on of course in all parts of India, and that memorable journey to the United States when she took the US by storm.

I vividly recall her first performance in Delhi in what was then the Constitution Club on Curzon Road. With no setting, no lighting, on a bare floor she danced and she took each one of the members of the audience with her by the sheer power of her presentation and the abandon with which she could deliver movements. Despite recognition and fame, and equal amount of critical evaluation, she persevered on the path that she had undertaken, to explore the depths of what she was dancing by making notations, by recording her rare repertoire of music. The archives that she leaves behind is invaluable and I think that it is our duty as her friends to see that that archive and specially her huge notations are preserved and worked on.

She was both prolific as also creative in many spheres. As painter one could see the same both stringent and finesse of lines, and as a musician when she could break forth into music along with Vasanti. As a human being generous to the core, her hospitality knew no bounds but at the same time guarding her privacy was equally important to her. Some of her dances had been captured in still photography of Sunil Janah and the documentation and films. But there is so much more to do. She will always stand tall, towering and alone in the whole field of dance, particularly Bharata Natyam and Mohini Attam. Her Kathakali had her own individual style, and when she went on to explore this new field of dance known by its various names today—Bhama Nrityam, Vilasini Nrityam, emerging out of what we generally identify as Kuchipudi—she had an equally important contribution to make. For me she was a dancer, painter and musician, but most of all a friend with whom I communicated freely and continuously for more than half a century. Even if we met rarely, there were frequent telephone calls, long phone calls. Her concern for everyone and her desire to reach out to anyone who needed her help, was her natural self.

And I could go on and on recalling those palpable moments of communication. She did not create a School in the sense of a 'Shantha Rao School of Bharata Natyam', but she leaves behind a legacy which beckons us all to re-look at some of our presumptions.

That apart, on this day I can only pay my humble tribute to this, where I began, a great, great born-dancer and a beautiful human being.

40.

Tribute to Periya Sarada

Periya Sarada teacher's unique and impressive contribution to Kalakshetra, the institution, has made her name synonymous with the institution next only to Rukmini Devi and Sankara Menon.

For six decades she has assiduously pursued the path of training herself and training generations of dancers, dancer teachers, musicians and scholars. From humble beginnings she has grown like a mature tree which has given strength and sustenance to all those who have sought her guidance and support.

It was her good fortune to be in close association with the 'greats' in music—Tiger Varadachari, Papanasam Sivan, Veena Krishnamacharya and others. Her close association with them enabled her to assist them in the unforgettable musical compositions for the dance-dramas Kumarasambhavam, Kutrala Kuravanji, Andal Charitram, Gita Govindam, etc. Almost more important was her tireless work in writing down the music as it was being composed.

Few people would have had the rare opportunity to work with Balu Bhagavathar of Melattur. He was an unparalleled human repository of the Bhagavatamela tradition. Periya Sarada's close association with Balu Bhagavathar resulted in the edited versions of Dhruva Charitram, Usha Parinayam and Rukmini Kalyanam. Through this effort a new direction was given to the presentation of these compositions in a contemporary stage context.

She effortlessly combined theory and practice, *sastra* and *prayoga.* This is evident from the works she has edited, such as the three volumes of the Sangita Ratnakara, published by the Adyar Library. It was only one who was fully immersed in the 'practice' (*prayoga*) who could edit the complex and sometimes ambiguous passages of the Sanskrit text.

But Periya Sarada is teacher first and last. Little wonder that she has always been addressed as Periya Sarada teacher by one and all.

In the field of music she has been associated with the greats. In the field of dance she has been the teacher of the greats of this century whose immaculate precision has been acclaimed by the young and old within Tamilnadu and India, as also abroad. These include the well-known and universally respected dancers—Sarada Hoffman, Yamini Krishnamurthi, Adyar Lakshman, Krishnaveni, C.V. Chandrasekhar, the Dhananjayans and of course Leela Samson, the present Director. Each of them have brought distinction to the institution in their varied distinctive ways and have done Periya Sarada proud.

Periya Sarada has rendered a yeoman service to the methodologies of teaching by devising a method of writing down Bharatanatyam in notation form. This is now being followed in the Kalakshetra. Equally important is her contribution in drafting a syllabus and method for teaching dance theory.

For all these multifaceted yet interconnected contributions, Periya Sarada has received admiration and love from her contemporaries as also her students. For me knowing Periya Sarada for over five decades has been a privilege. Each meeting has been a learning experience. Few carry monumental scholarship, creativity and critical insights with such grace, dignity and humility.

I am glad and happy that a volume has been prepared by Sundariji and others to honour her. She deserves this in full measure. Once again, as I have said, it is a pleasure and privilege to write these few lines.

41.

Dance: A Discourse of Peace on Carl Wolz

From the first memorable meeting in Hawaii in the early sixties to the meetings in Hong Kong, Japan, and Europe, Carl Wolz was a kindred spirit, who saw and experienced himself and the world through dance, and dance through the corporeal frame, which can transcend the physical to go beyond.

I recall the several conversations in Hawaii, but more so those on the beaches with the constant ebb and flow of the tide, when we saw together the dance of the waves and tides. His sensitivity to the traditional Hawai'ian dances, when women of large proportions could dance as light as a feather, was more than obvious. And of course Japanese traditions engaged him, to know and experience the stillness of movement. How beautifully and delicately he describes the spirit of Zen in *noh* in his article in a CORD publication! He had internalised Japanese language and culture and its dance traditions. It was this command which was the secret of his success in Japan. I watched him teach in Japan and bring new life to the all too familiar movement patterns. And in all this negative possibility of becoming the other or immersing himself into the other, he was himself—the soft spoken, profoundly devout American of Missouri, profoundly devoted to his mother and the mother earth of his birth. This was evident in his choreography, which moved beyond Julliard and Balanchine. I was particularly moved by the characteristic understatement of the piece entitled *Prayer and Apotheosis*. Equally moving, although very different in quality, was the choreography in *In an Autumn Garden*. And Carl was totally dedicated to notation.

And then there was Carl Wolz, the moving, energizing spirit in the Hong Kong conference. He had laid the foundation stone of the Asia-Pacific Dance Alliance and later the World Dance Alliance. It was an extraordinary effort to not only gather together so many diversities of the Asian dance traditions but to succeed in creating a space for real dialogue and interaction, not only through the word, but more importantly through the sharing of movement, vocabularies, choreography, and notation. For me it was a deep learning experience of enduring value. Carl nurtured a young generation of dancers and dance researchers from all parts of Asia. This he sustained in the subsequent meetings in Korea, Taipei, and Singapore. For all this and more, the world of dance spread over several continents will ever be beholden to him for having created a bond of friendship, love, passion for all that is 'precious' and almost 'sacred', beyond national boundaries and individual identities. Truly this was the world of diversities held together in a circle of bonding and interlocking. I said I cannot reconcile myself to his physical absence, but I am ever conscious of his presence through the mission he carried and the results, which will outlast us all.

How did he do so? Or, how can Dance do so? 'Dance', the oldest and the youngest of art expressions, is the most 'personal', subjective, and yet at the same moment it makes the demand to depersonalise the body, the subjective, and uplift the human to another level. 'Dance', through the very instrumentality of the 'body', the most physical and material, has the capacity to transcend the body, the body as it gets disembodied. The art makes the paradoxical demand of making the personal subjective, the most impersonal and significantly universal.

Undoubtedly each distinct style, school, 'genre', is located in 'space' and 'time'. It is contextual and embodies particularly of content, and specificity of culture, but in the last analysis its efficacy lies in its capacity to transcend person, social context, specific content, and all else, a libretto, a music score to make connection at a level where the very culture from which it emerges is not as important as the quintessential experience of peace and tranquility. Each dance composition presents a spectrum or emotive states through movement of the whole body or only apart, limbs or face. Through the very manipulation of the body or bodies in space and time, the experience of stillness and tranquility and peace is communicated. This is the experience of all great dance performances, be they ballet or modern dance or any of the Indian dance forms, or the dances of Korea or Japan. Dance then is the instrumentality of 'peace' at a deep psychical level, almost a spiritual experience when at its best and most chiselled.

Dance has a capacity of healing. Pertinently the announcement of the international conference in Japan in 2002 said that the conference would focus on both the role of dance in keeping tradition alive and as a catalyst of cultural, environmental, and political change. 'We will investigate dance as a healing agent in a cataclysmic environment and explore representation of identity across international individual cultural and temporal borders.'

The power of dance for healing and integration was impressively demonstrated through the workshops and seminars. Dance has the potential to heal the emotional and psychical scars of natural earthquakes and tsunamis, as also assuage the physical and emotional wounds of ethnic conflicts, wars and many other types of violence. Through the movement of the body, the ruptures of the heart and the mind can be healed. It can and has in many instances played a pivotal role in making a culture whole and bringing about re-integration and rejuvenation.

At another level, dance is an instrumentality of peace through cross-culture and across border communication. It is and has been more effective than international conferences with verbal discourse in bringing about peace. The experience is direct and instant, precisely because the corporeal physical frame is the instrument. It is also meaningful at a level of networking at an organisational level because here hierarchies are eschewed. In today's world it is not a matter of exploring or savouring exotic cultures. The world-wide movement through the initiative of the Asia-Pacific Dance Alliance, and then the World Dance Alliance, is now succeeding in gathering together diverse dance vocabularies, each with its own distinctiveness and individuality, but with the avowed goal of sharing a common pursuit of creating peace and harmony in the world through dance. Despite the rhetoric of globalisation, there is an intense anguish about the many ruptures and fractures of humanity's own making. Dance at both individual as also collective levels can be the strategy of respecting and loving differences and yet bringing peace with oneself and the world. Dance is indeed the instrumentality of 'healing' and restoration, peace and harmony, if only, if only our world of national boundaries and political ideologies will remember that to be human is the easiest and the most difficult. Dance can and has uplifted the human soul to another dimension so that we can ensure a more harmonious human order for the future.